DATE DUE

DEMCO 38-296

Weapons Under Fire

Garland Reference Library of Social Science
Volume 1047

Weapons Under Fire

Lauren Holland

Garland Publishing, Inc.
New York & London
1997

Library of Congress Cataloging-in-Publication Data

Holland, Lauren H.
    Weapons under fire / Lauren Holland.
        p.   cm.— (Garland reference library of social science ; v. 1047)
        Includes bibliographical references and index.
        ISBN 0-8153-2067-1 (case : alk. paper) — ISBN 0-8153-2068-X
    (pbk. : alk. paper)
        1. United States—Armed Forces—Weapons systems.   I. Title.
    II. Series.
    UF503.H65   1997
    355.8'0973—dc21   97-21805
                                        CIP

For the figure on page 69, from Alexander Kossiakoff, in Franklin A. Long and Judith Reppy, *The Genesis of New Weapons: Decision Making for Military R&D*, every effort was made to contact the copyright holder of this source. We were unable to do so and would welcome any further information.

Figure on page 72 from *The Politics of United States Foreign Policy* by Jerel A. Rosati, copyright © 1993 by Holt, Rinehart and Winston, Inc., reproduced by permission of the publisher.

Printed on acid-free, 250-year-life paper
Manufactured in the United States of America

For Nick

Contents

Tables and Figures xi

Preface xiii

Acknowledgments xv

Introduction xvii

Approaches to the Study and Explanations of Weapons Decisions xxi

Organization of the Book xxv

HIGHLIGHT

Polaris: A Case of Rational Decision Making xxx

CHAPTER 1

Explaining the Military Procurement Process 3

If Not Rational, Then What? 4

CHAPTER 2

Charting Military Policy: The View from the Presidency 25

Nature of the President's Powers 26

Forging Linkages Between Foreign, Defense, and Military Policy:

The Role of the President 29

Foreign and Defense Policy in the Post–World War II Period:

An Historical Overview 30

Presidential Influence: A Reassessment 51

HIGHLIGHTS

Skybolt: The President Takes a Stand and Alienates Everyone 58

Trident: Eight Presidencies and Still Plying the Waters 60

TFX: The Defense Secretary Stands Up and Takes a Fall 62

CHAPTER 3

Strategic Planning in the Pentagon: Can It Happen? 65
Making Weapons Decisions: A Theoretical Perspective 66
A Clash of Models: An Empirical Test 81
Conclusion 90

HIGHLIGHTS
Cheyenne: When Everything Goes Wrong 99
Skipper: Beating the Odds 101
Bradley: The Quintessential Hybrid 103
F-16: The Air Force Prevails in the End 105

CHAPTER 4

Prometheus Unbound: Technology and Weapons Development 107
The Role of Technology: A Theoretical Consideration 108
Testing the Claims of the Technology Argument 124
Conclusion 132

HIGHLIGHTS
Aegis: Too Sophisticated to Identify the Enemy? 138
Thor-Jupiter: The Technical Rush to Obsolescence 140
ALCM: A Weapon Looking for a Mission 142

CHAPTER 5

The Role of Congress in Weapons Acquisition Decisions:
Process and Policy Considerations 145
Congressional Powers: Vast or Limited? 146
Congressional Involvement: Potential or Actual? 147
Does Activism Mean Influence? 153
Assessing Congressional Involvement: Positive, Negative, or Neutral? 155
Congressional Influence: A Prospective 164
Conclusion 167

HIGHLIGHTS
F/A-18 (Hornet): Congress Gets Stung 174
M-1: Congress Builds a Tank 176
DIVAD: "Sargeant York Can't Shoot" 178

CHAPTER 6

The Role of the Public 181
A Public Role: The Theoretical Debate 182
A Public Role—Pest or Panacea? An Empirical Test 189
Conclusion 201

HIGHLIGHTS
B-1: The Bomber That Couldn't Be One 209
MX: A Missile in Search of a Home 211
M-16 Rifle: The Army's Attack on Democracy 213

CHAPTER 7

Conclusion 215

General Propositions 216
Implications 220
A Reform Impetus 223
Reform Measures 226

HIGHLIGHT
F-22: Business as Usual 232

APPENDIX A

Methodology 235

Dependent and Independent Variables 235
Selecting the Cases 236
Collecting the Bibliographic Sources 238
Generating the Data 238

APPENDIX B

List of Questions and Coding Form 241

Acronyms and Glossary 245

Selected References 249

Index 261

Tables and Figures

Tables

I.1 Weapons Systems by Representative Criteria xxiv
1.1 Weapons Systems by Performance Criteria 5
3.1 Structure of the Pentagon: Who Rules? 82
3.2 Does Military Need or Organizational Position Prevail? 85
3.3 Compromise (Concessions) by Performance Problems 89
4.1 Impetus for Weapons Systems 126
4.2 Weapons Systems by Scope of Participation 127
4.3 Scope of Participation by Performance 129
4.4 Technological Sophistication by Performance Problems 131
5.1 Congressional-Executive Relations on
     Major Weapons Systems 151
6.1 Nature and Scope of Public Involvement/Influence 191
6.2 Public Involvement by Performance Problems 199
6.3 Public Involvement by Cost Overruns 199
6.4 Public Involvement by Schedule Delays 199

Figures

3.1 How Nuclear Weapons Decisions Are Made 68
3.2 The Cycle for Major Weapons Acquisition 69
3.3 Department of Defense Policy Processes 72

PREFACE

For forty-five years, in the aftermath of World War II and America's inauguration of the nuclear age, fear of Soviet aggression and Communist expansionism provided the primary impetus for the shape of America's force structure and posture. During this time, every rifle, missile, tank, submarine, and plane that was built was justified as promoting America's national security in light of the Communist threat.

There is no longer a Soviet Union. The threat of Communism has evaporated. Regional conflicts prevail among the diverse ethnic groups that once composed the nations of the Warsaw Pact. Yet America continues to build the same weapons conceived for use against the Soviet Union and its allies during the period of the Cold War. In part, the security–weapons mismatch is understandable given the life cycle of most major weapons systems (five to fifteen years) and the capacity for redesigning weapons for new applications. The stellar performance of the M-1A1 tank in the Persian Gulf during Desert Storm is one example of the second phenomenon.

Another part of the explanation can be found in Congress and the Pentagon. In Congress, the Cold War mentality prevails. During the fall of 1995, the U.S. Congress approved funding for a new fleet of B-2 (Stealth) bombers that even the Pentagon disclaimed because the plane's mission, to penetrate Soviet air defense and attack hardened targets, is no longer relevant. For its part, the Pentagon, guided by a two- (regional or one-half) war strategy, (Quadrennial Defense Review, May 1997), is seeking billions for a third Seawolf attack submarine (originally conceived to track and destroy Soviet ships) and a new RAH-66 Comanche helicopter (originally conceived to defeat the Soviet's Hokum helicopter). Congress already has approved $1.5 billion for the submarine and $300 million for development of the helicopter. During the spring of 1996, congressional

Republicans sought (unsuccessfully) to revive a scaled-down version of the Star Wars missile defense system.

As the media clamor to portray current legislative politics as wasteful and parochial and Pentagon activities as business as usual, students of defense policy run to defend their more scientific explanations of why and how America comes to the decisions that it does to build the weapons. It is becoming increasingly difficult for the scholarly community to defend against the claims that the "Pentagon Gets a Free Ride" and "Military Pork Continues." This defense, however, is the task that I have set out for myself in this now timely book.

In my search for a reconciliation of the divergent views from the academic and media communities, I have found that there is a middle ground. There is a lot of pork in legislative politics, malfeasance in the Pentagon, and negligence in the defense industry. But there are also good intentions, a great deal of competence, and serious efforts to match America's military capabilities to credible future threats. Validating the middle ground requires looking further than the House Committee on National Security's actions on the B-2 bomber, President Clinton's campaign promise to support the Seawolf submarine, and the Pentagon's use of a concurrent and risky management strategy for the $71.6 billion F-22 fighter aircraft program. It necessitates a dissection of the decision-making process for a representative sample of major weapons systems to invalidate the claims that pork and malfeasance are both pervasive and determinate. This book attempts just such a comprehensive analysis.

ACKNOWLEDGMENTS

A number of people assisted in writing this book. Those with whom I held confidential interviews—thirty people serving in the Pentagon, Congress, and academia—contributed enormously to the information in it. Most of the formal, personal interviews were conducted in the fall of 1988 and again during the summer of 1991. Of the several graduate and undergraduate students assigned to me as research assistants, one deserves particular mention. Crae Franklin collected voluminous numbers of government publications and secured additional information while on a research trip to Washington, D.C., during the summer of 1991. The National Science Foundation provided me with the time, resources, and confidence to make researching this book possible; my gratitude to them is indescribable. The suggestions offered by the five anonymous reviewers commissioned by Garland Publishing were insightful and kind. My colleagues Susan Olson and Dan McCool offered timely encouragement. Senior Editor David Estrin was nothing less than exuberantly persistent. Finally, I wish to thank my son Nick who (despite his youth) has been a constant source of love, joy, and humor and a persistent reminder that there are more rewarding, fulfilling, and challenging things to do than write a book.

INTRODUCTION

Weapons in the United States are under fire. The "evil empire" has collapsed and the Berlin Wall has come down. Few firearms are currently being discharged against America's enemies. But weapons are under fire. They are under fire from the media, which is concerned with the amount of money "overspent" on military spare parts, and with the persistent crashes of prototype aircraft. They are attacked by some members of Congress, who speak out against the enormous amounts of funds being committed to major weapons systems for which there are no longer military rationales and that fail to perform credible missions. They are assaulted by an American public that no longer finds a defense buildup credible in the current international environment nor cost-effective in the current economic environment.

So why does the United States continue to devote billions of dollars to the purchase of military hardware? One popular retort, a reason proffered by members of the military community, is that although the international environment has changed, and the Soviet threat has receded, new and uncertain threats on the horizon necessitate a different, but no less ominous, military force. Today, few citizens buy this rationale. Ask an American why the United States continues to invest billions of dollars in military hardware, and the likely response will point to greed—a greedy defense industry, a greedy military, and a greedy Congress. Again, the response from the professional community is that the American public does not fully understand the nation's defense needs nor the difficulty in meeting these needs, because the public is ignorant of the process of building and deploying weapons systems. The public is neither privy to the classified information that confirms the threats that weapons systems are intended to protect us from nor can it appreciate the technical and scientific uncertainties (and the requisite costs) that complicate the process of acquiring advanced military hardware.

Nonsense. It is not necessary to be a scientist, weapons technician, or military specialist to understand whether the weapons that America builds are necessary or justifiable. Military hardware decisions are ultimately political decisions, products of a democratic process in which the people are a critical link. The public not only has a right to understand weapons procurement decisions, it has an obligation to do so. If the American public understood the uncertainties and complexities that cloud the process of making military hardware decisions, it might be less, not more, critical. As products of the American political process, weapons systems are compromise decisions that reflect the bargaining and negotiation that occur among several different actors and agencies. Weapons are not optimal solutions to clearly definable military problems. There is not one best weapons system that can meet a military threat in a definitive way. Rather, there are lots of possible solutions being promoted by actors and agencies acting politically, which is to say, acting to secure governmental support for a particular military perspective.

In this regard, making military hardware decisions is not that much different from making decisions in other public policy areas such as education, crime, transportation, or welfare. In these areas as well, definite solutions to problems are not available, in part because the nature of the problems themselves is obscure or imprecise. What is the crime problem? The high rate of recidivism? The lack of rehabilitation of criminal offenders? Police brutality? Poverty? What is the education problem? Inappropriate curriculum? Poorly trained and underpaid teachers? Crowded classrooms? Lack of sufficient parental support? What is the national security problem? Here too the problem is obscure and imprecise, and the answers abound, especially now that the Soviet Union is no longer the threatening hegemony of the Cold War period. The absence of a clear and precise understanding of the nature of societal problems complicates (if not compromises) the process of finding solutions.

The inability to define with precision the nature of societal problems is a condition of several forces, two in particular. One relates to the democratic structure of the American political system. The conflicts that exist over resolving basic societal problems are exacerbated in a democratic society, which recognizes different points of view as credible and legitimate. Democracies institutionalize conflict, bargaining, negotiation, and compromise. Compromise decisions are suboptimal ones.[1] Decision-making by democratic procedures is also inefficient, time-consuming, expensive, and protracted.

A second factor complicating policy-making relates to the constraints on making governmental decisions in both democracies and nondemocracies. Regardless of how a country structures its decision-making apparatus, the process of making policy is complicated by intangibles, unknowns, and uncertainties. To compensate, policymakers seek to bound the uncertainties and intangibles with standard ways of operating, although some degree of spontaneity and innovativeness is sacrificed in the process.[2]

The intangibles, unknowns, and uncertainties that complicate policy-making in the American political system are particularly troublesome in the area of defense policy. There are few certainties in military hardware production but lots of unknowns and intangibles. There are the uncertainties concerning the nature of the military threat now and in the future. Who could have predicted the fall of the Berlin Wall or the dramatic changes brought about by Mikhail Gorbachev's perestroika and glasnost? Which countries are likely to pose the greatest threats in the next ten years? What sorts of threats are there likely to be? What responses are likely to work in a different strategic environment in the post–Cold War era?[3] These are difficult questions to answer, even assuming that a country has the resources requisite to making rational decisions. No country does. There are limits on how much can be spent, how much time can be invested, and how many individuals can be assigned to the task of collecting intelligence information, for example. There are also limits on how much can be known about the international environment for rational decision-making to be credible. Too, there are the uncertainties associated with the application of new scientific principles never before applied to the development of weapons technology. If an MX missile had been launched in retaliation for a Soviet first strike, would it have hit its intended target? No one knows with certainty. What about the technology demanded of Star Wars or Brilliant Pebbles?[4] The scientific community is still divided on the issue of whether space defense is scientifically feasible. How realistic is it to project robotics into future war scenarios? There is no way to know for sure.

In addition to the intangibles associated with threat assessment and technological development, there are the uncertainties that derive from many of the strategic principles that have historically guided our defense policy-making, such as the concept of deterrence. Why did it work? What will work in the future? What exactly was it about the military buildup in the post–World War II period that effectively maintained a balance of power?[5] There are also the uncertainties associated with weapons development. To what extent can the final cost of advanced military hardware be accurately predicted? Is it possible to anticipate the length of time it will take to build and deploy a major weapons system? Ninety percent of advanced weapons systems in the post–World War II period have experienced significant cost overruns, and 85 percent have experienced schedule delays.[6] What are the military consequences of weapons projects consistently encountering schedule delays and cost overruns?

Finally, there are the uncertainties of who will win elections and what prevailing ideological orientations will dictate foreign policy. Why was the United States willing to risk American lives in Somalia and Haiti, while eschewing a similar commitment in Bosnia-Herzegovina until the Clinton administration? Would the fate of the Stealth bomber and the V-22 Osprey aircraft programs be different if George Bush had been re-elected?[7] Would Utah and Nevada be housing MX/MPS if Jimmy Carter had been elected to a second term? Would the Berlin Wall have fallen during a time when Michael Dukakis was president? There are many uncertainties in weapons procurement decision-making, and thus many risks.

The risks parallel the uncertainties. In the absence of certainty in intelligence information, wrongly conceived decisions are risky. It is impossible to accumulate all of the intelligence data requisite to making completely accurate predictions about current and future military threats. Invariably, those who collect and analyze the data carry a bias. President Kennedy's Cuban Missile Crisis decision to invoke a naval blockade rather than bomb newly deployed Soviet missiles in Cuba (1962), President Carter's attempt to rescue American hostages held in Iran (1980), President Reagan's decision to place an American "peace keeping" force in Lebanon (1983–1984), and President Bush's military commitment to force Iraqi leader Saddam Hussein to withdraw from Kuwait (1990–1991) were actions that carried unpredictable consequences. In the first case, Soviet leader Nikita Khrushchev "blinked first," but he resolved never to be vulnerable to American military power again. The hostage rescue was aborted, and 256 Marines were killed in Lebanon. Desert Storm was over quickly, but was it necessary?[8]

It is also impossible to predict with confidence the probable success of new and developing technology. Unqualified optimism is dangerous, especially when it affects the performance capabilities of a weapons system in an actual combat situation. Will a weapon perform as expected? If it does not, what are the risks to the lives of military personnel and, in the case of strategic weapons, to Americans? Consider the poor performance of the first series of M-16 rifles and the F-111 fighter planes used during the Vietnam War, and the revised (critical) evaluative judgments of the Patriot missile and Apache helicopter used in Desert Storm. Were defense analysts aware of the provocative nature and subsequent risks of America's decisions to develop the atomic bomb and the MIRV and to pursue cruise missile technology?[9]

There are also risks associated with the inability to predict how the political winds are likely to blow in any given election year and what effects their direction will have on the administration's defense policy agenda and on Congress's military funding commitments. The Lazarus-like quality of the B-1 bomber and the chameleon-like quality of the MX missile program have been a result of constant changes in political commitments. What if either weapon had been actually needed during the period when they continued to be in various stages of research and development? The uncertainties and subsequent risks of a political leader such as Ronald Reagan reading the political landscape in a threatening manner and engaging in a massive military buildup are well documented. Not even President Reagan could anticipate fully Gorbachev's reactions to his administration's belligerent foreign policy posture. Nor could Gorbachev anticipate the dramatic events in Eastern Europe. What if the reaction of the Soviet Union had been to invade and restore order among the Warsaw Pact nations (as occurred in Czechoslovakia in 1968) rather than to maintain a policy of noninterference? It is also impossible to know how other countries will respond to American actions. More uncertainty, more risks. To understand how and why America builds the weapons it does, then, it is necessary to understand these risks and uncertainties and how they affect the decision-making process.

Approaches to the Study and Explanations of Weapons Decisions

This is a book about how the American government makes the decisions that result in the production and deployment of major weapons of destruction in an environment of uncertainty. Operating on the assumption that every citizen has a right to comprehend and ultimately understand the forces that lead to military hardware decisions, this book seeks to remove the mystery (although not necessarily the intrigue) that has cloaked and, therefore, shielded defense policy from the public for so long. Keeping the military hardware inventory stocked costs the American public close to $80 billion a year (1997), and consumes the time and creative energies of thousands of civilian and military personnel. The people have a right to feel secure and to understand what security costs.

Hundreds of valuable and insightful studies have been published describing and explaining the process by which America acquires military hardware. Some of these studies find explanatory value in the predominant influence of bureaucratic politics or organizational momentum. Thus, weapons decisions are said to reflect efforts by the military services to secure continued funding for programs that reaffirm traditional military roles (organizational survival). Or, alternatively, weapons systems are characterized as compromise decisions that result from the bargaining that is a prerequisite to widespread government support.[10] A few writers assert that the technological imperative sparks and too often distorts the weapons development process.[11] From this perspective, weapons systems are promoted that feature irresistible technological features that are not militarily necessary. Some authors point to the impact of the follow-on imperative or the specter of the military-industrial complex in explaining the deployment of military programs. Thus, it is said that the decision to produce a new weapons system is timed to replace the end of a production cycle at a major defense industry plant. Or, weapons systems are made for basically economic rather than military reasons.[12] Still others are more sanguine about decisions that are the products of the warp and the woof of democratic politics. Hence, the decisions that are made are cogent and direct given the pluralistic nature of the political process.[13] In contrast are those who subscribe to some version of the rational actor or action-reaction theories. For these scholars, weapons systems are conceived as solutions to clearly identified and defined military threats.[14] Thus, weapons development is a rational process of meeting these threats.

The research in this study complements the prolific scholarship on military policy in five important ways. First, rather than focusing exclusively on one dimension of the process, it conceptualizes the process as a complex (multidimensional) and convoluted one. Thus, the book combines an investigation of the technical dimensions (i.e., technological complexities) of a weapons system (such as throw-weight, fire power, and so on), the "politics" of the system, and the strategic value (mission capabilities or doctrinal rationale) of a weapon, toward offering a broader examination of military policy. In so doing, the research builds upon the different levels of analysis completed by students of weapons procurement and attempts to reconcile their varying explanations. Consider, for example, the different levels at which the accounts of the TFX controversy are conducted by Robert Coulam (1977) and Robert Art (1968) and the generally different accounts of the ABM and MIRV procurement when viewed through the lenses of the action-reaction theories versus the bureaucratic politics model.[15]

Second, the study is sensitive to the fact that policy-making is a sequential (although not necessarily unilateral) process and that different theories and explanations may have explanatory value at different stages. Therefore, while strategic factors may have explanatory value at the concept formulation stage (Milestone 0), bureaucratic or political forces may have explanatory value at the production stage (Milestone III). To know that the technological imperative provided the impetus for the atomic bomb or that the follow-on imperative provided the initial impetus for the B-1 bomber and the F-15 fighter plane may be inadequate for understanding their subsequent development.

Third, an attempt is made to measure systematically whether there is a pattern in the relationship between the forces that influence weapons decisions and the quality of the decisions and, therefore, the performance of the weapons systems themselves. It needs to be asked whether it makes a difference which forces and actors are responsible for a particular procurement decision. Are weapons systems that were spawned by the technological imperative less capable or reliable than those that were dictated by a clear military (doctrinal or strategic) need? Do actors responding to bureaucratic and organizational forces tend to contribute to the deployment of weapons systems that are more often found to experience cost overruns and schedule delays? On balance, do legislators who engage in close micromanagement disrupt or improve military decision making and ultimately the quality of weapons systems?

Fourth, rather than selecting and applying one paradigm to one or a related group of national security decisions, this study goes further in its deliberate (but coherent) pluralism in examining the application of a variegated paradigm (three sets of conditions) to several (nineteen) cases of defense decisions (see Table I.1). Moreover, the large number of cases and the variations among them provide a more significant pool of data from which to generalize about procurement matters. Most studies focus narrowly on several cases in one military service or on a smaller set of only highly visible, controversial items. In this study, military projects were selected to represent the three primary services, a variety of organizational arrangements, a spectrum of mission objectives, several weapon types, a time frame spanning the post–World War II period, as well as different levels of technological sophistication, military consensus, and political support. (See Appendix A for a discussion of the cases and how they were selected.)

TABLE I.1

Weapons Systems by Representative Criteria

Criteria		
Name	**Service**	**Type**
Skybolt*	AF	Air-to-Ground Missile
Thor-Jupiter	AF/Army	IRBM
TFX	AF/Navy	Fighter Plane
Polaris	Navy	Submarine
MX	AF	Missile (ICBM) System
B-1	AF	Strategic Bomber
Cheyenne*	Army	Helicopter
C-5A	AF	Transport Plane
M16	Army	Rifle
Trident	Navy	Submarine
Bradley	Army	Armored Personnel Carrier
A-10	AF	Close Air Support Plane
F-16	AF	Fighter Plane
M-1	Army	Tank
Aegis	Navy	Air Defense System
Cruise	AF	Air-Launched Cruise Missile (ALCM)
DIVAD*	Army	Anti-Aircraft Cannon
F/A-18	Navy	Fighter Plane
Skipper	Navy	Air-to-Ground Munition

*Indicates systems that were canceled.

Finally, this study applies the controversial approach of empirical analysis to military politics. For many, any attempt to reduce the complexities and intricacies of weapons procurement matters to quantifiable entities is heresy. But after all, the process itself is quantified. Planes fly, tanks move, and aircraft carriers proceed at designated numerical speeds—not just fast and slow. And performance test results are projected in numerical form—not just excellent, fair, or poor. In further defense of this approach, it is because of the complexities of the weapons acquisition process—complexities that yield the various and sometimes inconsistent analyses—that such an approach is justified. Importantly, empirical analysis is used as a heuristic device, with the policy-making process built up again in subsequent chapters as the information about the case studies is woven into the analysis of how weapons decisions are made.

Every nation seeks the procurement of weapons that can be relied upon to advance cogent and realistic national security needs without jeopardizing other economic and social ones. In the United States, the relationships between military hardware, national security goals, and social and economic policy are in acute flux. The challenges of the 1990s are staggering: redefining military needs in light of changes in the strategic environment, reworking force structure and manpower in light of changes in the economic environment, and reassessing the relative value of social and military needs in light of changes in public attitudes. The future defense of the country depends on how the United States meets these challenges. This book offers a diagnosis of the military procurement challenge, as well as some prescriptions for meeting it.

Organization of the Book

The next chapter considers the dilemma that characterizes the weapons procurement process. In particular, it provides theoretical answers to the questions of why the United States builds the weapons it does, and why these weapons encounter performance problems, schedule delays, and cost overruns. Dissatisfaction with the official or rational explanation for military hardware acquisition has generated three alternative "answers." These explanations suggest that the choice and performance of weapons systems are influenced by (1) the uncertainty and complexity associated with the making of military procurement decisions, (2) the availability of advanced technology, and (3) a political process in which disputes are resolved among actors and agencies in the executive branch and Congress through bargaining and coalition-building.

Chapter 2 considers the role of the president in foreign and defense policy-making and examines two prevailing assumptions in the national security literature. First, there is the explicit assumption that the role of the president in national security policy is paramount, because he has the formal and especially the informal powers to dictate foreign, defense, and even military affairs. Second, there is the implicit assumption that foreign, defense, and military policy are linked in logical and important ways. The president sets foreign policy goals to which the military respond with defense policy and military hardware decisions that the president must approve. Ideally, this relationship promotes a force structure appropriate for meeting the threats to America's security.

The chapter begins with a discussion of the sources of and limitations on the president's national security powers. The issue of whether there is a logical relationship between foreign, defense, and military policy follows. The exact nature of the president's role in these three policy areas is explored more fully, drawing upon an historical examination of how various presidents have employed their powers to actually influence foreign and military policy in the post–World War II period. On the basis of this analysis, several conclusions are derived about presidential influence.

Chapter 3 examines the role of the Pentagon in making military hardware decisions. While defense analysts generally agree that the Pentagon controls military hardware decisions during the preliminary stages of the acquisition process, they are divided over how the Pentagon makes its decisions. Knowing how military decisions are made is essential for understanding the nature of those decisions and the weapons that these decisions produce. Three explanations predominate. One, the rational argument, describes decision-making as a judicious process that responds to well-defined military threats and produces weapons systems with the capabilities to meet these threats. The pragmatic and political explanations for weapons procurement challenge the underlying assumptions of the rational argument, presenting instead a view of military decision-making that is beset by risks and uncertainties and driven by organizational, bureaucratic, and political forces.

The chapter presents a testing of these contrasting explanations. It begins with a brief overview of how decisions are made in the Pentagon from the rational perspective. It then moves to an elaboration of the theoretical critique that the pragmatic and political arguments provide. In an effort to determine the validity of the three sets of explanations, the basic assumptions on which the analytical approaches diverge are tested empirically. Data are drawn from the nineteen cases in this study. The chapter concludes with a consideration of past and current reform efforts to inform the issue of whether the pattern of military policy-making described in this chapter will be appropriate in the post–Cold War period.

Chapter 4 considers the role of the scientific community in the decisions to build and deploy major weapons. Two theoretical positions prevail on the role of science and technology in military policy-making. The first or extreme position is a reaction to the assumption of the rational perspective that military forces are predictive in hardware decisions. Instead, technology is posited as determinant both as the initial impetus for weapons procurement and as the primary force driving the design and performance requirements of military hardware. According to this position, technology is a force impervious to political control, causing the production of unnecessary weapons whose only advantage is their technical sophistication. The second or moderate position responds to the rational claim that the military decision-making process is a sequential, objective search for the best weapon capable of responding to a military threat. Instead, technical considerations must compete with military and bureaucratic claims when weapons decisions are made. Weapons specialists too must compromise in order to attract allies from within the Pentagon and Congress to build a coalition in support of their preferred weapons ideas. From this perspective, technology is important but not determinant. The consequences for the performance of weapons systems can be either positive or negative. While the performance of some weapons has been literally compromised, other systems have benefited from the spur to innovation that competition, bargaining, and negotiation promote, contributing to the most sophisticated military arsenal in the world.

In this chapter, both positions are first analyzed theoretically, and then tested empirically relying upon the data provided in the nineteen case studies of weapons acquisition decisions. A concluding section considers the future role of technology in military hardware development.

Chapter 5 considers the role of Congress in weapons procurement decisions. The chapter first examines the nature of congressional powers to establish the parameters of potential legislative influence. Congress's actual role in military procurement matters is then assessed, drawing upon past studies, a set of interviews in the Pentagon and on Capitol Hill, and data collected on the nineteen weapons acquisition cases. This same data source is used to determine whether the legislative involvement that is manifest means influence over military hardware decisions. The normative implications of the findings are then considered particularly as the discussion informs the debate between advocates of the rational and political perspectives over the value of legislative involvement in national security matters. The chapter concludes with a consideration of the future role of Congress in light of the end of the Cold War and institutional changes that the Republican Party leadership have forecast.

In an effort to complete the picture of the decision-making process for military hardware decisions, chapter 6 assesses the role of the public. The chapter begins with an elaboration of the theoretical debate over the role of the public in the making of defense and foreign policy. Advocates of the Guardianship Principle contend that it is in the public interest (and more rational) for decisions on technical matters, such as the choice of military hardware, to be made by an elite group of military experts; the public is neither interested nor informed enough to contribute productively to the defense policy debate. Advocates of the Equality Principle counter with the claim that a policy-making process that confines decision-making to an elite violates the principles upon which democracy stands. The two theoretical positions are then tested empirically by examining the data gathered on the nineteen weapons acquisition cases in this study and by comparing decision-making in the United States with that in the late Soviet Union.

A concluding chapter brings together the different perspectives about how weapons decisions are made and why some weapons encounter problems. A preliminary effort is made to link in a logical and systematic manner the various causes and consequences of military hardware conception and development. The relevance of the study's findings are assessed in light of the dramatic changes in international relations that have occurred since the late 1980s. Of particular concern is the extent to which the United States, given past and current patterns of military policy-making, is equipped to make the force posture and structure decisions requisite to meeting the challenges of the post–Cold War era. Brief case histories (entitled "Highlights") of the weapons systems analyzed in this study are located throughout the book to illustrate the main points of the chapters.

Notes

1. See Deborah A. Stone, *Policy Paradox and Political Reason* (Glenview, Ill.: Scott, Foresman and Co., 1988), for a different argument.
2. See John Steinbrunner, *The Cybernetic Theory of Decision* (Princeton: Princeton University Press, 1974). Also see Matthew Evangelista, *Innovation and the Arms Race* (Ithaca: Cornell University Press, 1988).
3. Donald M. Snow addresses these questions in *National Security: Defense Policy for a New International Order* (New York: St. Martin's Press, 1995).
4. A key component of President Reagan's defense policy was a system called Star Wars that could intercept ballistic missiles targeted for the United States. President Bush down-scaled the program and renamed it "Brilliant Pebbles." Production funds for space-based defense were canceled during the first two years of the Clinton administration. The fiscal 1996 defense authorization bill includes funds for a national missile defense system. For a useful discussion see Donald B. Baucom, *The Origins of SDI, 1944–1983* (Lawrence: University Press of Kansas, 1992).
5. See John Lewis Gaddis, *How Relevant Was American Strategy in Winning the Cold War?* (Carlisle Barracks, Pa.: Strategic Studies Institute, 1992).
6. Norman Augustine cited in David C. Jones, in *National Security Affairs: Theoretical Perspectives and Contemporary Issues*, eds. B. Thomas Trout and James E. Harf (New Brunswick, N.J.: Transaction Books, 1982), 279. Also see Michael E. Brown, *Flying Blind: The Politics of the U.S. Strategic Bomber Program* (Ithaca: Cornell University Press, 1992), 14–15.

7. The Stealth (B-2) bomber is the latest in a series of strategic bombers produced by the United States. The V-22 Osprey aircraft is a weapon designed for use by the Marine Corps that can convert from a helicopter to a fixed wing plane, thus combining the advantages of both types of aircraft. Both weapons programs became controversial during the 1980s, the B-2 bomber for strategic, technical, and fiscal reasons, the Osprey for strategic and political reasons. President Bush supported the B-2 bomber and opposed the V-22, only to have his positions reversed by Congress, which cut production funds for Stealth and restored them for Osprey. President Clinton cut production funds for the B-2, and the House of Representatives restored them. Both Congress and President Clinton support Osprey.

8. For more information on these foreign policy crises see Roger Hilsman, *The Politics of Policy Making in Defense and Foreign Affairs: Conceptual Models and Bureaucratic Politics* (Englewood Cliffs, N.J.: Prentice-Hall, 1993).

9. The development of nuclear weapons has raised a number of ethical and moral issues that continue to divide the academic and lay communities alike. One such issue concerns the moral implications of the United States being the first country to successfully test and use the atomic (or fission) bomb, and that country's success in sustaining the lead in subsequent thermonuclear developments such as MIRV and cruise missile technology.

10. Morton Halperin, *Bureaucratic Politics and Foreign Policy* (Washington, D.C.: The Brookings Institution, 1974); Graham Allison, *Essence of Decision: Explaining the Cuban Missile Crisis* (Boston: Little, Brown, 1971).

11. Ralph Lapp, *Arms Beyond Doubt: The Tyranny of Weapons Technology* (New York: Cowles, 1970); Herbert F. York, *Race to Oblivion: A Participant's Guide to the Arms Race* (New York: Simon and Schuster, 1970); Solly Zuckerman, *Nuclear Illusion and Reality* (New York: Viking, 1982); and Marek Thee, "Science-Based Military Technology As a Driving Force Behind the Arms Race," in *Arms Races: Technological and Political Dynamics*, eds. Nils Petter Gleditsch and Olav Jnolstad (London: Sage, 1990).

12. James R. Kurth, "The Military-Industrial Complex Revisited," in *American Defense Annual*, ed. Joseph Kruzel (Lexington, Mass.: D.C. Heath, 1989); Steven Rosen, ed. *Testing the Theory of the Military-Industrial Complex* (Lexington, Mass.: Lexington Books, 1973); Mary Kaldor, "The Weapons Succession Process," *World Politics* 38 (July 1986).

13. Samuel P. Huntington, *The Common Defense: Strategic Programs in National Politics* (New York: Columbia University Press, 1961). Also see Daniel Wirls, *Buildup: The Politics of Defense in the Reagan Era* (Ithaca: Cornell University Press, 1992).

14. Kenneth N. Waltz, *Theory of International Politics* (Reading, Mass.: Addison-Wesley, 1979); George W. Rathjens, "The Dynamics of the Arms Race," in *Progress in Arms Control?* eds. Bruce M. Russett and Bruce G. Blair (San Francisco: Freeman, 1979); Barry R. Posen, *The Sources of Military Doctrine* (Ithaca: Cornell University Press, 1984); Richard Rosecrance, "Reply to Waltz," *International Organization* 36 (Summer 1982): 682–685.

15. Rathjens, *Dynamics of the Arms Race;* Graham Allison and Frederic Morris, "Armaments and Arms Control: Exploring the Determinants of Military Weapons," in *Arms, Defense Policy, and Arms Control*, eds. Franklin A. Long and George W. Rathjens (New York: W.W. Norton, 1976); Halperin, *Bureaucratic Politics;* Ronald L. Tammen, *MIRV and the Arms Race: An Interpretation of Defense Strategy* (New York: Praeger, 1973).

HIGHLIGHT

Polaris
A Case of Rational Decision Making

Toward the end of the Eisenhower administration, the first Polaris nuclear submarine was successfully launched—on time, at cost, and with a performance record that demonstrated its capacity to do what it was originally designed to do. Several factors account for the success of this program, the absence of one of which might have bound Polaris in the web of constraints that has plagued military hardware development and compromised weapons systems since that time. Foremost, the program benefited from policy decisiveness, that is, agreement on the need for a new weapon to bolster America's strategic retaliatory force, challenged by Soviet development of an ICBM. The disagreement that transpired among and within the services was not over the need for an invulnerable retaliatory strike, but over the best way to accomplish it. Even the philosophical debate over whether to embrace the "minimum" or "finite" deterrence posture failed to weaken enthusiasm for a nuclear submarine that was viewed as less vulnerable and more flexible than strategic bombers. In addition, the concept of a nuclear triad effectively neutralized the opposition to a Navy program from the Air Force, thus removing quite early one potentially bothersome hurdle to deployment. Both Eisenhower (massive retaliation) and Kennedy (counterforce policy and flexible response) found the Polaris eminently suited to advancing their respective foreign and defense policy goals and strategies. In short, the Polaris was conceived to meet a well-defined and widely accepted military need.

Polaris was also the beneficiary of the fortuitous development of the needed technology during its procurement life, management autonomy, unparalleled resource opportunities, widespread support, and limited opposition. Despite the technical risks and uncertainties raised by the need to integrate a number of component subsystems in the Polaris, the requisite technology emerged. Moreover, the placement of the Polaris program in the Special Projects Office (an independent office in the Navy) accorded managers considerable autonomy, enhanced by the innovative decision to set flexible rather than rigid performance goals and options to accommodate any changes and modifications that might need to be made during the program's acquisition life. Finally, advocates of Polaris were able to effectively neutralize potential opposition. Once the Navy overcame its initial resistance to Polaris (for technical and organizational reasons), there were no "scathing congressional investigations," "hostile" newspaper accounts, or "incriminating" GAO reports. In short, the development of Polaris is a textbook case of successful weapons procurement.

Primary Sources: James Barr and William E. Howard, *Polaris!* (New York: Harcourt, Brace, 1960); Harvey M. Sapolsky, *The Polaris System Development: Bureaucratic and Programmatic Success in Government* (Cambridge: Harvard University Press); J.J. Dicerto, *Missile Base Beneath the Sea: The Story of Polaris* (New York: St. Martin's Press, 1967).

Weapons Under Fire

CHAPTER 1

Explaining the Military Procurement Process

Every nation must contend with potential and real threats to its territorial integrity and make decisions about how to defend itself. The defense decisions that the nuclear nations make are particularly ominous since they invariably result in the production or purchase of massive weapons of destruction. The military hardware decisions that are made also raise fundamental questions about the wise investment of scarce public resources that might have been applied to solving social and economic problems, the risks that accrue to those who use and those against whom the weapons are intended for use, and the moral dilemma of holding the world suspended in a web of nuclear proliferation. One can only hope that such profound decisions be made in a truly rational manner. In America they are not.

The process that the United States relies upon to make the decisions to build and deploy major weapons systems is not a rational one, if "rational" is defined as the sequential, objective search for the most legitimate response to a viable national security concern in the strategic arena. The uncertain environment within which military hardware decisions are made, the irresistible lure of advanced technology, and the democratic nature of the American political process make rational decision-making difficult if not unacceptable.[1]

Inevitably, the outputs of this process are not rational either, although they may be "good, worthwhile, or desirable."[2] The weapons systems that are built are not necessarily the most appropriate responses to foreign policy challenges. Rather, they are compromise decisions. In most cases, the United States manufactures and deploys weapons capable of performing a certain mission or of meeting a security need or threat, but weapons that are nonetheless flawed. In some cases weapons are produced that are unnecessary given that their performance capabilities are redundant with other systems, or even obsolete (such as the B-1 bomber).[3] In other cases weapons have performance capabilities that are either excessive or insufficient for meeting national security needs, meaning that some mission requirements (such as deterrence) are overmet, while others (such as air lift) go unmet.[4]

This chapter considers the dilemma that characterizes the weapons procurement process. In particular, it provides theoretical answers to the questions of why the United States builds the weapons it does, and why these weapons encounter performance problems, schedule delays, and cost overruns. Dissatisfaction with the official or rational explanation for military hardware acquisition has generated three alternative "answers."[5] These alternative explanations suggest that the choice and performance of weapons systems are influenced by (1) the uncertainty and complexity associated with the making of military procurement decisions, (2) the irresistible lure of advanced technology, and (3) a political process in which disputes are resolved among actors and agencies in the executive branch and Congress through bargaining and coalition-building.

If Not Rational, Then What?

In 1988 the General Accounting Office (GAO) reported to Congress that since 1960, the Department of Defense (DoD) routinely "has had to deal with the problems of cost growth, schedule slippage, and performance shortfalls in the acquisition of major weapons systems. . . ."[6] In 1995, GAO concluded that the Pentagon was still engaging in "wasteful practices" that resulted in "many new weapons systems cost[ing] more and do[ing] less than anticipated and experienc[ing] schedule delays. Moreover, the need for some of these costly weapons, particularly since the collapse of the Soviet Union, is questionable."[7] Defense contractor Norman Augustine found that "over the last thirty years our major weapons systems have met performance goals 70 percent of the time, but have met schedules only 15 percent of the time and cost estimates only 10 percent of the time, even after accounting for inflation."[8] Evidence from the Rand Corporation documents a similar pattern.[9]

The data in this study also evince a pattern in the post–World War II period of performance problems, schedule delays, and cost overruns in the development and deployment of military hardware. (See Table 1.1 for a summary.) Of the nineteen cases studied, just over half (53 percent) were classified as meeting their performance goals (at their initial operational capacity [IOC] date) and 47 percent as failing to meet these goals. (Of the latter, a third of the systems were eventually canceled.) In addition, close to 60 percent of the weapons encountered serious cost overruns and schedule delays.

TABLE 1.1

Weapons Systems by Performance Criteria

	Criteria		
Name	**Performance Problems** y/n	**Cost Overruns** y/n	**Schedule Delays** y/n
Skybolt	yes	yes	yes
Thor-Jupiter	yes	yes	yes
TFX	yes	yes	yes
Polaris	no	no	no
MX	no	no	no
B-1	yes	no	no
Cheyenne	yes	yes	yes
C-5A	yes	yes	yes
M16	yes	no	yes
Trident	no	yes	yes
Bradley	yes	yes	yes
A-10	no	no	no
F-16	no	yes	no
M-1	no	yes	yes
Aegis	no	no	yes
Cruise	no	no	no
DIVAD	yes	yes	yes
F/A-18	no	yes	no
Skipper	no	no	no

What is it about the weapons acquisition process that causes weapons programs to encounter schedule delays, cost overruns, and performance problems? The answers abound. Most commonly, studies by de-

fense analysts find explanatory value in the predominant influence of bureaucratic politics or organizational momentum. The second-most-cited
explanation for military procurement decisions is a strategic one. A less
common, but no less convincing, set of studies points either to the impact
of the follow-on or to the technological imperative on the development
of weapons systems. Finally, there are those students of military policy-
making who subscribe to a political model.

Rather than reiterating and then testing the core assumptions of each
conceptual framework, the discussion that follows draws upon the diverse literature to fashion three cogent and comprehensive perspectives on weapons development and performance. Each perspective is
grounded in a different set of conditions (pragmatic, technical, or political) upon which its view of military policy-making is constructed.

Each argument is a reaction to the rational perspective traditionally used
to explain defense policy behavior. The rational argument, formalized in balance-of-power theory, action-reaction models, and game theory, finds explanatory value in military need, which is the impetus for the development of
military hardware. Weapons systems, then, are rational answers to military or
national security problems. The government rationally calculates the threats
to the security of the country and formulates strategies to meet these threats.
The weapons systems developed are then logical extensions of this process.
Each weapon can trace its origin to a military need. Obviously, the rational
argument is inaccurate; otherwise, weapons would be completed and deployed on time, at cost, and able to perform their mission or meet the threat
that originally justified their conception. But what accounts for the absence
of rationalism in the making of weapons decisions?

Pragmatic Argument

The answer from the pragmatic perspective is that rational decision-making, even in the military policy area, is impossible to execute. As a result,
despite considerable efforts to regulate the decision-making process for
procuring major weapons,[10] the process remains flawed. The procedural
flaws cause flawed decision-making and, therefore, the deployment of
some marginally useful systems.

Rational decision-making is compromised for three reasons. First,
the making of military policy, particularly strategic forecasting and intelligence estimating, is uncertain and difficult. Strategists and analysts are
unable to understand fully the strategic environment and the exact nature of a military threat that is anticipated but may never arise. Since

weapons take from five to fifteen years to be deployed and can be in inventory for as many as twenty (in some cases thirty) years,[11] military planners must anticipate a threat well in advance. In some cases, a weapon may be conceived to serve an anticipated defense need, but by the time the weapon is produced, the need is no longer pressing. Understandably, defense strategists and military analysts are inclined to err on the side of the worst-case scenario and to try to meet several possible military threats to compensate for strategic uncertainties. This approach can result in a weapon being assigned excessive, unrealistic, or ambiguous performance expectations. The additional capabilities are garnered at great expense, causing the weapon to encounter cost overruns.[12]

A classic example is the thirty-year development of the B-1 bomber.[13] Originally conceived during the 1960s as a high-speed, high-altitude manned strategic bomber replacement for the B-52, the B-1 was canceled by the Carter administration during the 1970s in lieu of the "more cost-effective" air-launched cruise missiles.[14] It was revived by the Reagan administration, redesigned for low-level flight, and renamed the B-1B. As late as 1988, the Congressional Budget Office (CBO) was questioning the ability of the B-1B to penetrate Soviet airspace and deliver nuclear weapons as part of a second strike-force.[15] Today, its anticipated use is as an aircraft capable of carrying conventional weapons, including cruise missiles. Even before its original strategic mission was invalidated by the breakup of the Soviet Union and the Warsaw Pact, persistent changes in its design and mission stretched out production, causing many of the bomber's capabilities to be unnecessary in light of the development of the B-2 (Stealth) bomber. The price of the B-1 bomber has increased 290 percent during its development life.[16]

A second reason the military decision-making process is not rational is that defense planners and military strategists professionally cannot ignore nonmilitary concerns in making weapons decisions. In too many cases of weapons procurement decisions, organizational survival is at stake. It is impossible to separate out the competition that goes on concerning weapons decisions among the military services over budget, promotion, approval, and power. In most cases sufficient intra-agency socialization has convinced military and nonmilitary actors alike that what will benefit their stature is also most in the public interest. The public interest may be compromised in the process, as the competition is resolved in mutual concessions that submerge these fundamental disagreements. The results can be redundant weapons systems such as the Navy's D-5 (Trident II) and the Air Force's MX missiles, both of which provide the same

improvements in ballistic missile accuracy and increases in yield or payload. The Trident II and MX alike were developed as missiles with multiple, independently targetable reentry vehicles (MIRVs), with the same
hard-target kill capability to make them more effective in attacking hardened targets such as Soviet Intercontinental Ballistic Missile (ICBM) silos.
Several unsuccessful efforts were made during the 1970s to encourage the
two services to collaborate in designing and developing their missiles.[17]
During the Clinton administration, the MX missile system was canceled
as superfluous, although the D-5 missiles were retained.[18]

A third condition hindering rational decision-making is that people
disagree about both the need for and uses of military hardware. Weapons
may be instruments or tools to secure defense and military policy goals and
objectives, but strategists and defense planners hold differing opinions on
the value and nature of these goals and objectives. Inevitably, weapons decisions reflect these differences. For example, much of the governmental controversy associated with the MX missile system, Trident II missile, Bradley
personnel carrier, M-1 tank, and Stealth bomber, to name a few, stemmed
from disagreements over the missions assigned to and capabilities of each
weapon. Informing these disagreements were differences of opinion on
fundamental national security issues such as what was perceived as necessary to sustain deterrence and the nature of a warfighting doctrine.[19]

The most fundamental differences in the post–World War II period
occurred over Soviet intentions and the best way to meet the Soviet
threat. The controversy over the hard-target capabilities of the MX and
Trident II missiles once again is illustrative. Advocates of improved ballistic missile accuracy consistently argued that a hard-target or counterforce
capability was necessary to retain essential equivalence with Soviet forces
and thus deter a Soviet strike. The Soviets would be deterred by the
knowledge that the United States could accurately target and effectively
destroy Soviet ICBMs and military support facilities. Moreover, the Soviets would be forced to divert funds for improving the offensive capabilities of their weapons to improving their defensive capabilities, if the
United States had a hard-target capability, thus ultimately reducing the
Soviet threat to American ICBMs.

Opponents countered with the charge that ballistic missile improvements would encourage the Soviets to strike first in a crisis situation and,
therefore, were destabilizing. According to this argument, since the increased accuracy and yield achieved in the MX and Trident missiles were
greater than what the opponents perceived to be demanded by a retaliatory
(second strike) force, the increased capabilities were unnecessary unless the

United States planned to launch a first strike against Soviet forces, contrary to official policy. Knowing this, the Soviets might be more tempted to launch their ICBMs on warning of attack, thus increasing the chances that a nuclear war would be linked to human error or computer malfunction.[20]

Once again, the United States is engaged in a major evaluation of its strategic and military policies in light of changes in Russia and Eastern Europe and in response to the Persian Gulf War. More than at any time since the end of World War II, the United States is confronted with the challenge of fashioning a consensus on how to define and respond to national security threats in a newly complex and changing global environment. It is not surprising, therefore, that the defense community is divided over what security contingencies to prepare for and which weapons systems will promote America's national security objectives. An example is the controversy over the Pentagon's QDR (May 1997). According to the pragmatic argument, resolving these differences, together with the uncertain, turbulent, and uncontrollable nature of foreign affairs, will compromise the search for an optimal force structure.

In sum, the pragmatic argument is an attempt to explain the absence of rationalism in a situation of uncertainty and limited resources. It assumes that defense planners and analysts are well-intentioned individuals who are motivated by military concerns but compelled to compromise given the constraints on rational decision-making. It suggests that the international system and America's security and status determine military hardware decisions. However, there is a fundamental absence of consensus on where the threats in the international system lie and what is necessary to sustain America's security and status. There are also limits to what can be known about America's position in the world, today and in the future. Moreover, there are conflicting demands on policymakers, which allow nonmilitary concerns to enter into the formulation of foreign and defense policy. These conditions make rational decision-making impossible. Bargaining and negotiation substitute, resulting in compromise decisions that support some marginally useful weapons systems. Too, the process of resolving basic disagreements over the military threats and the methods to meet them is time consuming and ultimately expensive, contributing to schedule delays and cost overruns.

Technical Argument

The second argument explains the weapons procurement process in terms of the technical dimension of military hardware development.[21]

The role of technology in weapons procurement is twofold: it can either provide the original impetus for the procurement of a military project (technological determinism) or it can influence the subsequent development of weapons conceived for military or political reasons (technological influence).

In the first instance, technology can substitute for military need as the original impetus for the conception of a weapons system. In all such cases, the weapons are new ones, rather than upgrades of existing programs or follow-on systems. In notable cases, such as radar and, less clearly, the atomic bomb, the consequences are said to have been laudable ones. In other cases, where the principal stimulus to innovation has come from either the industrial or the research and development communities, the excitement of using new technology has influenced the production of military hardware with performance capabilities that are greater than those necessary to realize a military mission. According to Colin Gray, "the interstate adversary can always be invoked to dignify and provide some rationale for a research programme that scientists wish to carry out anyway."[22] Such systems, characterized as being gold plated, are expensive to build and maintain, exacerbating the problem of cost overruns. This approach also increases the likelihood that while the completed weapon may perform as expected, some of its capabilities, while nice to have, would not necessarily be decisive in a combat situation.

The decision to develop MIRVs is cited by several defense analysts to illustrate the influence of technology on weapons development. According to one study, the scientists and technicians who conceived MIRV in 1962 were working without the guidance of a specific mission requirement or strategic doctrine.[23] Dr. John Foster, director of defense research and engineering from 1965 to 1973, asserts that the initial decision to develop MIRVs was made by weapons scientists and the military services in the absence of evidence of a Soviet ABM threat.[24] Once invented, MIRV was successfully "sold" to the Department of Defense.[25] Only later were the prevailing strategic doctrines of counterforce and assured destruction used to rationalize MIRV to actors outside the scientific community. While "the simple desire to bring to fruition an interesting and elegant technological concept" was only one of several forces producing the MIRV decision, it was the technical aspects of MIRV that proved to be the most provocative to the Soviets, who also developed MIRV technology and then deployed it on their "heavy" SS-18 missiles, giving them a "theoretical" first-strike capability against American ICBMs.[26] According to Matthew Evangelista, the "supporters of the U.S. MIRV . . . appear not to have thought through the [destabilizing] consequences" of Soviet MIRV development,[27] a "precarious" situation that possibly could have been avoided by including MIRV in the SALT I talks.[28]

The second instance, in which technology, rather than being the original impetus, is a contributing force to the development of major weapons systems, is more common, but no less potentially disruptive. It is particularly disruptive in cases where the technology is highly advanced, as is true of the majority of major weapons systems in the American force structure. The lure of advanced technology can be decisive at any of the several formal review stages of military hardware development referred to as the Milestone Review Process. Technology can prove significant when a system's military requirements or performance parameters are being set, a prototype is being tested, a system is undergoing full-scale develop-ment, or a weapon is being produced. The perceived cozy relationship among decisionmakers in the scientific, industrial, and military commu-nities has led some scholars to the conclusion that a military-industrial complex is operating in the defense policy area.

The effects of technology are not necessarily only negative. The tech-nological sophistication of American weaponry did provide for a mostly theoretical but decided military advantage over the late Soviet Union dur-ing the period of the Cold War. Advanced technology is also cited as a cru-cial factor in explaining the efficiency with which the Americans and their allies won the war against Iraq in Desert Storm and in accounting for the low casualty rate on the allied side. Computer technology (robotics, digi-tized battlegrounds, and information warfare) is being celebrated as a way for the United States to maintain its superior global military stature.

On the other hand, America's obsession with technological advances has been a costly endeavor, purchased at the expense of nonmilitary needs. Too, a number of weapons currently in the force structure are con-sidered gold-plated ones, their missions capable of being performed by larger numbers of less sophisticated systems.[29] Pierre Sprey compares nine expensive weapons systems in the U.S. inventory during the 1980s against cheaper alternatives in support of the argument that "expensive, complex weapons are generally [less] effective" than cheaper alternatives in larger numbers.[30]

Highly complex and technically sophisticated weapons systems also tend to be more difficult to operate, and they break down more often, con-tributing to reliability and maintainability problems, a relationship exem-plified by tactical aircraft.[31] In the "consolidated guidance" for the 1981 budget, Defense Secretary Harold Brown identified the growing complexity

of tactical aircraft as a major factor "in an increasing difficulty in maintaining the combat readiness of our air crews and their equipment."[32] Brown
also released a chart documenting a significant inverse relationship between weapon complexity and system reliability. Norman Augustine has
found that as a general rule, "the last ten percent of performance sought
generates one-third of the cost and two-thirds of the problems."[33]

It is also the case that the high costs that advanced technology ex-
tracts limit the number of weapons that can be purchased, jeopardizing
the performance of the weapons as part of a total system. The MX missile
and B-1 bomber projects encountered considerable cost overruns that
were influential (although not necessarily determinant) in Congress's decisions to fund a number of units at a level well below the amount requested by the military. In the case of MX, Congress agreed to fund a
quarter of what President Carter requested and only half of what President Reagan asked for. The question is whether the United States had
enough MX missiles and B-1 bombers to sustain essential equivalence
with the Soviet Union in the period of the Cold War. In short, advanced
technology is a liability at several stages and levels.

Technology can also influence procurement at the requirements
stage. In some cases the performance requirements (or parameters) delineated by the planners and strategists demand new technology so challenging that the development of such systems is uncertain. One oft-cited
example is the Strategic Defense Initiative (SDI). For forty years, the
United States has been working on developing a viable missile defense
system. What has sustained this program (canceled by Clinton but revived in 1996 by Congress), despite concerns that the technical challenges
were insurmountable, were the strategic advantages of the threat of missile defense in negotiations with the Soviet Union and "the technological
spin-offs" that space-based defensive systems promised.[34]

The risks that uncertain technological development raise are obvious. The most serious situations are those in which military strategy depends upon the development of a weapon that then fails to materialize
because the technological challenges are too great. DIVAD (Division Air
Defense gun) illustrates this problem. The technical challenge posed by
the DIVAD gun was not in the development of new technology but in the
technological challenge of integrating a number of tried and tested components. (Importantly, the same challenge plagued the B-1B program.)
DIVAD was conceived during the 1970s as a response to the threat posed
by advanced, low-flying Soviet attack aircraft and helicopters to American soldiers in combat. "[Soviet] aircraft would be coming in and deliver-

ing guns, gunfire, napalm, rockets, or, the helicopters might be standing off and delivering antitank precision munitions."[35] DIVAD was designed to track and destroy Soviet aircraft in order to provide the requisite anti-aircraft protection for frontline tanks and troops while in battle. The weapon was canceled in 1985, after a series of tests proved it unworkable, at a time when the principal antiaircraft mobile gun, the Vulcan, was considered to be obsolete.[36] In other words, if the United States had been engaged in an actual combat situation with the Soviets or their allies, American tanks and troops would have been highly vulnerable.

Advanced technology may also be a problem during the testing stage of the procurement process. The most complex systems are the least susceptible to "live" tests. Therefore, the uncertainties associated with innovative technology are exacerbated. In addition, for both important and trivial reasons, as scientific and technical discoveries are made, weapons systems in various stages of development and production are modified to accommodate the most recent technological advances. In some cases, such as the M-1A1 tank, the improvements have been important ones.[37] In other cases, the "improvements" have been achieved at the expense of other capabilities (as in the case of the F-16) or have endowed a weapon with military capabilities that are not worth their cost, that is, have caused a weapon to be gold plated. The Bradley personnel carrier and the F-15 fighter plane illustrate the latter phenomenon.

Advocates of the technology argument are particularly vindicated by current advances in computer technology, robotics, and virtual reality that threaten to change not only the nature of America's force structure but the manner in which war is waged. Encountering the enemy on a digitized battlefield without actually being there (with robotics, laser-guided smart weapons, backpack computers, and high-tech rifles that shoot around corners) and immobilizing the enemy by injecting a virus into the aggressor's computerized telephone system are examples given of the tail wagging the dog. The biggest threat is the vulnerability of the United States to cyberattacks from errant Third World nations that purchase the technology cheaply, essentially leveling the playing field. The United States is particularly susceptible to computer viruses that are intended to disrupt the communications network that binds a nation. Instead of an arms race, the United States may find itself engaged in a computer technology race with uncertain, but potentially devastating, consequences.

In sum, the technical argument makes several predictions about military decision-making and the attendant problems of cost overruns, performance difficulties, and schedule delays. Foremost, it predicts that weapons decisions will be made in line with the needs of technicians and the interests of weapons scientists. An ancillary assumption is that weapons scientists work closely with a military service and a defense industry in promoting the application of technical breakthroughs. The impact of technology can be found at any one of the several stages of weapons procurement, from conception to production. Technology can provide the original impetus for innovative systems, or it can lead to significant modifications of systems already in the inventory (upgrades). Moreover, technology can have negative or positive effects on the development of major weapons systems. Negative effects include the problems associated with weapons systems for which there is no preexisting military need, and those that arise in highly advanced and ambitious weapons systems, such as performance failures, cost overruns, and schedule delays. Positive effects of advances in technology include the production of some highly innovative and ultimately indispensable weapons that have contributed to the military strength and stature of the United States.[38] In the future, advances in technology (such as the introduction of robotics in the field) are expected to make military combat more efficient, reduce the risks of war, and, in the case of "information warfare," even preempt actual combat.

Political Argument

The third argument suggests that the primary impetus for weapons development is neither military nor technical but political. Behind each weapon is a group of legislators responding to constituent demands, bureaucrats seeking to perpetuate their organization, executive officers reacting to governmental pressures, and defense contractors struggling for economic survival. Democracy credits all of these groups with a role in making public policy. Unfortunately, each group's needs cannot be met by the same set of military policies. Moreover, conflict is not confined to groups in different sectors of the government and defense industry. Defense companies compete for contracts; the military services compete for funding to support preferred weapons systems; the Joint Chiefs of Staff (JCS) and the Office of the Secretary of Defense (OSD) compete over which set of military priorities will prevail; the secretary of defense and the president's national security advisor compete over which assessment of the international environment will be compelling; legislators from various states differ on the value of military spending; and the Defense Department competes with other national governmental units for funds to support their programs. Conflict and competition are inevitable. In a democracy, conflict is mediated through certain norms, rules, and procedures. Most important is the norm of coalition-building, which requires groups to make concessions and seek compromise in order to build a winning (working) majority.

The democratic nature of the American policy-making process institutionalizes conflict, bargaining, and compromise. It also recognizes as valid the pull of nonmilitary forces on political actors in military policy-making. Legislators are required to run for public office, bureaucrats are required to secure adequate budgets to maintain their credibility, defense industrialists are required to secure a profit for the company and its stockholders, and the president's personal advisors are required to serve their employer. In practice this means that no set of actors can afford to ignore the pull of nonmilitary forces. In fact, it is sometimes more rational (and, therefore, the incentives are greater) for some actors to act contrary to military forces when professional survival is at stake.

For practical reasons, then, the process by which America makes its weapons decisions is best described as a series of compromise decisions engendered by the multitude of individual and organizational actors operating at various stages of the procurement process, and at different levels and in various arenas of government. Since weapons acquisition in the United States is a developmental or sequential process, decision-making is cumulative. Preliminary decisions concerning the military need for and design features of a particular weapons system must be confirmed by subsequent sets of actors as the process builds toward a congressional funding decision. Advocates of this argument often employ the term "momentum" to describe the support or opposition that builds for or against a weapons system as it progresses through the stages of the acquisition process to ultimate deployment in the field.

The consequences of making military policy politically are compromise decisions. Some compromise decisions produce highly workable weapons, benefiting as they have from the checks and balances, accountability, and fragmentation and decentralization of governmental power that are the hallmarks of American democracy. In such cases, the political process works in its intended way. Preliminary errors of judgment are corrected by subsequent actors whose cumulative insights serve to continuously improve the quality of military hardware. A notable example is the M-1 tank.

During its twenty-year development, the M-1 Abrams tank has been plagued by allegations of poor reliability and maintainability, high development costs, and excessive fuel consumption from a variety of

sources, including military, legislative, and public ones. As a result, the
tank has undergone extensive testing at various stages of development
from prototype to "current product-improved future variations, in vir-
tually all earthly environments from arctic to desert. . . ."[39] Consequently, most of the problems discovered in the early prototype stage
have been corrected, according to supporters.[40] The military and some
senior staff personnel in Congress now assert that the Abrams tank
meets or exceeds all of its combat performance specifications except
track life.[41] In short, the main army tank has evolved from a much-ma-
ligned to a highly praised weapons system. The Pentagon touts the M-
1A1's main gun and targeting system. The M-1, IPM-1, and the M-1A1
have all won the Canadian Army Trophy international gunnery competition. Data from the Gulf War indicate that the M-1A1's main weapon
performed well at long ranges and that improvements in crew protection were effective in minimizing death in action.[42] While critics (most
notably the GAO and the Project on Government Procurement) continue to find fault with the M-1, they readily admit that the tank has
made "achievements in the areas of crew protection, accuracy and le-
thality. . . ."[43] Recent military testimony before Congress rebuts much
of the initial optimism about the performance of American military
hardware in the Persian Gulf, without invalidating the vastly improved
condition of the Army's main battle tank, especially the M-1A1 series.
In sum, the tank has benefited from the input of various actors during
its development life.

The democratic process can also produce compromise decisions that
result in weapons systems with capabilities that are redundant, obsolete,
excessive, or insufficient for meeting national security needs. In some extreme cases, the process produces weapons with performance expectations that are only vaguely related to military need but are expected to
garner support.[44] In an effort to gain the organizational, executive, and
congressional support necessary to put a weapons systems into production, advocates sometimes package the project in a way that anticipates
both support and opposition. In these cases the compromises reached
during the coalition-building process have been made at the expense of
the quality of the weapon itself.

A classic example is the Bradley personnel carrier/fighting vehicle, a
weapon that is "all things to all people."[45] The Bradley (also called the
M-2) was conceived in 1964 as an "austere" replacement for the M-113
personnel carrier. It developed into a complex motorized infantry combat vehicle (MICV), featuring components advanced by various agen-

cies and actors whose support was requisite for program approval. Its firing ports, cannon, and antitank guided munitions (ATGMs) were promoted by systems analysts in the OSD. The M-2's TOW (tube-launched, optically tracked, wire-guided) antitank missiles were touted by armor officers, the House Armed Services Committee (HASC), and Defense Secretary James R. Schlesinger. General William DePuy raised the concern that the addition of TOW missiles would "add an unacceptable amount of weight to a vehicle which already exceeded the . . . limit."[46] The infantry branch queried whether an MICV with TOW would "require complete reorganization of the infantry force structure," since there would be room for only seven instead of nine crew members.[47] According to one study, the Bradley's mission to deliver troops to the forward area of the battlefield and go fast enough to keep up with the M-1 tank put the vehicle in a position unsuitable for performing its other mission of firing antitank weapons.[48]

Bargaining, negotiation, and compromise are most likely to take place in cases where the policy-making process involves a large number of actors whose interests conflict and who each has a stake in the decision to build a particular weapon. In such cases, the incentives to be actively and aggressively involved are considerable. The most common situations are those in which a military hardware decision is likely to produce a redistribution of power among or within the military services (such as the Antiballistic Missile [ABM]), affect large numbers of congressional constituents (such as the MX missile system), be unacceptably costly (such as the MBT 70), or have been politicized by some controversy surrounding its research and development (such as DIVAD).

The political controversy over the MX missile system has been unprecedented in its scope and intensity. The MX program has enlisted the involvement of more actors and agencies over a twenty-year period than any other weapons system in America's procurement history.[49] In addition to the formal actors traditionally involved (such as the Air Force and other agencies in DoD, weapons scientists and technicians, defense contractors and subcontractors, and military experts in Congress), the MX provoked the participation of individuals and organizations outside the defense policy-making apparatus. These included citizens' groups opposed to deployment of MX/MPS in their states for environmental, religious, cultural, economic, social, and strategic reasons (Utah, Nevada, Kansas, Nebraska); the Mormon Church, which effectively mobilized members in Utah and Nevada; and legislators and senior officials in the Ford and Carter administrations formerly uninvolved and uninterested in defense policy but who found the MX destabilizing, dangerous, and unnecessarily expensive.[50]

Advocates of the political argument recognize the difficulty of separating out military and nonmilitary motivations, since in most cases those involved in the defense process achieve a compatibility between the two. For example, the services defend as militarily indispensable weapons that are essential to their traditional missions, despite considerable controversy concerning the future military utility of heavy armored forces (Army), manned strategic bombers (Air Force), and aircraft carriers (Navy). During the Cold War, the services also justified the pursuit of gold-plated weapons systems as militarily necessary to match the quantitative superiority of the Soviets and to compensate for a fixed force structure. Members of Congress defend as militarily essential systems that will benefit their constituents, such as the Marine Corps's Osprey V-22 plane and the Navy's F-14. Industrialists rationalize the practices of underestimating costs (the buy-in phenomenon) and overestimating capabilities in order to secure a contract competitively. The phenomenon of invoking military need to justify nonmilitary benefits is institutionalized by the structure of the defense system, which rewards and thus encourages devotion to organizational, institutional, and professional norms.

The effect of having so many participants with varied incentives seeking specific capabilities involved in the defense process is that too many sets of interests must be met by a single weapons system. The constant need to engage in consensus-building and to garner political support can result in the production of hybrid, compromise, or consensus projects that invariably are neither the best nor the most appropriate solution to a particular military problem. This argument is used in part to explain the factors that produced an overly large and powerful (albeit quite workable) Trident submarine and that have kept the B-1 bomber program alive.[51] The Bradley personnel carrier has been cited as a good example of what "consensus-building during the requirements process" can do, which in this case has meant loading "too many capabilities into the same system [resulting in the] vehicle's strange combination of capabilities."[52] In too many cases, a policy commitment is made not because "it is in fact the most rational means for achieving an agreed-upon objective or . . . in the true national interest, but rather [because] enough of the people and organizations having a stake in the policy and holding power agree to [it]."[53]

Adherents to this position do not contend that every time a large number of advocates rally around a weapons system, it is bound to succeed politically but fail technically and strategically. They do not suggest that the origin of every weapons system can be traced to selfish motivations or that nonmilitary actors inevitably have an adverse influence on the procurement process. They do, however, maintain that the performance of a weapons system is likely to be affected by the number, status, and position of individuals with an interest in the project.

In sum, the political argument makes several predictions about military decision-making and the attendant problems of cost overruns, performance difficulties, and schedule delays. Foremost, it predicts that weapons decisions will be made for political reasons. In essence, the weapons acquisition process is a political one composed of several different sets of actors all motivated by different forces. Such a process results in conflict, which is worked out by compromise. Compromise results in hybrid weapons. The broader the scope of participation, the greater the degree of conflict over a weapons system, the more likely it becomes that the completed weapon will encounter performance problems, schedule delays, and cost overruns.

In the chapters that follow, the explanatory power of the three arguments will be tested. How effectively does each perspective explain how the United States decides military procurement issues and why major weapons systems encounter problems? What does each explanation tell us? What do they overlook? Is one explanation sufficiently rich to "explain" the weapons acquisition process, or do we need a variety of perspectives applied at different stages of the process? How well do the three explanations link the process to the outputs of the system, weapons decisions? Does one approach explain cost overruns, another performance failures?

In an effort to answer these questions, the procurement process is broken up into components that reflect the sources of conflict among the three explanations. More precisely, the rational, pragmatic, and political perspectives diverge in their views on the nature of the roles of the president and his advisors, the Pentagon, Congress, and the public in procurement matters. The rational and technical perspectives diverge in their views on the nature of the role of technology in military politics. In the evaluation that follows, the different perspectives are used as heuristics to glean insights that can be applied toward constructing a preliminary theory of weapons decision-making.

Notes

1. Deborah A. Stone, *Policy Paradox and Political Reason* (Glenview, Ill.: Scott, Foresman and Co., 1988).

2. Ibid., 8.

3. A recent example is the B-1 bomber, whose strategic mission was replaced with a conventional one with the development of the B-2 (Stealth) bomber and the elimination of the Soviet threat. The Clinton administration then canceled further production of the Stealth in light of the absence of a real future mission. In the FY 1996 DoD budget, Congress appropriated additional funding for the bomber program, despite opposition from the Pentagon.

4. Stephen Van Evera and Barry R. Posen, "Reagan Administration Defense Policy: Departure from Containment," *International Security* 8 (1983): 3–45. For example, despite the expansion of America's air- and sea-lift capabilities during the 1980s, it still took several months to transport the necessary material, personnel, and military hardware to the Persian Gulf during Operation Desert Shield. It is unlikely that future antagonists will be as patient as Saddam Hussein.

5. The definition of rational decision-making used in this chapter combines elements of the realist or balance-of-power theories and the rational-actor model. Exponents of the realist or balance-of-power explanation assert that foreign and defense policy decisions (including procurement ones) are externally determined by the nature of international politics and the character of the international system. Applied to weapons decisions, this generalization suggests that policymakers initiate military hardware projects that are legitimate responses to actual or potential national security concerns in the strategic arena, such as the appearance or projected development of a new weapon in an adversary's military arsenal. Exponents of the rational-actor model assert that the *process* that is relied upon to make policy decisions is a rational one, which is to say, a process in which "individuals consciously formulate goals, gather information about alternative means to achieve them, evaluate the alternatives, and choose the ones most likely to succeed." Stone, *Policy Paradox*, 249. This explanation describes the internal dynamics of decision-making. The first perspective explains why weapons systems originate; the second explains why they have certain operational qualities. Together the two perspectives suggest that weapons decisions are fully researched, fully debated, and fully analyzed responses to clearly defined, clearly identified, and viable threats in the international environment. For a more complete discussion of these various models see the discussion in Michael E. Brown, *Flying Blind: The Politics of the U.S. Strategic Bomber Program* (Ithaca: Cornell University Press, 1992), 4–6, and the discussion in Stone, *Policy Paradox*, especially 249–264.

6. U.S. General Accounting Office, *Major Acquisitions: Summary of Recurring Problems and Systemic Issues: 1960–1987* (Washington, D.C.: Government Printing Office, GAO/ NSIAD-88-135BR, September 1988).

7. U.S. General Accounting Office, *Defense Weapons Systems Acquisition* (Washington, D.C.: Government Printing Office, HR-95-4, February 1995).

8. Norman Augustine, currently CEO of Martin Marietta, a major defense manufacturer, quoted in David C. Jones, in *National Security Affairs: Theoretical Perspectives and Contemporary Issues*, eds., B. Thomas Trout and James E. Harf (New Brunswick, N.J.: Transaction Books, 1982).

9. See Robert Perry et al., *System Acquisition Strategies* (Santa Monica, Calif.: Rand Corporation Report, R-733-PR/ARPA, June 1971), v, 1–11; Edmund Dews et al., *Acquisition Policy Effectiveness* (Santa Monica, Calif: Rand Corporation Report, R-2516-DR&E, October 1979), 27; Michael Rich and Edmund Dews, *Improving the Military Acquisition Process: Lessons from Rand Research* (Santa Monica, Calif: Rand Corporation, R-3373-AF/RC, February 1986); and Jeffrey A. Drezner and Giles K. Smith, *An Analysis of Weapon System Acquisition Schedules* (Santa Monica, Calif: Rand Corporation, R-3937-ACQ, December 1990). For a general overview see Brown, *Flying Blind*, 15.

10. Rationalize means (a) to effect a match between foreign policy (or political) goals, force structure, and military strategy (war plans), in the most cost-effective manner possible, and (b) to facilitate the selection of weapons systems with capabilities that can perform missions that are developed in response to military threats. The planning, programming, and budgeting system, the milestone review process, and the defense budget process are examples.

11. Brown, Flying *Blind*, 5.

12. Center for Strategic and International Studies, *U.S. Defense Acquisition: A Process in Trouble* (Washington, D.C.: Georgetown University, 1987).

13. Nick Kotz, *Wild Blue Yonder: Money, Politics, and the B-1 Bomber* (New York: Pantheon Books, 1988), 115 f; James Fallows, *National Defense* (New York: Random House, 1981), 168 f; Brown, *Flying Blind.*.

14. Quoted in "Carter Blocks Production of B-1," *Aviation Week and Space Technology*, 4 July 1977, 14–16.

15. U.S. Congressional Budget Office, *The B-1B Bomber and Options for Enhancements* (Washington, D.C.: Government Printing Office, #Y 10.2:B 63, August 1988).

16. Greg Williams, *Weapons Unit Costs.* (Washington, D.C.: Project on Government Procurement, 11 June 1990). Also, GAO/ NSIAD-95-151, 18 July 1995.

17. Richard Burt, "Sea-and-Land Missile Sought by Pentagon," *New York Times*, 24 April 1978, A11.

18. See Les Aspin, *The Bottom-Up Review: Forces for a New Era* (Washington, D.C.: Department of Defense, 1 September 1993).

19. James H. Dixon et al., *National Security Policy Formulation: Institutions, Processes, and Issues* (New York: University Press of America, 1984); David C. Hendrickson, "American Strategy: Past and Future," 1–36; and Scott D. Sagan, "Change and Continuity in U.S. Nuclear Strategy," in *America's Defense*, ed. Michael Mandelbaum (New York: Holmes and Meier, 1989), 279–317.

20. Jonathan E. Medalia, *Trident Program* (Washington, D.C.: Congressional Research Service, #IB73001, 11 June 1987). Also see Colin S. Gray, *Weapons Don't Make War: Policy, Strategy, and Military Technology* (Lawrence, Kans.: University Press of Kansas, 1993).

21. Herbert F. York, *Race to Oblivion: Participant's Guide to the Arms Race* (New York: Simon and Schuster, 1970); Marek Thee, "Science-Based Military Technology As a Driving Force Behind the Arms Race," in *Arms Races: Technological and Political Dynamics*, eds. Nils Petter Gleditsch and Olav Jnolstad (London: Sage, 1990).

22. Colin Gray, *The Soviet-American Arms Race* (Westmead, England: Saxon House; Lexington, Mass.: Lexington Books, 1976).

23. Scilla McLean et al., *How Nuclear Weapons Decisions Are Made* (New York: St. Martin's Press, 1986), 78.

24. Dr. John Foster Jr. was director of defense research and engineering from 1965 to 1973. See Lapp, *Arms Beyond Doubt*, 81; Graham Allison and Frederic Morris, "Armaments and Arms Control: Exploring the Determinants of Military Weapons," in *Arms, Defense Policy, and Arms Control,* eds. Franklin A. Long and George W. Rathjens (New York: W.W. Norton, 1976); Morton Halperin, *Bureaucratic Politics and Foreign Policy* (Washington, D.C.: The Brookings Institution, 1974); Ronald L. Tammen, *MIRV and the Arms Race: An Interpretation of Defense Strategy* (New York: Praeger, 1973).

25. Ibid.

26. Rathjens, *Dynamics of the Arms Race*, 37; Matthew Evangelista, *Innovation and the Arms Race: How the United States and the Soviet Union Develop New Military Technologies* (Ithaca: Cornell University Press, 1988), 8.

27. Evangelista, op cit., 8.

28. McLean, *How Nuclear Weapons Decisions Are Made*, 82.

29. According to McNaugher, while the debate over which weapons are gold-plated ones is indeterminate, "the developmental patterns [associated with major weapons development] suggest that the nation's acquisition process systematically errs in the direction of gold plating weapons." Thomas L. McNaugher, *New Weapons Old Politics* (Washington, D.C.: The Brookings Institution, 1989), 132.

30. Systems compared include the M-60A1/M-1; Oerlikon 35–mm/DIVAD, F-16A/F-15 A/C; and A-10/F-15E. (The first weapon is the cheaper alternative; the second is the more expensive one that the U.S. elected to buy.) It should be noted that Sprey measures effectiveness relying upon "actual combat and field test evidence," rather than "mechanistic computer models of combat" or "technological promises." Pierre Sprey, "The Case for Better and Cheaper Weapons," in *The Defense Reform Debate: Issues and Analysis*, eds., Asa A. Clark IV, et al. (Baltimore: The Johns Hopkins University Press, 1984), 193, 197.

31. Harold Brown, cited in the *International Social Science Journal* (May 1980): 29.

32. Harold Brown, quoted in Richard A. Stubbing, *The Defense Game: An Insider Explores the Astonishing Realities of America's Defense Establishment* (New York: Harper and Row, 1986), 154.

33. Norman Augustine, *Augustine's Laws* (New York: American Institute of Aeronautics and Astronautics, 1982), 41. Also, McNaugher, *New Weapons Old Politics*, 6–10.

34. Baucom, *The Origins of SDI,* 198.

35. Major General James P. Maloney, U.S. Army, *20/20, ABC NEWS*, transcript, 13 December 1984.

36. Ibid.

37. Materials provided by Public Affairs Office, AMSTA-CT, Art Volpe, U.S. Army Tank Automotive Command (TACOM), for *Army Magazine* (October 1990).

38. B.R. Inman and Daniel F. Burton Jr., "Technology and U.S. National Security," in *Rethinking America's Security: Beyond Cold War to New World Order*, eds. Graham Allison and Gregory F. Treverton (New York: W.W. Norton, 1992), 117–135.

39. TACOM, information sheet, n.d.

40. See, for example, the comments of Representative Melvin Price (D-Ill.), *Congressional Record* (23 June 1982), 3904–3905.

41. Personal interviews.

42. It should be noted that the M-1A1 and the M-1 continue to come under criticism. The GAO continues to express concerns regarding the tank's survivability, affordability, performance capabilities, and general effectiveness. The Project on Government Procurement provides evidence that the M-1 continues to be plagued by maintainability and fuel efficiency problems.

43. Greg Williams, *Issue Paper, M-1 Abrams Tank Performance in Desert Storm* (Washington, D.C.: Project on Government Procurement, 17 June 1991), 5. GAO/NSIAD-90-57, 28 February 1990.

44. Kotz, *Wild Blue Yonder;* Franklin C. Spinney, *Defense Facts of Life: The Plans/ Reality Mismatch* (Boulder, Colo.: Westview Press, 1985); Fen Osler Hampson, *Unguided Weapons: How America Buys Its Weapons* (New York: W.W. Norton, 1989).

45. McNaugher, *New Weapons Old Politics*, 129.

46. Quoted in Daniel J. Kaufman, *Organizations, Technology, and Weapons Acquisition: The Development of the Infantry Fighting Vehicle*, Ph.D. dissertation. (Cambridge, Mass.: Massachusetts Institute of Technology, May 1983), 319.

47. Ibid., 259.

48. McNaugher, *New Weapons, Old Politics*, 130.

49. Lauren H. Holland and Robert A. Hoover, *The MX Decision: A New Direction in U.S. Weapons Procurement Policy?* (Boulder, Colo.: Westview Press, 1985).

50. Ibid.

51. The argument is not that these systems are unworkable, but that they have capabilities that are unnecessary for performing the assigned mission or military task.

52. McNaugher, *New Weapons Old Politics.*

53. Roger Hilsman, *The Politics of Policy Making in Defense and Foreign Affairs: Conceptual Models and Bureaucratic Politics* (Englewood Cliffs, N.J.: Prentice-Hall, 1993), 72.

CHAPTER 2

Charting Military Policy

The View from the Presidency

A core assumption of the rational explanation for military hardware decisions is that national security needs dictate or, at a minimum, guide military strategy. For both legal and practical reasons, the people look to the president to identify, articulate, and/or validate what is necessary to insure America's national security.[1] The military, economic, and diplomatic threats to America's integrity, for which the use of weapons is threatened or employed, become, then, the impetus for military hardware development. The logic of this relationship is quite simple. The president sets foreign policy goals to which the military respond with defense policy and strategy and military hardware decisions that the president must approve. Ideally, this relationship promotes a force structure appropriate for meeting threats to America's security.[2]

This chapter considers the accuracy of the rational explanation from the perspective of the presidency, guided by the theoretical insights of the pragmatic, technical, and political arguments. The chapter begins with a discussion of the sources of and limitations on the president's national security powers. Of particular concern are the practical and organizational constraints on presidential authority. The issue of the nature of the relationship between foreign, defense, and military policy and strategy follows. Next, the actual role of the president in these three policy areas is explored more fully, drawing upon an historical examination of how various presidents have employed their powers to actually influence foreign and military policy and strategy in the post–World War II period. The objective of this analysis is to determine the extent to which presidential *involvement* in foreign and defense policy-making generally has allowed president's to *influence* weapons acquisition decisions, and the nature of this influence. The argument is not that presidents are or should be involved in the decisions to start weapons research and development efforts or in the decisions about performance requirements or technological attributes. But neither should weapons decisions be made irrespective of presidential oversight. In fact, it is presidential direction that can lend coherence to military policy and legitimacy to weapons decisions. In other words, presidential involvement should be significant enough to maintain a reasonable linkage between America's foreign and defense policy objectives and the lethal means available to meet these objectives. Without this linkage, there is an unacceptable disconnection between military hardware and commitments.

Nature of the President's Powers

Although the Founders created a constitutional system in which making foreign policy would be a shared (legislative-executive) endeavor, presidents have dominated the process in the post–World War II period. The president derives much of his authority to decide issues of foreign and national security policy, including questions of military hardware, from the U.S. Constitution. Additional sources of presidential influence in foreign and national security affairs are legislative mandates, federal court decisions, and the unique institutional position of the president in the executive branch.

Constitutionally, the president has the power to supervise and manage wars, negotiate treaties, enter into diplomatic relations with foreign countries, appoint executive officials, veto legislation, and make sure that the laws are faithfully executed. Practically, his superior access to information, extensive staff, exposure to the mass media, organizational acuity, and singular authority contribute additional power. With the Budget and Accounting Act of 1921, Congress gave the president crucial budgetary powers (including priority-setting and managerial responsibilities) that have contributed to presidential dominance during the preliminary stages. Through their control over the executive budget, presidents can shape national security policy. Despite statutory efforts during the 1970s to reverse a legislative pattern of deference to the president in the formulation and conduct of national security and foreign policy, Congress has been reluctant to make full use of its newly acquired defense powers.[3] (The role of Congress in national security and defense policy will be discussed more fully in chapter 5.) The federal courts have been broad in their interpretation of the president's foreign and national security powers.[4] The American public views the president as "the most legitimate actor in the making of foreign policy."[5] In short, the president is recognized as having both the authority and the responsibility for the "structure" of the armed forces and the national security system, a "coherent" national security policy, and an "effective" defense establishment.[6]

President Harry Truman once observed that the scope and breadth of an American president's national security powers were so great as to "have made Caesar, Genghis Khan, or Napoleon bite his nails with envy."[7] But as President Truman found out while in office, making effective use of presidential powers means battling institutional, political, and legal constraints. Foremost, the president cannot act alone. The enormity of the task, the convoluted nature of the American policy-making process, the system of checks and balances, and the additional demands on his time mean that the president must rely upon a network of advisors in deciding national security policy. The president sits at the head of a national security system whose members are charged with advising him as to the nature of the military threats to the United States and its vital interests and the means available for responding to them. The president's willingness to guide, coordinate, and supervise the decision-making process is what gives national security policy its coherence. Key actors include the national security advisor (ANSA), defense secretary, secretary of state, chairman of the Joint Chiefs of Staff (CJCS), and additional members of the National Security Council (NSC) and its staff.[8] The president also relies upon the advice of the Office of Management and Budget (OMB) (formerly the Bureau of the Budget) in formulating the defense budget; depends on the Senate to ratify treaties and approve presidential appointments; and looks to Congress generally to "declare" wars, fund programs, and act upon his recommendations.

So dependent have some presidents become on their personal advisors that questions have been raised about the extent of presidential influence on foreign policy and national security matters. The Iran-Contra affair is a recent example. One author has suggested that, while the president is recognized as having a "central position" in the making of national security policy, "in practical terms [he] becomes as much the object of the bureaucratic political process as its controller."[9] This situation is particularly evident in cases where bureaucrats have their own agenda. President Kennedy's order to the State Department to begin negotiations for the removal of Jupiter missiles from Turkey prior to the Cuban Missile

Crisis is one example. President Carter's cancellation of production funds for the B-1 bomber program is another. Even Congress and the American public, when sufficiently mobilized, can thwart the president's efforts in national security policy, as evidenced by the multifaceted and subsequently ill-fated MX missile system.

In military policy, the mismatch between the life cycle of a weapons systems (five to fifteen years) and a president's term of office (four to eight years) can further limit presidential discretion. Presidents inherit weapons systems in various stages of development. Even modifications of existing weapons exceed the average tenure of a modern president. Presidential influence is further constrained by the lengthy periods of time involved in both the defense budget planning process and the weapons procurement process. A presidential term begins in January, at which time both processes are well advanced. Planning for the defense budget begins in October and takes twenty-one months, culminating with a congressional defense appropriations bill in late spring or summer. (Chapter 3 includes a complete discussion of both processes.) Thus, presidents inherit both weapons systems and military budgets.

Whether the technology to make the requisite modifications is available is another issue with which presidents must contend. Moreover, one president's priorities may be preempted by another whose foreign policy goals differ. Modifications in national security objectives must adjust to the realities of this force structure, rather than the reverse. The Carter administration tried to alter U.S. maritime policy from a navy configured primarily for power projection to one configured for sea control, but was limited by decisions made in the 1950s and 1960s, which led to a navy with twelve aircraft carriers.

Many scholars have argued that a president's success in controlling the foreign and national security policy network (and the strategies and policies, including weapons, they inherit) is contingent upon the effectiveness of his organizational powers and the quality of his appointments.[10] A president acquires control over the process and, therefore, policy by selecting the key players, establishing the rules of the game, organizing the decision-making system, setting the public agenda, and even (as Moe argues) politicizing the bureaucracy.[11] In this way, the president positions himself in the center of a policy-making network that funnels information and ultimate decisional power to him. By being the "ultimate coordinator," the president becomes the "ultimate persuader" and "ultimate decider." "The national security process can do no more than bring its product to the threshold of the Oval Office where the president takes over and his personal methods replace those of the bureaucrat."[12] "Coordinating the capabilities represented by [the several] agencies and departments, and bringing them to bear on the several dimensions of the national interests, can be seen as the operational essence of foreign and national security policy-making. Access to and control of these establishments become, therefore, necessary conditions for the successful conduct of foreign and national security policy."[13]

The influence that presidents exercise over military hardware decisions derive from their enormous foreign and defense policy powers. The president can establish the national security objectives that then guide the military in making weapons decisions. Technically, no military project can go into production and deployment without presidential support. At crucial points in a weapon's life cycle, the president can invoke his budgetary powers to insure that his strategic preferences are being met in a piece of military hardware. A president enhances his ability to influence weapons decisions through the control that he exercises over the decision-making process, which, again, can be organized to his advantage. In short, while the president does not always "make" weapons decisions, he can influence them through his control over foreign and defense policy (policy oversight), influence over defense funding decisions (fiscal oversight), and authority over the organization of the decision-making apparatus (administrative oversight).

Forging Linkages Between Foreign, Defense, and Military Policy: The Role of the President

In theory, national security policies and strategies should not only serve the nation's foreign policy goals, but also "provide the basic guidelines and framework for decisions on force levels, programs, and weapons systems and for the development of operational plans for the use of military force."[14] In short, national security policy should be tied logically to both foreign and military policy. Given his prominent role in foreign and defense policy, the president has the power and position to forge the necessary linkages. Through forging these linkages, the president determines the full range of national security policies.

Students of national security policy recognize that presidents do not influence foreign and defense policy equally. Rather, most presidents concentrate their decision-making energies on foreign policy, while deferring defense policy to their national security advisors and analysts in the Pentagon. There is the implicit assumption, however, that even military hardware decisions are ultimately presidential ones, given the logical and important relationships between foreign, defense, and military policy delineated above. The president secures his control through his budgetary and administrative powers. The president is the "ultimate decisionmaker" because "he sets the tone for policy" and "is ultimately responsible for implementing" that policy.[15]

The theoretical discussion of presidential powers in the last section catalogues the potential for presidential influence over military hardware decisions. But what have presidents actually done with their powers, and what have been the consequences for weapons development? Answers can be gleaned from an historical examination of presidential administrations during the period of the Cold War. Of particular concern is whether the foreign and defense policy goals that presidents have established have effectively guided military decision-making; whether presidents have used their funding powers to influence weapons decisions; and whether presidents have been successful in securing the defense policy goals that they have sought.[16]

Foreign and Defense Policy in the Post–World War II Period: An Historical Overview
Truman and Eisenhower (1945–1961)

Truman

A number of presidential administrations in the post–World War II period are credited with significant changes in foreign and defense policy, particularly in matters of strategy and arms control. (Of the range of national security policy decisions that an administration makes, those regarding strategy and arms control are the most closely linked to military hardware decisions.) The Truman administration (1945–1952) authored the Truman Doctrine (1947), which promised economic and even military support to nations resisting communism, and set the tone and foundation for the strategy of containment. Along with its domino-effect corollary conceived during the Eisenhower administration, the objective to contain Communism (containment) provided the guidance for all subsequent foreign and national security decisions in the post–World War II period.[17] During Truman's presidency, the means used to implement containment ranged from economic (Greek-Turkish Aid Program, the

Marshall Plan, and the Berlin airlift 1948) and diplomatic (creation of NATO in 1949) to military (Korean War 1950). Many of these policies directed subsequent military hardware decisions, by specifying the categories of weapons needed (although not the exact type of weapon or precise number of units required). The success of NATO, for example, committing the United States to collective security with its European allies and relying as it did on America's monopoly of nuclear forces as a deterrent to Communist aggression in the region, required a stockpile of nuclear bombs and strategic air forces. NATO also embraced a permanent line of defense in Europe (even in peacetime), dictating a requisite level of American military power. The objective of containing Soviet expansionism also signaled the transition in American foreign policy from isolationism to internationalism (even interventionism), signaling further changes in military investments.[18]

If the question is, Does the president determine national security policy and if so to what extent? then the answer from the Truman administration was, Yes and considerably. By relying upon a "formalistic" management and decision-making system in which the president was positioned at the apex, Truman insured that he would be the "ultimate decider." According to one study, "it was Truman himself who chartered the United States' course during the turbulent, formative years of the Cold War."[19] Truman's penchant for presidential control was enhanced by the passage of the National Security Act of 1947, establishing the Department of Defense (DoD), the Central Intelligence Agency (CIA), and the NSC. Shortly thereafter, the NSC staff began an extensive study (NSC-68) of the military threats to the United States and the capabilities available to meet these threats. NSC-68 provided the basis for the formulation of America's first comprehensive defense policy (New Look) during the Eisenhower administration.

In terms of military hardware policy, Truman was less deliberate. With the exception of the hydrogen bomb, President Truman initially offered little specific guidance on weapons development, thus enhancing military discretion and competition, albeit within the guidelines implicit in containment and related policies that dictated what categories of weapons to build. Without clear guidance as to how containment or deterrence was to be achieved, however, the military services fought over roles, missions, needs, and requirements. Moreover, despite the implicit need for increased military commitments, Truman did not immediately increase defense spending to meet his foreign policy pronouncements. On the contrary, the president imposed tight budget ceilings that had the effect of fueling interservice competition. In sum, while Truman, through his intimate and successful involvement in making national security policy, established the parameters and boundaries of military hardware development, the responsibilities for the conception, research and development, and production of weapons systems devolved to the military services.

Eisenhower

A similar pattern emerged under President Eisenhower, to whom revisionist accounts accord considerable influence over both foreign and defense policy during his administration. While Eisenhower did delegate more authority to his advisors and cabinet members than did Truman, he is credited with a number of important foreign and defense innovations that narrowly circumscribed subordinate decisions, including ones on weapons procurement. Most notable was the New Look at defense policy, which sought to contain Communism through deterring Soviet aggression without compromising America's economic strength. This meant reducing defense spending by prioritizing our commitments. The United States was prepared to use ground forces to protect its vital interests in certain regions, such as Western Europe and Japan, and to provide material assistance and training to nations in other areas resisting Communism where American interests were deemed less vital. At the core of the New Look policy was the nuclear strategy of massive retaliation (which relied on the use of air power) to deter Soviet expansionism beyond the line of containment through the threatened use of American nuclear power "by means and at places of our own choosing." The doctrine of massive retaliation directed that enough nuclear weapons with sufficient capability be built to sustain deterrence. The assumption was that the Communists would be deterred by the knowledge that the United States had the capacity and the willingness to drop nuclear weapons on Moscow or Peking if either Russia or China used conventional force against other countries such as Korea.

The consequences for weapons development were significant. Spending on conventional weapons was reduced, while spending on nuclear weapons (particularly strategic bombers) was increased. Tactical nuclear weapons development was accelerated (the weapons introduced into the European theater), and the targeting precision of nuclear weapons was improved.[20] The precise number of weapons that was "sufficient" and the exact sorts of attacks that would justify massive retaliation were left intentionally unspecified to heighten the risks and thus deter Communist aggression. Nonetheless, 255 Titan and Atlas ICBMs, 540 Minuteman ICBMs, and 19 Polaris submarines were approved during the Eisenhower administration.

Eisenhower provided further ammunition for reductions in procurement funding with his commitment to a one-war capability (something he began to reconsider during his second term). On the other hand, the administration's actions to secure bilateral (with South Korea and Taiwan) and multilateral (SEATO, CENTO) agreements incurred additional funding commitments for diplomatic and economic purposes.

As long as the Americans retained their nuclear monopoly, the strategy of massive retaliation worked, and spending on weapons procurement was curtailed. The Soviets' acquisition of an intercontinental ballistic missile (ICBM) (and, therefore, retaliatory) capability discredited massive retaliation. The likelihood that the United States would risk a nuclear war to protect its vital interests beyond American borders was not credible. To bolster deterrence in light of Soviet missile development, the Eisenhower administration, during its second term, increased support for conventional weapons.

To secure the control over international affairs that he sought, Eisenhower adopted a formalistic management system that insured that he would receive the information, policy options, and analyses requisite to orchestrating the policy stance of his administration.[21] Decision-making became "the exclusive preserve of the president and Secretary of State John Foster Dulles."[22] Policy formulation, implementation, and evaluation, however, were lodged in a highly structured NSC. Eisenhower increased the role of NSC (which operated with a clear chain of command), pushed reforms to advance unified advice from the Joint Chiefs of Staff, and succeeded in acquiring the statutory means to increase the power of the secretary of defense (Defense Reorganization Act of 1958).[23] In sum, Eisenhower did make extensive use of his foreign and defense policy powers, but from a position at the head of a chain of command that progressively narrowed the range of presidential discretion, but not guidance. While advice flowed from bottom to top, decision-making flowed from top to bottom.

Like Truman, Eisenhower's involvement in procurement matters was indirect but nonetheless influential. Although the administration made little use of its funding powers to compel the military services to make specific hardware choices (such as how many or the prescribed capabilities of bombers and tactical weapons), the administration's policies signaled an emphasis on certain categories of weapons systems (first strategic air forces and tactical weapons and then additional conventional ones). The exception was Defense Secretary Neil McElroy who, during his twenty-six months of service, did try to restrict specific weapons programs.[24]

Kennedy and Johnson (1961–1969)

The Kennedy administration, while embracing containment and deterrence, abandoned the New Look and massive retaliation policies. With the Soviet acquisition of nuclear weapons, massive retaliation was seen as provocative and unworkable, confronting the United States with the inconceivable dilemma of "humiliation or all-out nuclear war." Instead, Kennedy sought a flexible response capability that would allow the United States and its allies "to deter or fight at any and all levels, from low-intensity operations to nuclear war. . . ."[25] The objective was to respond to Communist actions on the same terms in which they were executed. Together with the principle of "forward strategy," committing NATO to pushing the Communists as far east as necessary in an actual engagement, "flexible response" constituted a new defense strategy.[26]

The strategy of flexible response was used to justify increases in both conventional and nuclear forces. Flexible response, by moving our commitments away from an exclusively nuclear solution to include conventional military threats as well, justified an inventory of weapons deemed appropriate for any possible military engagement, although the nature of the balance between conventional and nuclear weapons was never made clear. Conventional forces were important to provide the requisite flexibility implicit in the new doctrine, and nuclear forces were important to deter or (as a last resort) meet Communist aggression. This latter objective was formalized in the doctrine of "controlled response" (to reflect McNamara's brief belief that a nuclear war could be controlled and limited) and then "assured destruction" during the Johnson administration (later MAD—Mutually Assured Destruction—when the Soviets achieved nuclear parity, giving them the capacity to meet a retaliatory strike from the United States with a third strike of their own).[27] "Assured destruction" meant that a Soviet first attack should not occur if U.S. fire power were great enough to guarantee retaliation. The doctrine led to the diversification of America's strategic forces into the triad of ICBMs, nuclear submarines, and strategic bombers. Kennedy accelerated and expanded the Polaris submarine program and increased both Minuteman (ICBM) procurement and SAC (Strategic Air Command) ground alert capabilities. (President Johnson continued Kennedy's strategic plans: by 1967, the United States had 1,000 Minutemen ICBMs, 54 Titan silo-based ICBMs, 656 SLBMs on 41 Polaris subs, and about 600 long-range bombers.)[28] The nuclear threshold was raised further by building up American armed forces to be able to fight two (major)-and-one-half (one minor) wars. The Green Berets (Special Forces) were expanded to provide the United States with an unconventional warfare capability, anticipating Kennedy's commitment to introduce American forces more directly into the Third World.[29]

At the same time, however, Kennedy, and then Lyndon Johnson, sought ways to reduce Soviet-American tensions and build a peaceful relationship between the two countries. Under Kennedy, for example, the United States became the primary sponsor of the United Nations.[30] Kennedy was also successful in negotiating the Partial Test Ban Treaty of 1963. In the midst of the Vietnam War, Johnson worked to achieve more cooperative relations with the Soviet Union and to expand political, economic, and cultural ties with Soviet satellites in Eastern Europe. In the aftermath of the Glassboro summit conference (June 1967), a Nuclear Nonproliferation Treaty (1968) was signed by the Soviets, Americans, and fifty-nine other countries.

In addition to making strategic and doctrinal changes, Kennedy supervised the execution of changes in structure and administration. Foremost, the national security policy-making apparatus was restructured. Following the Bay of Pigs, Kennedy relied less on the JCS and the State Department and more on NSC for policy analysis, and turned also to ad hoc groups (such as the ExComm in the Cuban Missile Crisis) for policy formulation.[31] Kennedy's defense secretary, Robert McNamara, reorganized the Pentagon to make it more efficient and responsive to the president. The collegial style of policy-making that Kennedy embraced placed him at the center of a group of loyal advisors, including Secretary of State Dean Rusk, McNamara, and ANSA McGeorge Bundy.[32]

Johnson, who inherited the Kennedy foreign policy team, relied less on NSC and more on small and informal advisory forums such as the "Tuesday lunch," and his personal advisors, particularly his ANSAs, McGeorge Bundy and then W.W. Rostow.[33] Despite Johnson's apparent lack of initial interest and experience in foreign affairs, the president alone selected the course of action from a list of policy options provided by his ANSA and other key advisors.[34] (One infamous example is Johnson's role in selecting bombing sites during the Vietnam War.) Where the collegial style of policy-making worked for Kennedy, it failed for Johnson, whom observers accuse of fostering unanimity through coercion and "other steps designed to maintain a preconceived viewpoint consonant with the president's known inclinations."[35] Unlike Kennedy, who allowed the process of decision-making to unfold before making a policy commitment, Johnson preempted that process with his preconceived opinions. Both men, however, were actively involved in making foreign and defense policy, with varying degrees of success.

Unlike his predecessors, Kennedy made concerted efforts through his defense secretary to direct and dictate (even micromanage) military decisions. Robert McNamara was personally involved in linking weapons decisions with strategy, realigning our strategic forces, and sizing our strategic forces against the Soviet threat. McNamara even translated strategies, such as assured destruction, into actual quantitative goals and evaluated the extent to which individual weapons programs contributed to strategic objectives. Efforts were also made during the Kennedy administration (and later during the Carter administration) to strengthen presidential influence over military matters through budgetary means. McNamara instituted the programming, policy, and budgeting system (PPBS), in part to provide him with an effective way to tie military planning and funding decisions together. McNamara's involvement in weapons acquisition decisions led to the cutting back, canceling, or phasing out of a number of programs, including the Thor and Jupiter ballistic missile programs, the B-70 bomber, and the Skybolt missile.[36] McNamara also tried to bring our conventional forces (which constituted the bulk of annual defense spending) in line with military requirements, but with less success. He mandated a force-structure level for each service, but did not set any funding ceilings. The absence of funding limits allowed the military departments to recommend gold-plated systems, since force structure levels did not dictate performance parameters. The services pursued weapons with varied capabilities that allowed them to stay within the limits of the force structure levels, while at the same time compensating for the reductions in numbers with increases in the quality and accoutrements ("bells and whistles") of military hardware. The MBT-70 tank, Cheyenne helicopter, SAM-D (Patriot) air-defense missile system, F-14 interceptor aircraft, and F-111 and F-15 fighter planes were all begun during the Kennedy administration. Eventually, the tank and helicopter programs were canceled by Congress, the F-111 failed to develop into the biservice plane intended by McNamara, the Navy version (F-111B) was canceled by Congress, the F-14 and F-15 were deployed with capabilities and costs in excess of those originally intended, and the Patriot missile took several years to mature.

Although force structure ceilings were set during the Kennedy administration, the decisions were as much political as military. For example, the decision to cap Minuteman missiles at 1,000 was not made solely on military grounds. One additional incentive was to compensate the Air Force for the cancellation of the B-70 bomber program and the B-52-launched Skybolt missile program. Another was to make the funding request palatable to Congress. Frederick Hartmann and Robert Wendzel also point out that the policy of assured destruction, which was declared by the civilian leadership, and "the actual employment policy of the military more and more went their separate ways. Despite assured destruction, the SIOP (the single integrated operational plan) was essentially unchanged, with counterforce targets, flexible options, controlled responses, and sequential attacks all remaining in it."[37]

Nixon and Ford (1969–1977)

Spurred on by political expediency and domestic turmoil, the Nixon administration achieved far-reaching changes in foreign and national security policy. The administration's successes were due in part to another dramatic restructuring of the national security policy-making apparatus, in particular, the pivotal placement of Henry Kissinger, who dominated foreign policy. By normalizing relations with the People's Republic of China, Nixon and Kissinger were able to shift official policy to the one-and-a-half war strategy, which, of course, immediately diminished the perceived forces/strategy imbalance. With the Nixon Doctrine, which retrenched our foreign commitments (particularly in the Third World) and transferred to our allies more responsibility for their own military security, Nixon was able to bring down defense spending, in line with public sentiments in the aftermath of the Vietnam War.[38] (The armed forces were reduced, and an all-voluntary military service system installed, for example.) While still guided by the need to forestall Soviet expansion, a rhetoric of detente was also preached.[39] Detente sought to prevent military conflict by expanding the linkages between East and West in order to create a sense of a common fate.[40] Detente, which was central to the Nixon Doctrine, also dictated a reduction in nuclear arms and in tensions with the Soviets and signaled recognition that Communist states had legitimate security interests that they had a right to protect (although the containment concept was not totally abandoned).

The administration's commitment to the doctrine of nuclear sufficiency (rather than superiority), in combination with arms control efforts, diminished the frenzied pace of arms competition. By "sufficient," the Nixon administration meant "essential equivalence," an expedient position given the Soviet Union's status of strategic parity and, in some cases, superiority, and irreversible advances in the United States in missile and warhead accuracy. While the Soviets had more and bigger missiles, the Americans had more accurate and reliable missiles. The move to MIRV ballistic missiles, for example, was justified as necessary to counter Soviet numerical superiority in launchers.

The technological advances in missile and warhead accuracy achieved during this time gave new meaning to targeting decisions and reduced the number of multiwarhead rockets needed to execute a devastating nuclear strike. In response, the Nixon administration issued National Security Decision Memorandum 242 with a commitment to a more flexible targeting capability. The United States retained the assured-destruction force requirements forged earlier, including the emphasis on deterrence through an American second-strike capability, and added the limited nuclear options strategy (LNOs) to bolster deterrence by developing ways to meet limited Soviet provocations.

In an effort to formalize and stabilize nuclear parity, the SALT I negotiations were begun in 1969, and the ABM Treaty and the Interim Agreement on Certain Measures with Respect to the Limitation of Strategic Offensive Arms were signed in 1972. SALT I placed limits on delivery vehicles (such as missiles and bombers) and prohibited other actions that would alter the existing military equilibrium between the two nations (such as freezing ICBMs at the 1972 level), but failed to restrict overall nuclear firepower. For Nixon, who subscribed to the principle of realpolitik, arms control was not an ethical goal or an end in itself, but a practical component of an integrated set of foreign and defense policies that sought to promote the national (material) interests of the United States and other nations (including the Soviet Union) through the creation of a stable international order. The purpose of SALT I (like its successor SALT II), for example, was to secure a strategic balance between the Americans and Soviets by preserving the second strike capability of each nation. To secure SALT I, Nixon came to support the Trident submarine and missile system as a bargaining chip in arms control negotiations, although he personally opposed the nuclear submarine program.

The Nixon administration made major contributions in the realm of foreign and defense policy, and credit belongs to the president, who dominated the policy-making process. By elevating and expanding the role of NSC (headed by Kissinger), circumventing the existing foreign policy bureaucracy, and working through interdepartmental groups chaired by Kissinger, Nixon insured that the foreign policy apparatus was responsive to his will. The system was also highly centralized and structured, more so than those of Nixon's predecessors. Importantly, Nixon was able to effect the substantive and organizational changes in foreign affairs without the Cold War consensus that had guided foreign policy in the post–World War II period (but had been shattered by the Vietnam War). The absence of a consensus had both a liberating and politicizing effect on foreign policy. In the absence of a consensus, foreign policy was in flux, and innovative ideas were aired. But politics no longer stopped at the water's edge. President Ford basically kept Nixon's foreign policy team and continued his policies, but abandoned Nixon's heavy-handed style.

During Nixon's first term, the military services were given considerable autonomy to make weapons decisions within set funding ceilings, with little specific guidance from the president or his defense secretary, other than the implicit ones contained in the Nixon Doctrine and related policies. Secretary of Defense Melvin Laird's response to a 1971 systems analysis study's conclusion that our conventional forces actually exceeded our military needs was to increase military requirements, rather than decrease our forces.[41] Nixon's second-term defense secretary, James Schlesinger, was more involved in procurement matters. Because he continued the practice of establishing budgetary ceilings within which the military services could operate independently and autonomously, with only minimal policy direction,[42] Schlesinger's attempts to bring America's strategic arsenal and strategic priorities in line had only minor effects on America's force structure. For example, in his drive to strengthen the conventional capabilities of NATO, Schlesinger failed to establish quantitative goals, leaving that decision to the services.[43] Not unexpectedly, the only major defense program that Nixon canceled was the Air Force's Manned Orbiting Laboratory. (The MBT-70 was eliminated by Congress during Nixon's term.)

Henry Kissinger explains the reluctance of most post–World War II presidents to use their budgetary powers to dictate major weapons systems in the following way.

[While] it may seem strange that a [procurement] decision . . . of such consequence could be made by a department of the government without White House clearance . . . the White House faces a serious decision in determining at what point to intervene in the budgetary process. Our defense budget is larger than the entire expenditures of any European country. In early phases [OMB] can have considerable influence—but only on the gross totals. . . . [The DoD and the military services] are acutely sensitive about what they consider their prerogative in making the initial recommendation about how to divide up approved funds among the services. . . . The White House saw the outlines of the detailed defense program only during the summer before it was put into final form in October. By then the services had made their various trade-offs. . . . The unresolved issues were kept to a minimum and were usually highly technical, satisfying Presidential insistence on having the last word without enabling his staff to undertake a serious strategic review.[44]

Carter (1977–1981)

President Jimmy Carter entered office determined to make foreign policy decisions informed by moral concerns. Carter's emphasis on human rights and nuclear disarmament deviated sharply from traditional U.S. national security policy.[45] As a broad foreign policy objective, Carter sought to build better economic and political relations with both the industrialized and the Third World countries. For Carter, this meant working with the developed countries to solve the problems of global poverty and abuses of human rights in and the economic exploitation of lesser developed countries. Believing that essential equivalence and an approximate strategic balance existed between the United States and the Soviet Union (PRM-10), Carter concentrated his national security policy efforts on achieving a reduction in nuclear forces (through a SALT II agreement) and conventional forces in Europe (through the Mutually Balanced Force Reductions Treaty—MBFR). At the same time, Carter worked to enhance deterrence less by building up our defense capability than by improving existing weapons programs and endorsing a flexible targeting approach called "countervailing strategy," the core of which was "limited nuclear options."[46] According to Carter's defense secretary, Harold Brown, this targeting approach would allow the United States to respond to Soviet aggression "at a level appropriate to the type and scale of a Soviet attack. . . . We must be able to . . . attack, in a selective and measured way, a range of military, industrial, and political control targets, while retaining an assured destruction capacity in reserve." (Presidential Directive [PD] 59)[47] To meet Soviet quantitative superiority and bolster the range of counterforce options that were the essence of the countervailing strategy, Carter approved funding for research, development, and deployment of MX missiles in a mobile basing (MPS) mode, endorsed continued production of the Trident submarine, supported development of air-launched cruise missiles (ALCMs) (in lieu of the B-1 bomber), and renewed interest in a ballistic missile defense system. The president also promoted research efforts to further enhance missile accuracy and strengthen the survivability of our strategic command, control, and communications system (C^3I). In short, Carter immersed himself in the details of the full range of national security decisions from foreign policy to military procurement ones.

Unfortunately for Carter, the Soviets were neither deterred in their foreign actions (Africa, Cuba, Afghanistan) nor restrained in their military buildup. The Soviet invasion of Afghanistan in December 1979 doomed Senate approval of the SALT II treaty, which the Carter administration had successfully negotiated. (SALT II set limits on strategic launchers, including MIRVs, placed restrictions on advances in weapons technology, and established parity in the strategic weapons held by the Americans and Soviets.)[48] Carter reacted to Afghanistan by increasing defense spending, which the American public had previously demanded be reduced. Nor were the Soviets the only military power indifferent to changes in American foreign policy during Carter's reign. Hostilities in the Middle East (such as the taking of American hostages by rebellious Iranians) led the president to issue the Carter Doctrine committing the United States to defend with force the security of the Persian Gulf and its oil (deemed a vital U.S. interest) and thus once again widening the gap between available military forces and foreign policy commitments. The Carter Doctrine, announced in January 1980, shifted the planning strategy of the United States from one-and-one-half wars to one-and-two-half wars. Plans were constructed to provide for the simultaneous occurence of a major war with the Soviet Union and two regional conflicts. To help implement this policy, the Rapid Deployment Force (RDF) was authorized to defend American interests in the Gulf. Additional new policy directives were issued in Presidential Directive 18. Carter's PD 18 has been described by one insider as producing a strategic program that was "long on abstractions and short on specifics."[49] According to Snow, despite Carter's good intentions, in the end his strategic and particularly conventional force policies deviated only slightly from that of his Republican predecessors.[50]

Carter and his successor Ronald Reagan have been sharply criticized for the substance of their foreign policies and the manner in which these policies were conceived, formulated, and implemented, and for selecting foreign policy advisors with limited experience. Crabb and Mulcahy assert that the "widely" held judgment is that the foreign policies of Carter and Reagan were "poorly conceived," "disastrously managed," lacking in "conceptual coherence," and (in some cases) "unnecessarily provocative."[51] The authors begin with the assumption that it is the constitutional responsibility of the president to provide "direction for the nation's foreign policy" and "to adopt a decision-making model appropriate to his . . . style of governance" and conclude that the president is then responsible for the policies that result.[52] From this perspective, Presidents Carter and Reagan are faulted for the excesses of their administrations, Carter for overmanagement and Reagan for undermanagement.

Despite a limited background in foreign affairs, Carter insisted on being involved in the details of policy development, even at the preliminary stages. To insure a broad range of views from his senior advisors (from which he could then make decisions), Carter relied on a collegial model of making foreign policy. What thwarted the success of this model was Carter's failure to lend a "clear sense of vision" or provide guidance sufficient to coordinate the disparate views of his advisors. The result was policy fragmentation and a process unable to respond efficiently to national security challenges.

In the procurement area, the Carter administration tried with limited long-term success to use funding to dictate military hardware decisions. In an effort to increase presidential influence through budgetary means, Harold Brown introduced the annual consolidated guidance document (CG) in 1977 and zero-based budgeting (abandoned in 1981). Brown also strengthened the Office of Systems Analysis within the DoD to give him more control over military matters. Despite management changes in the Pentagon, Carter was unable to prevail. In response to his cancellation of production funds for the B-1, cutting of funds for the F/A-18, and acceleration of funds for the cruise missile program, Congress countered with sufficient appropriations to keep the B-1 in research and development (R&D) until Reagan resurrected the program and restored funds for the Navy fighter plane. Carter also tried to cancel production of the Bradley personnel carrier; delete procurement of the sea-launched cruise missile (SLCM), the nuclear cruiser, and a conventional carrier; cut funding for the FB-111 strategic bomber; delay full-scale development of MX; and terminate the AMST intratheater airlift program.[53] Once again, Congress later restored funds for the Bradley, an aircraft carrier, SLCM, and MX. In the end, Carter was forced to embrace weapons systems (such as MX and Trident) that he opposed, in order to gain support for SALT II, which he later withdrew from Senate consideration. Defense Secretary Harold Brown's efforts to bring service programs more in line with our foreign policy were further complicated by Carter's interests in nuclear disarmament and human rights policies.

Reagan (1981–1989)

Throughout the post–World War II period, until the fall of the Berlin Wall, there was a broad consensus that the Soviet Union constituted the biggest military threat to America's national security. Debate raged, however, over the exact nature of this threat and the best means for meeting it. On these points, Ronald Reagan was unambiguous; the Soviet Union was the "Evil Empire," an entity whose presence was a moral affront to Americans. In dangerously provocative language, Reagan warned of the need to be prepared to fight the Soviets in several theaters (Southwest Asia, NATO, and the Pacific) simultaneously in a global war. Aides spoke of a war-fighting capability that could contain a nuclear exchange. At the same time, the Reagan Doctrine extended the policy of containment to justify efforts to seek and pursue opportunities to roll back Soviet influence. The administration exhibited a renewed willingness to pursue U.S. objectives with military force. For example, increased funding was secured for insurgency groups in Communist countries such as Nicaragua and Angola, and military action was initiated in Grenada. The Reagan administration also sought a shift away from mutually assured destruction to a policy of assured survival. Toward this end, the administration proposed a massive research effort to develop a defense system based in space that would prevent missiles from reaching the United States. The hawkish rhetoric was accompanied by dramatic increases in defense spending, an enormous military buildup, and some important shifts in national security policy (such as the Strategic Defense Initiative (SDI) or Star Wars, the Reagan Doctrine, and the transition from a defensive to an offensive conventional strategy).[54] For the most part, however, the Reagan administration merely expanded or enhanced the importance of programs begun during previous administrations. Examples include moves to upgrade RDF to the Central Command (CENTCOM), promote Special Forces (because of its unconventional warfare role), deploy Pershing II and ground-launched cruise missiles (GLCMs) in Europe, and accelerate Carter's procurement program (consisting of the MX, Trident II D5 missiles, Stealth, ballistic missile and civil defense, and improvements in C^3I), to which Reagan added the (previously canceled) B-1B program.

Fortunately for the administration, the Soviet Union was in no economic condition to keep up with the buildup that Reagan's policies endorsed. Under Mikhail Gorbachev (and his policies of perestroika, glasnost, and "new political thinking" in foreign policy), Soviet-U.S. relations improved. These improvements, coupled with unmanageable budget deficits in America and public perceptions of wasteful military spending (spare parts scandal) and malfeasance (Iran-Contra), led Congress to resist a continued military buildup. "In real terms, defense budget authority actually declined for the next four years, with procurement hit particularly hard."[55] Eventually, Reagan was forced to soften his rhetoric and consider arms control options. Despite a wobbly start, the Reagan administration made considerable progress toward securing strategic and intermediate-range missile agreements first with the Strategic Arms Reductions Talks (START) and then the Intermediate Range Nuclear Forces (INF) talks. The INF treaty was ratified in 1988, requiring the withdrawal and destruction of all nuclear missiles with intermediate ranges (300–3,400 miles).

Even with the overarching global view and clear (albeit broad) set of ideological goals that President Reagan articulated, foreign policy-making was fragmented and in "drift and disarray" for a number of reasons. Foremost was Reagan's policy-making style. Reagan preferred to make policy decisions by merely endorsing a consensus already reached among his key advisors. Otherwise, the president was "detached and uninvolved" in the process. Without supervision from the president, there was nothing but broad platitudes to guide policymakers. Reagan's advisors were often divided over major foreign and defense policy issues ranging from the Middle East to relations with the Soviets. While the secretary of state and secretary of defense were embroiled in a power struggle, the NSC was conducting national security policy independently (Iran-Contra). According to Carter's ANSA, Zbigniew Brzezinski, Reagan's failure to impose "a systematic top-down decision-making system either on the executive branch as a whole or on his associates" resulted in a decision-making process that "at the very top [was] institutionally more fragmented than at any point since World War II."[56]

In addition to broad grants of authority, Reagan also appears to have delegated responsibility, a situation that prompted the Tower Commission to fault the president for "major deficiencies" in his "management style."[57] Contributing further to drift in policy-making was the fact that Reagan's advisors were inexperienced and poorly informed, and the internal operating procedures of his bureaucracy, especially within the NSC (which was expected to coordinate foreign policy-making), were "poorly defined and loosely supervised." Amazingly, despite all of this, Reagan was able to achieve a remarkable level of foreign policy coherence in the end, primarily because his key policymakers already shared a "common world view,"[58] and his policy agenda was "simple, straightforward," and "readily explicable to the public."[59]

Reagan had a profound effect on the rate and size of military procurement. Under his "guidance," military spending increased for all categories of conventional and strategic forces. A clear and precise rationale for these increases and the implications for military hardware development were absent, however. In fact, the Reagan administration has been accused of embracing strategic concepts so broad or demanding (such as horizontal escalation) that they could be used to support almost any new weapons program, which is exactly what happened.[60] In testimony before Congress on the fiscal year 1986 budget, Defense Secretary Casper Weinberger stated in the annual report that "America's most basic national security objective is to preserve the United States as a free nation at peace, with its fundamental institutions and values intact."[61] The strategy was described foremost as intended to "deter aggression" and, second, if deterrence fails, to "seek the earliest termination of conflict on terms favorable" to the United States and its allies. (The national security objectives and defense strategy of the United States are contained in the annual report that the defense secretary submits to Congress for funding.) Conveniently, the point at which these objectives were fulfilled could not be calibrated. The difficulty in quantifying America's basic national security objectives, in combination with the visions of global war, account for the administration's failure to close the forces/strategy gap, despite a plethora of procurement activity. The administration devolved power to the services to make weapons decisions within certain funding ceilings and then provided unequivocal support, resulting in monies for the development of SDI, a 600-ship navy, and modernization of all three legs of the nuclear triad, in addition to improvements in (or upgrades of) existing conventional systems and the development of new ones in every class and for each service.[62] The only major weapons system canceled during Reagan's term was DIVAD (for technical reasons), although the administration supported the antiaircraft gun in principle.

Bush (1989–1993)

Throughout his four-year presidency, George Bush was in the difficult position of presiding over the most dramatic and profound changes in the international environment in forty years. The volatile and uncertain conditions of the global situation partially explain the administration's inability to respond to these changes and challenges with equally profound and creative foreign and national security policy shifts. The Soviet threat evaporated, the Warsaw Pact disbanded, Germany reunited, and democratization movements emerged all over the world. At the same time, regional threats surfaced, and nationalistic and ethnic unrest reemerged, particularly in the nations that once belonged to the Warsaw Pact. The Bush administration responded with some reductions in defense spending, plans for a major restructuring and downsizing of the military, and visions of a New World Order, signaling an emphasis on international cooperation rather than conflict.[63] After forty years of relying upon military strength to secure our foreign policy goals, the New World Order called for greater emphasis on diplomatic and economic strategies. In accordance, the administration began a redefinition of foreign and national security policy that would place more emphasis on building America's economy (to make the United States competitive internationally), and on using this country's military and political power to encourage the spread of democracy and implementation of market economies throughout the world.[64] America's strategic bombers were taken off alert status, and the launch on warning option was abandoned. Bush also continued the commitment to arms control. The CFE (Conventional Forces in Europe) talks were begun in 1989, and START was signed in 1991.

Desert Storm and Somalia, however, were clear indications that for Bush, military power was still a viable tool for realizing America's foreign policy goals. In fact, the defense planning guidance for the fiscal years 1994 to 1999, issued during the Bush administration, de-emphasizes the idea of cooperative and collective security and promotes the idea of a world order dominated by the United States and the logic of a balance of power.[65] That document (supplemented in May 1994 with the defense planning guidance for fiscal years 1996 to 2001, but still classified today) begins by establishing as "our first objective . . . to prevent the reemergence of a new rival, either on the territory of the former Soviet Union or elsewhere, that poses a threat on the order of that posed formerly by the Soviet Union." The United States, according to the Pentagon's plan, is prepared to use military force to protect the vital interests of our country and those of our allies, or where foreign action "could seriously unsettle international relations."[66] The strategy document anticipates a military force configured to meet lower-level threats at lesser costs, relying more on the ability to reconstitute additional forces when needed. The document is accompanied by a set of "'illustrative' scenarios" that identify likely future foreign conflicts that could involve American military combat forces. These include regional wars against Iraq and North Korea, a Russian attack on Lithuania, and a number of other smaller contingencies. Needless to say, this document sparked considerable controversy among defense analysts, Congress, and America's allies, resulting in the document's revision by the Pentagon to eliminate passages suggesting a commitment to a Pax Americana.[67]

Bush entered office with considerable experience and interest in foreign affairs and a commitment to a hands-on management style. The national security team that Bush pulled together (Secretary of Defense Richard Cheney, ANSA Brent Scowcroft, and Secretary of State James Baker), while skilled, hard-working, and collegial, shared a common Cold War–era mind-set that stymied their propensity to be creative and innovative in redirecting America's foreign and defense policy orientation. Without these broader policy changes, the status of America's force structure remained relatively unaltered, despite concerted efforts by Cheney and Colin Powell, chairman of the JCS. Bush shared with his advisors a recognition that the world was changing, but he was unable to articulate a new set of ideological goals or formulate a coherent vision for the post–Cold War period, a shortcoming that continues to plague the Clinton administration. The consequence was a reactive (rather than anticipatory) approach to foreign and defense policy issues, solving problems as they arose.[68] John P. Burke adds that Bush's inclination to rely on a "small circle of trusted senior advisors," rather than on the formal foreign policy-making apparatus, narrowed "the foreign policy advice net," accounting in part for the administration's caution, with the important exception of Desert Storm.[69] Even here, despite the ambitious nature of Bush's response to Saddam Hussein's invasion of Kuwait, the administration has been criticized for failing to anticipate Hussein's move. In short, Bush was an experienced, albeit cautious and conventional, foreign policy president who embraced a hands-on management style that placed him at the center of an informal circle of equally cautious and conventional advisors. The result, as Burke predicted, was a series of "missed opportunities and undue constraint" during a time of rapid international change.[70]

Not unexpectedly, these patterns—the erratic nature of global relations, the absence of a coherent set of foreign policy objectives, and the predominant Cold War mind-set among key advisors—were not conducive to radical changes in weapons procurement either. Under the direction of Cheney and Powell, plans were undertaken "for major program and force reductions and major changes in the joint command structure of the armed forces."[71] On military hardware matters, however, Bush continued implementing Reagan's strategic modernization program, with some congressionally mandated restrictions on Stealth and SDI, and Cheney continued the practice of delegating responsibility for making weapons decisions to the military services, with funding decisions lodged in the Pentagon's Comptroller's Office. In two important instances, however, Cheney took an important stand against weapons systems supported by the military (and Congress), the Marine Corps's Osprey V-22 tilt-rotor aircraft program and the Air Force's F-22 fighter plane. Not unexpectedly, both systems are currently alive and well.

Clinton (1993–2001)

Bill Clinton entered the presidency with a commitment to refocus America's energies on domestic problems. During his campaign, Clinton reminded the voters that the lesson to be learned from the collapse of the Soviet Union was that "we must take care of our own people and their needs." In this sense, then, "foreign and domestic policy are inseparable." Clinton, like Bush, promised to place greater emphasis on the economic and diplomatic instruments of foreign policy and less on the military ones. As such, he said he would increase use of America's economic strength to achieve political goals such as democracy and human rights in other countries. By the end of his first term, however, Clinton had committed military forces to a U.N. peacekeeping operation in Bosnia-Herzegovina (1995–1997), sent troops to Haiti to restore President Jean-Bertrand Aristide to power (October 1994), expanded and then completed the military operation in Somalia (1995), increased military strength in the Persian Gulf (autumn 1996), and inaugurated a major restructuring of the Pentagon and America's military force structure. It was not that the administration failed to try economic sanctions and diplomacy first in each of the forementioned instances of America's use of military force. But in the end it was American military capabilities that succeeded.

Despite notable foreign policy successes, the administration's national security actions were attacked regularly for lacking consistency and focus, and the president was criticized for his indecisiveness. If the Clinton administration's policies and policy-making apparatus are compared to those of his predecessors, then clearly there is fault to be found. Throughout his first term, Clinton did waffle on foreign policy challenges such as Bosnia, Somalia, and Haiti, mostly to build support for his domestic agenda and to appease congressional and Pentagon critics of his early foreign policy statements. However, it is important to recognize that foreign and defense policies, during both the Clinton and Bush administrations, were still being made without the benefit of a clearly identifiable set of threats, a commonly recognized hegemonic force, and the stability of the international order that characterized the post–World War II period. The Clinton administration can be faulted for the inappropriate use of a collegial decision-making model that, in the absence of a guiding presidential force, is unworkable in the current global context. At the same time, Clinton's highly experienced advisors (first Secretary of Defense Les Aspin, then William Perry, and then William Cohen; first Secretary of State Warren Christopher and then Madeleine Albright, and first ANSA Anthony Lake and then Samuel Berger) are not sufficiently ideologically grounded to compensate for the president's lack of a global vision.[72]

As the political perspective suggests, developing coherency is extremely difficult in a democracy under the best of circumstances. Thus, the degree of consistency that has characterized the making of defense and foreign policy during the 1990s is impressive. Of particular interest for the future of weapons procurement is the consistency with which the Weinberger principles[73] (conceived during the Reagan administration) continue to be applied and refined in advance of a use of military force; the emphasis on smaller, regional conflicts; the commitment to collective military action through the U.N. and NATO; and the willingness to use limited American force for humanitarian relief, drug interdiction, counterterrorism, and peacekeeping operations.[74] Foreign policy advisors also continue to subscribe to the same set of threats, from the former Soviet republics, the proliferation of nuclear weapons, historic tensions in the Middle East and the Korean Peninsula, terrorist attacks, and the ethnic violence in the former Yugoslavia.[75] Also, the status quo of threatening conventional military power in defense of "vital" U.S. interests and pursuing advances in weapons technology continues to characterize American defense policy.[76]

Clinton, like his Democratic predecessors, tried to use his presidential powers to encourage broad changes in military politics and management. In 1993, for example, the administration reduced the number of assistant secretaries in the Pentagon as one way to neutralize that department's bureaucratic power.[77] Clinton's first defense secretary, Les Aspin, introduced changes in the Pentagon commensurate with a review of America's defense needs and global changes in the post–Cold War security environment. Aspin's "bottom-up review," released on 1 September 1993, concluded that the United States should be guided in its force structure, personnel, and funding decisions by the need to maintain the capability to fight and win two major regional conflicts simultaneously (the two one-half war scenario). The analysis resulted in recommendations calling for major reductions in manpower, deferrals in modernization spending (such as for a new main battle tank), and a transition from an emphasis on heavy forces (such as tanks, heavy artillery, and mechanized infantry) to light forces (such as special forces and airborne infantry) for the Army. Moreover, the document raised questions about the continuing need for large numbers of Navy vessels, in particular, hunter-killer and nuclear submarines. The review also pointed up the absence of a justification for the two primary missions of the Air Force, placing in jeopardy land-based ICBMs and strategic bombers.

Acting upon Aspin's review, the Clinton administration pushed for a series of sweeping cuts in the defense budget (including the approval of the latest round of 105 military-base closures and consolidations) (July 1995), and directed the military to shift its emphasis to regional contingencies, and expedite plans to cut back combat units, fleets, and aircraft squadrons. A number of weapons systems were affected, including the Air Force's MILSTAR (Military Strategic and Tactical Relay), the Army's RAH-66 Comanche attack helicopter, the Army's Patriot PAC II missile system and the Navy's A-6 bombers, and air force fighter/ interceptor planes and navy ships generally. Those weapons systems retained or restored included the C-17, more fast sealift ships, the V-22 tilt-rotor aircraft, the F-22 fighter, and "smart" weapons.[78] The MX missile system was canceled and tactical fighter wings cut. Congress continues to debate the future of the Stealth bomber. Generally, however, acquisition accounts have been less affected than manpower and overall force structure, which have carried more of the burden of the funding cuts. For example, Army active divisions have gone from eighteen in 1990 to twelve in 1995, close to the goal of ten divisions; Navy ships have declined from 546 to 373 (with a goal of 346); and aircraft carriers and carrier air wings have dropped from fifteen to eleven and thirteen to ten respectively.[79] Congressional Republicans continue to act to reverse some of Clinton's actions.

Presidential Influence: A Reassessment

The involvement of presidential administrations in the making and re-making of foreign and defense policy in the post–World War II period has been considerable. Truman, Kennedy, Johnson, and Nixon were the most directly involved in the full range of national security issues. Eisenhower, Carter, Bush, and Clinton did make the decisions for their administrations, but in so doing relied on a broad base of information and advice. Ford and Reagan appear to have been more inclined toward deference and delegation in national security matters. Similarly, the guidance that each administration has provided to the Pentagon in crafting military hardware decisions has varied as well. In some cases, presidential preferences have been clear and concise (Kennedy and Carter) and the commitment to executive oversight strong (Truman, Kennedy, and Carter). In other cases, presidential preferences, while clear, have been less well defined (Reagan) and the commitment to military autonomy and discretion strong (Nixon, Reagan, and Bush). Presidential administrations also have varied in their use of budgetary and administrative powers to influence weapons decisions, with the Republican administrations less and the Democratic administrations more inclined to micromanage the Pentagon. Not unexpectedly, varying levels of success have been realized by different administrations seeking to influence military hardware decisions. The Democratic administrations have encountered the most resistance from the Pentagon, but they are also the ones that sought to provide clear guidance to and limits on the discretion and autonomy of the military. In contrast, the Republican presidents have been more inclined toward deference in matters of military procurement.

Overall, while individual presidents, in most cases, have not "made" weapons decisions, presidential guidance of military hardware decisions has been considerable, providing the rationale requisite to building a meaningful force structure. Presidents have been able to provide the context for military decisions, an essential condition for success in light of the difficulties, uncertainties, and risks associated with weapons decisions.[80] In this sense, the rational argument for military hardware decisions is validated, with some important qualifiers predicted by the political and pragmatic perspectives. Foremost are the political (term limits), constitutional (shared powers; scope of presidential responsibilities), institutional (executive-bureaucratic relations), and structural (limited resources and time) limits on presidential power, precluding the tight administrative control needed to match military hardware decisions to foreign and defense policy goals and strategies. Despite considerable formal and informal power in national security matters, for practical reasons, presidents (even in crises) cannot act alone. They too must bargain and negotiate with other actors to build a coalition of support for their preferred policies, with the consequence being compromise in too many cases. Nixon's and Carter's grudging support for the Trident submarine and MX missile system, respectively, are illustrative. Presidents also must serve their own political constituency. Second, presidents find themselves vulnerable to circumstances beyond their control. The Soviet invasion of Afghanistan that doomed Senate confirmation of SALT II, the timely disintegration of the Soviet Union during the Reagan administration, the collapse of the Berlin Wall and breakup of the Warsaw Pact during the Bush administration, the launching of Sputnik during the Eisenhower administration: All of these events had profound effects on national security policy. Third, presidential influence is further constrained by the mismatch between the life cycle of a weapons system and the term of political office. Thus, the weapons that a president inherits already have built up a coalition of support (momentum) that is difficult for a temporary political actor to reverse. Finally, forging coherence in public policies in a democracy is difficult under the best of circumstances, such as those that characterized the period of the Cold War. When defense analysts and military actors are divided over fundamental policy questions of strategy and doctrine, as they currently are, the search for an optimal force structure is compromised.

Presidential guidance will become an even more important tool for building a coherent and viable set of foreign and defense policies in the post–Cold War period. Without a common enemy around which to build a consensus, the demands of national security policy-making are extreme. The uncertainties associated with the anticipated reactions of the Soviet Union pale in comparison to the unpredictability of the behavior of those nations that currently pose the greatest threats to America's security, such as Iraq, Iran, and North Korea. The challenges of collecting reliable intelligence information in closed societies, problematic during the Cold War, are even greater now that resources are being retrenched. The international scene is a volatile one, wherein threats change, and the fortunes of countries rise and fall on a regular basis.

The challenges of the post–Cold War period also mean that presidents are likely to devote more attention to the broader context of foreign and defense policy, while devolving military policy to the Pentagon. While the president will continue to establish the national security goals and strategies for which weapons are to be used, defense analysts and military planners in the Pentagon will make the decisions concerning which and how many weapons systems are needed to meet these objectives. Therefore, to adequately answer the question of why America builds the weapons it does, and why these weapons encounter performance problems, the analysis must look to the Pentagon, not to the president and his advisors.

Notes

1. See, for example, Cecil V. Crabb and Kevin V. Mulcahy, *American National Security: A Presidential Perspective* (Pacific Grove, Calif.: Brooks/ Cole Publishing Colo., 1991), Donald M. Snow and Eugene Brown, *Puzzle Palaces and Foggy Bottom: U.S. Foreign and Defense Policy-Making in the 1990s* (New York: St. Martin's Press, 1994), and Sam C. Sarkesian, *U.S. National Security: Policymakers, Processes, and Politics*, 2d ed. (Boulder, Colo.: Rienner, 1995).

2. In this chapter, the terms "foreign policy," "defense policy," and "national security policy" are defined as follows. "Foreign policy" refers to the full range of policies defining our relationships with other nations. "Defense policy" describes those foreign policies whose objective is the protection of the territory of the United States, its values and beliefs, and its vital interests abroad, such as oil. These can include military policies to deter, or if deterrence fails, to win a war; diplomatic policies such as arms control agreements; or economic policies such as embargoes. "National security policy" is used interchangeably with "defense policy." "Military policy" is used to refer exclusively to military solutions such as weapons decisions and war plans. See Sarkesian, *National Security*, chapter 1, for a discussion.

3. Barry M. Blechman, *The Politics of National Security: Congress and U.S. Defense Policy* (New York: Oxford University Press, 1990).

4. Robert Scigliano, "The Presidency and the Judiciary," in *The Presidency and the Political System*, ed. M. Nelson (Washington, D.C.: Congressional Quarterly Press, 1990).

5. Ralph G. Carter, "Congressional Foreign Policy Behavior: Persistent Patterns of the Postwar Period," *Presidential Studies Quarterly* 16 (Spring 1986): 329–359.

6. Daniel J. Kaufman, "National Security: Organizing the Armed Forces," *Armed Forces and Society* 14 (Fall 1987): 85–112.

7. Clinton Rossiter, *The American Presidency* (New York: Harcourt, Brace and World, 1960), 30.

8. The NSC refers to the formal statutory body established by the National Security Act of 1947. Although the membership has changed, it generally has included the president, vice president, important cabinet-level officials such as the secretaries of defense and state, and the director of the CIA.

9. James K. Oliver, "Presidents As National Security Policymakers," in *Rethinking the Presidency*, Thomas E. Cronin, ed. (Boston: Little, Brown, 1982), 392.

10. Stephen D. Krasner, "Are Bureaucracies Important? (Or Allison Wonderland)," *Foreign Policy* 7 (Summer 1972): 159–179.

11. See Terry M. Moe, "The Politicized Presidency," in *The New Direction in American Politics*, eds. John E. Chubb and Paul E. Peterson (Washington, D.C.: The Brookings Institution, 1985).

12. Roger Hilsman, *The Politics of Policymaking in Defense and Foreign Affairs: Conceptual Models and Bureaucratic Politics* (Englewood Cliffs, N.J.: Prentice-Hall, 1993.

13. Oliver, "Presidents as National Security Policymakers," 392.

14. Samuel P. Huntington, *Common Defense: Strategic Programs in National Politics* (New York: Columbia University Press, 1961), 235.

15. Scilla McLean, ed., *How Nuclear Weapons Decisions Are Made* (New York: St Martin's Press, 1986), 62.

16. In their book, Barbara Kellerman and Ryan J. Barrilleaux assess presidential leadership using the following criteria: "whether the president's goal was clearly articulated and communicated; how energetically he used his authority and exercised power and influence; which tactics of power, authority, and influence he employed; what motivated domestic and foreign constituencies to accept or reject his attempt to lead; which sources of power, authority, and influence were most effective; and whether implementation was in fact accomplished." See *The President As World Leader* (New York: St. Martin's Press, 1991), x.

17. According to George Kennan, the goal of the containment strategy was to discourage the Soviet Union from expanding beyond its borders. Foreign policy was seen as a zero-sum game, and unrest around the world was seen as the result of Soviet revolutionary activities. See George F. Kennan, "The Sources of Soviet Conduct," *Foreign Affairs* (July 1947): 566–582, published under the pseudonym "X".

18. Crabb and Mulcahy, *American National Security*, 71.

19. Donald M. Snow and Eugene Brown, *Puzzle Palaces and Foggy Bottom: U.S. Foreign and Defense Policy-Making in the 1990s* (New York: St. Martin's Press, 1994), 46.

20. NSC 162/2, approved 30 October 1953.

21. Snow and Brown, *Puzzle Palaces and Foggy Bottom*, 47.

22. Crabb and Mulcahy, *American National Security*, 89. It was Dulles who promised to not merely contain Communism, but to roll back Soviet influence by liberating nations such as Hungary (1956) under Soviet domination. When push came to shove, however, the U.S. failed to act.

23. Ibid., 98–99, 172–173. Also, Charles W. Kegley Jr. and Eugene R. Wittkopf, *American Foreign Policy: Pattern and Process* (New York: St. Martin's Press, 1987), 346.

24. Francis J. West Jr., "Secretaries of Defense: Why Most Have Failed," *Naval War College Review* (March/April 1981): 87.

25. Kennedy, quoted in Hartmann and Wendzel, *Defending America's Security*, 246.

26. Crabb and Mulcahy, *American National Security*, 108.

27. Both Snow and Hilsman reject the classification of MAD as a strategy, referring to it as a "description" and strategic situation, respectively. The Soviet Union never subscribed to the doctrine of MAD.

28. Hartmann and Wendzel, *Defending America's Security*, 248.

29. Ibid., 233, 303–304.

30. Kegley and Wittkopf, *American Foreign Policy*, 40.

31. Ibid., 385. Also, Hartmann and Wendzel, *Defending America's Security*, 100. Under Johnson, the JCS was partially rehabilitated and the NSC downgraded as Johnson preferred to rely upon the line departments, particularly the Defense Department.

32. Snow and Brown, *Puzzle Palaces and Foggy Bottom*, 48.

33. Crabb and Mulcahy, *American National Security*, 114–116.

34. Ibid.

35. Ibid., 125.

36. Ibid., Table 13, 270.

37. Hartmann and Wendzel, *Defending America's Security*, 249.

38. The Nixon Doctrine sought to redefine the nature of the assistance that Third World countries could expect from the United States by moving away from a commitment to direct military involvement to material assistance and training. In essence, the United States renounced the role of policeman of the world and replaced its active involvement overseas with the provision of economic and military assistance. See Donald M. Snow, *National Security: Defense Policy for a New International Order*, 3rd ed. (New York: St. Martin's Press, 1995), 87–88, and Kegley and Wittkopf, *American Foreign Policy*, 42–52, 64, 132.

39. Snow, *National Security*, 250.

40. Ibid., 105.

41. Richard A. Stubbing, *The Defense Game: An Insider Explores the Astonishing Realities of America's Defense Establishment* (New York: Harper and Row, 1986), 306.

42. Fen Hampson, *Unguided Missiles: How America Buys Its Weapons* (New York: W.W. Norton, 1989), 32; Stubbing, *The Defense Game*, 300f.

43. Stubbing, *Defense Game*, 324f.

44. Henry Kissinger, *Years of Upheaval* (Boston: Little, Brown, 1982), 266–267.

45. Stubbing, *Defense Game*, 343.

46. "Progressively during the Nixon, Ford, Carter, and Reagan administrations, U.S. doctrine and force procurement moved toward a posture that strove for deterrence through giving the president a range of counterforce options as well as countercity options. Eventually, during the Carter administration this eclectic strategy was given a name: the countervailing strategy. However, in spite of its name this strategy was still composed largely of MAD." Hilsman, *The Politics of Policymaking*, 324.

47. Quoted in Hartmann and Wendzel, *Defending America's Security*, 257.

48. For the Soviets this would have meant dismantling 270 strategic weapons.

49. Stubbing, *The Defense Game*, 361.

50. Snow, *National Security*, 90.

51. Crabb and Mulcahy, *American National Security*, 153ff.

52. Ibid., 155.

53. See Stubbing, *The Defense Game*, 350.

54. The transition from a defensive to an offensive strategy led to a new "maritime strategy" and "airland battle" doctrine for American ground forces in Europe. For a complete discussion of the strategic and doctrinal consequences of the transition see Michael M. Boll, *National Security Planning: Roosevelt Through Reagan* (Lexington: University Press of Kentucky, 1988), 229–230.

55. Ibid., 263.

56. Quoted in Carnes Lord, *The Presidency and the Management of National Security* (New York: The Free Press, 1988), 4.

57. Quoted in ibid., 183.

58. Snow, *National Security*, 60.

59. Louis W. Koenig, *The Chief Executive*, 5th ed. (New York: Harcourt Brace Jovanovich, 1986), 415.

60. See, e.g., the defense secretary's FY 1984 report. Both the Bush and Reagan administrations were criticized for not providing a strategic rationale for U.S. defense policies and managerial practices and thereby creating a vacuum into which weapons and personnel decisions could be made on the basis of organizational interests. This is not to suggest that the Reagan administration did not subscribe to certain strategic doctrines, only that there were limited efforts made to link the massive defense buildup to these strategic concerns. Some analysts take issue with this contention. *Congressional Quarterly,* for example, suggests that Reagan's support for MX in fixed silos and the deployment of Pershing IIs and ground-launched cruise missiles in Western Europe were calculated to advance our war-fighting capability. Moreover, efforts to improve C^3I and civil defense were based on efforts to improve the ability of the United States to endure a nuclear attack. The criticism, then, ought to be directed not at a lack of strategic thinking, but at the value of the strategic principles embraced by the Reagan administration. Another criticism is that the strategic concepts the Reagan administration embraced were so broad that they could be used to justify almost any new weapons program. On the other hand, similar criticisms can be leveled against all administrations. Also, the Reagan administration is not immune from the criticism that some principles were invoked to justify weapons developments that had only a peripheral relationship to each other. One example is the justification for both the MX missile and D-5 II missile having hard-target capabilities.

61. Quoted in Les Aspin, *Searching for a Defense Strategy* (Washington, D.C.: House Armed Services Committee, September 1987).

62. Modernization of the nuclear triad included deployment of the MX, procurement of the B-1B bomber and development of the B-2 bomber, B-52s with ALCMs, and more Trident submarines with the highly accurate Trident II (D-5) SLBMs. Additionally, qualitative upgrades were made in the F-15, F-16, and C-58; the C-17 and the (Stealth) Advanced Tactical Fighter were developed; and, additional purchases were made of the Los Angeles–class attack submarines and Aegis cruisers, SLCM platforms, carrier air wings, battleships, Nimitz-class carriers, Abrams M-1 tanks, Bradley IFVs, and AH-64 attack helicopters.

63. Paul Y. Hammond, "Central Organization in the Transition from Bush to Clinton," in *American Defense Annual*, 9th ed., ed. Charles F. Hermann (New York: Lexington Books), 163–164.

64. *Wall Street Journal*, 11 August 1988, 1.

65. The defense planning guidance, released every two years, is a classified document drafted by the Pentagon in conjunction with the National Security Council and in consultation with the president or his senior national security advisors. The planning document is "an internal Administration policy statement" that essentially shapes national security policy. It is distributed to military and civilian leaders in the Pentagon to guide them in making decisions on forces, budgets, and strategy.

66. "These threats are likely to arise in regions critical to the security of the U.S. and its allies, including Europe, East Asia, the Middle East and Southwest Asia, and the territory of the former Soviet Union. We also have important interests at stake in Latin America, Oceania, and Sub-Saharan Africa." "Various types of U.S interests may be involved in such instances: access to vital raw materials, primarily Persian Gulf oil; proliferation of weapons of mass destruction and ballistic missiles, threats to U.S. citizens from terrorism or regional or local conflict, and threats to U.S. society from narcotics trafficking."

67. Patrick Tyler, "Pentagon Drops Goal of Blocking New Superpowers," *New York Times*, 24 May 1992, L14.

68. Crabb and Mulcahy, *American National Security*, 203.

69. John P. Burke, "Presidential Influence and the Budget Process: A Comparative Analysis," in George C. Edwards III et al., *The Presidency and Public Policy Making* (Pittsburgh, Pa.: University of Pittsburgh Press, 1985), 71–94.

70. Ibid., 174.

71. Hammond, "Central Organization in the Transition," 164.

72. Snow, *National Security*, 97–98.

73. In brief, the United States will eschew a military commitment in the absence of (a) international support and cooperation, (b) public support, (c) clear political objectives, and (d) evidence that the mission(s) can be accomplished quickly with minimal casualties.

74. Clinton's first foreign policy actions were to provide air drops of supplies to Bosnia and to continue the U.S.-led relief effort in Somalia. Both were actions taken in cooperation with the United Nations and/or other countries to meet regional conflicts. The Somalia action in particular foreshadows a greater emphasis on peacekeeping and humanitarian missions. *Defense News*, 14 December 1992–20 December 1992: 8.

75. See comments by JCS Chairman Gen. Colin L. Powell, "U.S. Forces: Challenges Ahead." *Foreign Affairs* 72 (Winter 1992/1993): 32–45.

76. Quoted in *Defense News*, 26 October 1992–1 November 1992, p. 1.

77. Sarkesian, *U.S. National Security*, 84.

78. *Defense News*, 26 October 1992–1 November 1992, p. 1.

79. *Defense News*, 14 February 1994–20 February 1994, p. 1.

80. On the other hand, making foreign and defense policy decisions that narrow the gap between military threats and capabilities is further complicated by the uncertainty of intelligence data. Only retrospective judgment can validate the certainty of intelligence data, making such information obscure and therefore any analysis based on it risky. The reliability of intelligence information is further mitigated by the closed nature of the societies in which it is collected and the limited resources available to commit to collecting and analyzing it. The reliability of data interpretation, of defense analysis, is limited by human bias.

Skybolt
The President Takes a Stand and Alienates Everyone

President John F. Kennedy's decision in December 1962 to cancel the Air Force's Skybolt Missile Program "led to the most perilous crisis between the United States and Great Britain since the Suez affair," and was resolved only when the United States promised to share its Polaris submarine program with England (which sought a delivery system for its Vulcan nuclear bombers).[1] Yet the ballistic missile system had been deemed of dubious value even at its conception and had encountered excessive cost growth, highly visible technical problems, and performance shortfalls during its entire procurement life. Throughout 1959 and 1960, the Fletcher Committee (an independent advisory committee established to review and evaluate the program) recommended that it be discontinued. The Skybolt was both technically complex (the "most complex ballistic missile system [that] the U.S. had yet undertaken"), and militarily unnecessary.[2] With the shift during the Kennedy administration from "massive retaliation" to the strategy of "controlled flexible response," McNamara realized that Skybolt would contribute "only marginally to our strategic nuclear capability."[3]

The Skybolt, however, had powerful advocates. The Air Force conceived the missile program during the Eisenhower administration as an "answer to the Navy's Polaris FBM system, rather than as a national security requirement in its own right." The Air Force promoted the ballistic missile system (which would be carried on B-52s) as a way to sustain their organizational mission and reaffirm the value of manned bombers. International support was secured when British Prime Minister Macmillan was assured that Skybolt would provide his country with an independent nuclear status. Kennedy originally promoted Skybolt to fulfill a campaign promise to close the missile gap with the Soviets. Once Kennedy was in office, however, McNamara, applying systems analysis, determined that Skybolt was flawed, overpriced, and unnecessary. The military services responded by colluding in support of Skybolt to offset McNamara's efforts to dominate decision-making in a newly centralized Pentagon (1958 Reorganization Act). Thus, the Skybolt program became intertwined with the broader conflict over civilian and military control over procurement matters. The decision to cancel Skybolt provoked a lobbying campaign from Douglas Aircraft Company and allies in Congress. The defense secretary prevailed with support from the president, and the Air Force was compensated with an increase in their Minuteman force. The United States also embraced a policy of multilateralism (NATO interdependence) to further appease Great Britain. In sum, the Skybolt illustrates both the strengths and weaknesses of presidential influence in military hardware matters.

[1]Henry Brandon, "Skybolt"; in *Readings in American Foreign Policy*, eds. Morton H. Halperin and Arnold Kanter (Boston: Little, Brown, 1973), 403.
[2]Ibid., 405–406.
[3]Richard A. Stubbing, *The Defense Game* (New York: Harper and Row, 1986), 270.

Primary Sources: Brandon, "Skybolt," Stubbing, *The Defense Game;* Lord Harlech, "Suez Snafu, Skybolt Sabu," *Foreign Policy* 2 (Spring 1971); Kenneth N. Ciboski, "The Bureaucratic Connection: Explaining the Skybolt Decision," in *American Defense Policy*, eds. John E. Endicott and Roy W. Stafford (Baltimore: The Johns Hopkins University Press, 1977).

HIGHLIGHT

Trident
Eight Presidencies and Still Plying the Waters

The life cycle of the Trident submarine and missile program has spanned the tenure of eight presidents, seven of whom inherited the mammoth nuclear program in various stages of development. One tried unsuccessfully to cancel it; two supported it for reasons other than its strategic contributions to the nuclear triad; and only one saw the program as an indispensable part of his national security agenda.

The Trident submarine and missile program was conceived as a follow-up system to the Polaris/Poseidon submarine during the Kennedy administration, one that would increase America's nuclear capabilities and offset a Soviet military buildup. Richard Nixon entered office initially opposed to the weapons program for military reasons, but came to support it for political reasons. Trident first was used as a bargaining chip during the SALT I talks with the Soviets. Nixon then relied on Trident to appease congressional "hawks" who opposed SALT I as a concession to the Russians, as well as congressional "doves" who opposed the Trident, but supported arms control efforts. An additional incentive for his support of Trident was Admiral Thomas Moorer, who made JCS support for SALT I contingent upon accelerated funding for Trident. The showdown came in 1972 when Congress refused Defense Secretary Melvin Laird's request for production money for Trident until a final design was selected (consistent with Deputy Defense Secretary David Packard's "fly-before-you-buy" policy). Nixon prevailed, Trident survived, and SALT I was ratified in the end.

Ford's support for Trident was reduced by the Carter administration, which also found itself ultimately supporting the program for political rather than military reasons, in this case, to garner support for SALT II. From the beginning, Carter saw no military need to replace the Poseidon submarine (the successor to Polaris) (which he felt could continue to perform its strategic mission for some time) with an unnecessarily large submarine that was encountering performance failures and cost overruns. After delaying production of Trident, Carter, albeit reluctantly, was brought on board by JCS, when they threatened to withhold approval for SALT II.

Congressional opposition resurfaced once again, and public opposition emerged during the Reagan administration, when concerns were raised over construction problems, strategic and arms control implications (the destabilizing possibilities of the Trident II's hard-target capability), and environmental issues. Nonetheless, Trident thrived, an enormous nuclear submarine program being the centerpiece (along with the MX and B-1B) of an ambitious new strategic modernization program. Bush continued Reagan's modernization program which came under attack during the Clinton administration for military reasons (absence of the Soviet threat) and fiscal concerns (need to reduce defense spending).

Primary Sources: D. Douglas Dalgleish and Larry Schweikart, *Trident* (Carbondale, Ill.: Southern Illinois University Press, 1984); Fen Hampson, *Unguided Missiles* (New York: W.W. Norton, 1989); Barry E. Carter and John D. Steinbruner, "Trident," in *Commission on the Organization of Government for the Conduct of Foreign Policy* (Murphy Commission), vol. 4, appendix K (Washington, D.C.: Government Printing Office, June 1975).

HIGHLIGHT

TFX
The Defense Secretary Stands Up and Takes a Fall

The TFX controversy, more than any other military program, illustrates how difficult it is for the president and his defense secretary to overcome the organized efforts of the military services (using bureaucratic means) to secure their preferred weapons systems. Upon taking office, McNamara discovered that the Navy and Air Force were developing new, but separate, fighter planes. Beginning in 1959, the Air Force sought a multipurpose tactical bomber for deep-interdiction missions (TFX), and the Navy pursued a fleet air defense interceptor (F-6D Eagle Missileer) (i.e., a platform for long-range air-to-air missiles to protect the fleet). As part of the concerted efforts by the Kennedy administration both to rationalize the process by which America makes its weapons decisions and to effect a match between strategic and doctrinal goals and military hardware, McNamara mandated (in 1961) that the Air Force and Navy abandon their separate programs and participate in a joint one. In 1967, with the shift to flexible response, the services were told to develop a joint air-superiority fighter-bomber compatible with the objective of a limited nonnuclear war.

Both services, more enamored with the idea of massive retaliation (all-out war) and hostile to the idea of joining forces, acted to undermine McNamara's efforts. Foremost, the services delineated "unjustifiably demanding performance requirements" for their version of TFX that resulted in a plane expected to perform several different and incompatible missions, creating a technological nightmare that stretched the state of technical art.[1] The Air Force and Navy (somewhat surreptitiously) managed their individual programs in ways that resulted in two separate planes with some elements in common, but hardly interchangeable. The program was further complicated by charges of malfeasance in the award of the contract to General Dynamics that led to ten months of congressional hearings. The Air Force version (F-111), despite serious performance deficiencies, went into production, while the Navy version (F-111B) was canceled by Congress. The irony is that the F-111 went on to become a competent fighter plane that is still in inventory, both services eventually were funded for the planes they originally wanted before McNamara mandated jointness—the F-14 (Navy) and F-15 (Air Force)—and the F-14 and F-111B programs were almost identical in terms of performance requirements, contractor, and problems. In sum, the story of TFX is the story of how a plane designed for one service (Air Force) evolved first into a plane designed for use by all three services, then a plane designed for use by two services, and finally two versions of one basic plane for use by two services.[2]

[1]Alain C. Enthoven and K. Wayne Smith, *How Much Is Enough? Shaping the Defense Program, 1961–1969* (New York: Harper and Row, 1971), 263.
[2]Robert J. Art, *The TFX Decision: McNamara and the Military* (Boston: Little, Brown, 1968), 11.

Primary Sources: Art, *The TFX Decision;* Robert F. Coulam, *Illusions of Choice: The F-111 and the Problem of Weapons Acquisition Reform* (Princeton: Princeton University Press, 1977); Enthoven and Smith, *How Much Is Enough?*

CHAPTER 3

Strategic Planning in the Pentagon

Can It Happen?

If the president does not play the principal role in the decisions to conceive and develop major weapons systems, where does the power lie over weapons acquisition? Defense analysts generally agree that the Pentagon controls military hardware policy, at least during the preliminary stages of the acquisition process. However, analysts are divided over *how* the Pentagon makes its decisions. Knowing how military decisions are made is essential for understanding the nature of these decisions and the weapons that they produce. According to the rational argument, decision-making is a judicious process that responds to well-defined military threats and produces weapons systems with the capabilities to meet these threats. The pragmatic and political explanations for weapons procurement challenge the underlying assumptions of the rational argument, presenting instead a view of military decision-making that is plagued by risks and uncertainties, and driven by organizational, bureaucratic, and political forces.

This chapter tests these contrasting explanations. It begins with a brief overview of how decisions are made in the Pentagon from the rational perspective. It then elaborates on the theoretical critique that the pragmatic and political arguments provide. In an effort to determine the validity of the two sets of explanations, the basic assumptions on which the analytical approaches diverge are tested empirically. Data are drawn from the nineteen cases in this study. The chapter concludes by considering past and current reform efforts to inform the issue of whether the pattern of military policy-making described in this chapter will be appropriate in the post–Cold War period.

Making Weapons Decisions:
A Theoretical Perspective[1]

The Rational or Ideal Process

The president and his advisors set the foreign policy and national security objectives that commit the United States to certain strategies and courses of action (chapter 2). But the military means to fulfill these goals are conceived in the Pentagon. According to the rational perspective, the weapons acquisition process is an analytical one that produces decisions about military hardware that are reasonable choices, which are arrived at after reviewing all viable alternatives intended to maximize the fulfillment of well-defined strategic missions or to meet a perceived or anticipated military threat. Accordingly, the weapons procurement process within the Pentagon is arranged to maximize rational decision-making. The formal organization chart portrays a pyramid-type structure in which power flows downward from the Joint Chiefs of Staff (JCS) and Office of the Secretary of Defense (OSD) to the military services. The JCS, composed of senior military officers from each service, is responsible for formulating military strategy and advising the civilian leaders, the president, and the defense secretary. The advice that the JCS provides is supposed to be an overall military perspective achieved through the coordination of individual service positions and activities. Thus, the role of the JCS is to forge coherent military positions on important defense matters and advise the president and defense secretary of these positions. The chairman is appointed by the president, while the other members are selected by their individual military services. The role of the OSD, representing civilian control, is to make the four services more responsive to the president. It is the defense secretary's responsibility to develop a national military strategy to guide all military decisions (following presidential and congressional approval), including those on force levels, programs, weapons systems, and operational plans.[2] The services are then expected to implement the defense plans and policies made by their superiors.

A textbook portrait of the weapons acquisition process begins with a description of the planning, programming, and budgeting system (PPBS) and Milestone processes.[3] The formal process begins with a threat assessment produced by the combined activities of the CIA (Central Intelligence Agency), the DIA (Defense Information Agency),[4] the National Security Council (NSC),[5] and the secretary of defense.[6] The result is the National Intelligence Estimate (NIE), which is examined by the defense secretary together with budgetary targets from the Office of Management and Budget

(OMB) and the status of our current policy provided by the NSC. From this, the defense secretary, in conjunction with the JCS and the president, prepares the defense planning guidance document, in which our military priorities, goals, and strategies are spelled out. The four military services are then asked to respond to this report with specific force planning recommendations, which are reviewed by JCS. The services also provide their own independent blueprints for force planning called programme objectives memoranda boards or POMs. The POMs contain a five-year projected list of needed weapons systems, both old and new. The JCS review the POMs and issue a joint programme assessment memo that evaluates the extent to which the service needs, taken together, fulfill the mandate set out in the defense planning guidance document. The Defense Resources Board (DRB) (now the DPRB)[7] examines the POMs and the joint program assessment memo before forwarding all five documents to the defense secretary, who issues a programme decision memorandum. Each service reviews the memorandum before submitting funding requests to the OMB and the Comptroller's Office in the Department of Defense (DoD), where the programs are rank-ordered. Every newly conceived weapons system also must be reviewed and approved by an evaluation board (DSARC, now DAB) and the secretary of defense at critical stages in its procurement life cycle to avoid commitments to suboptimal systems.[8] Funding requests for new and upgraded weapons systems are made to the OMB and the Comptroller's Office in DoD. With presidential approval, a budget is forwarded to Congress.

The Pragmatic and Political Critiques

To many observers of the Pentagon, the process neither works in the ways delineated by this organizational description nor does it reliably produce optimal military hardware decisions. "There is no rational system [for achieving] coherent and enduring strategy, the forces to carry it out and the funding that should be provided—in light of the overall economy and competing claims on natural resources," the Packard Commission concluded after studying decision-making in the Pentagon.[9] "The absence of such a system contributes substantially to the instability and uncertainty that plague our defense program. These cause imbalances in our military forces and capabilities, and increase the costs of procuring military equipment."[10] As the commission and subsequent defense reformers discovered, the weapons acquisition process is beset with confusion, conflict, coalition-building, and compromise that obviate rational decision-making.[11] From the beginning, when the CIA, DIA, and NSC combine to

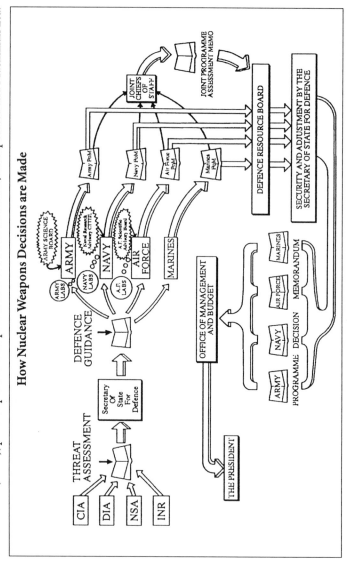

How Nuclear Weapons Decisions are Made

FIGURE 3.2

From Alexander Kossiakoff, "Conception of New Defense Systems and the Role of Government R&D Centers," eds. Franklin A. Long and Judith Reppy. *The Genesis of New Weapons: Decision Making for Military R&D* (New York: Pergamon Press, 1980), p. 73.

The Cycle for Major Weapons Acquisition

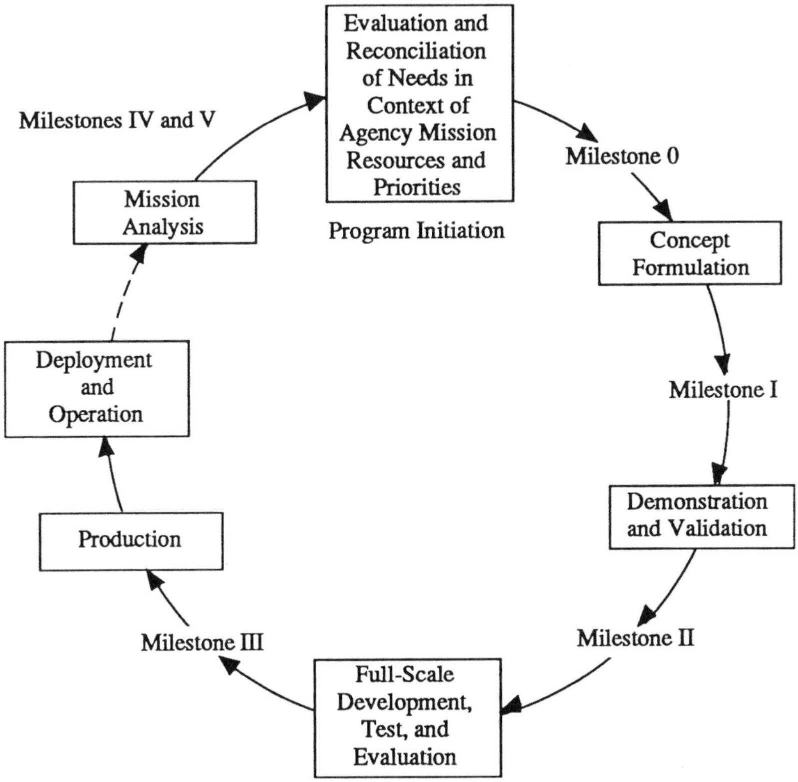

provide a threat assessment, the forces of ambiguity and conflict and, therefore, compromise are at work. Each agency may provide a different assessment that reflects ideological and parochial differences as well as organizational ones. As Fen Hampson notes, "[i]n the competition among different interests in the Pentagon and the rest of the bureaucracy, intelligence forecasts are used to advance key interests."[12]

Intelligence forecasting is further compromised by the difficulties associated with data collection, particularly in closed societies such as those that constitute the major threats to American interests. To compensate, analysts project future threats by looking at the past behavior, current capabilities, and amount of money spent by enemy nations.[13] Since it is extremely difficult to obtain reliable information on the actual intentions of these countries, the information upon which a threat assessment is made can be flawed and highly subjective. Consider, for example, the case of the M-1 tank, which was touted as a necessary response to the Soviet T-80 tank; or the F-15 fighter plane, which was defended as a counterweight to the Soviet MIG-25 Foxbat. In both cases Soviet capabilities were vastly overestimated. The reverse has been true as well, as evidenced by the shooting down of a U-2 spy plane piloted by Francis Gary Powers in 1960. According to a number of senior Soviet economists, during the Cold War, CIA estimates consistently erred on the side of understating military spending and overestimating the size of the Soviet economy.[14] This is extremely significant in light of the economic causes of the Soviet Union's demise.

The patterns of confusion, conflict, and coalition-building (as well as parochialism) that are manifest in producing the NIE continue throughout the procurement process, Pentagon critics contend, and are evident in the defense planning guidance report that the defense secretary issues, in the POMs that the military services issue, in the joint programme assessment planning memorandum that the JCS issue, in the programme decision memoranda that are submitted to the OMB and the president, and eventually in the budget submitted to Congress. At each stage of the process, actors seek to secure a position that benefits their organization's integrity and their own personal standing. For example, for reasons related to the control that the military services have over their promotion and tenure, the members of the JCS (with the exception of the chairman) have generally ignored cost constraints in the joint strategic planning document and cobbled the separate service wish lists in order to secure benefits for their own department. Similarly, in their competition for shares of the budget and a favored role in America's defense strategy, the military services have developed the POMs with little regard for the defense planning guidance.[15] Given the momentum that builds in support of a military program, propelled by parochial and organizational concerns, weapons systems are rarely terminated at the Milestone III decision stage for performance failures or excessive cost overruns.[16] As noted in chapter 2, the defense planning guidance document continues to support a status quo that reflects the preeminent role of America's multiservice military force to maintain a favorable balance of power in international relations.

Structural

In explaining how and why nonmilitary interests so readily intrude upon and disrupt the weapons acquisition process, advocates of the pragmatic and political explanations point to structural and cultural factors. Pre-eminent among the structural factors is the quasi-bureaucratic nature of the Pentagon. In other words, the three characteristics of a true bureau-cracy (specialization of functions, adherence to set rules, and a hierarchy of authority) that promote rational decision-making exist only in modi-fied form in the Pentagon.

The rational perspective envisions a highly centralized institution with clearly drawn lines of authority and a pervasive adherence to disci-pline, for purposes of command and combat expediency. The pragmatic and political challenges assert that the actual structure of the Pentagon is decentralized, with a multitude of actors and agencies sharing power over military matters. The decentralized nature of the Pentagon in part reflects the aversion Americans have to a tightly organized military force, as well as our attachment to the incompatible goals of efficiency and democ-racy.[17] While a rigid hierarchy with levels immune to scrutiny is incom-patible with the democratic procedures mandated by a republican form of government, the enormous size and complexity of the tasks the mili-tary is responsible for necessitate some formal structure. The combina-tion of deference to and decentralization of authority has created a unique organizational phenomenon that supports four separate and distinct, but internally disciplined, military services that are steeped in tradition.[18]

One recent study describes the process in the Pentagon "as three dif-ferent but overlapping systems," in which different combinations of ac-tors and agencies prevail[19] (see Figure 3.3). The decisions to use military force are made by the president, drawing upon the advice of his national security advisors and the chairman of the JCS. Questions of military strategy and tactics (essentially preparations for war) are resolved by the military services, the OSD, and the defense secretary. These include the development of nuclear doctrine, the size and scope of the country's force posture, and the nature and fate of highly visible, expensive, and contro-versial weapons systems. On matters concerning the day-to-day manage-ment of the military, the services prevail. These include the multitude of routine decisions that are made about personnel and equipment (includ-ing most weapons systems). Thus, on military hardware matters, the mili-tary services are paramount. As Rosati concludes, "decisions over which weapons to build, where they should be deployed, and how they will be used in combat are typically made within an individual service, 'rubber stamped' within the JCS, and usually approved within OSD. The presi-dent and the secretary of defense might exercise influence on those issues

FIGURE 3.3

Figure from *The Politics of United States Foreign Policy* by Jerel A. Rosati, copyright © 1993 by Holt, Rinehart and Winston, Inc., reproduced by permission of the publisher.

Department of Defense Policy Processes

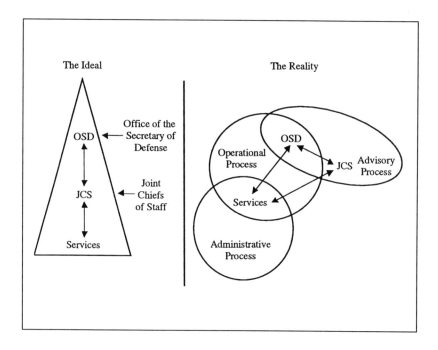

in which they are most interested and attentive. Otherwise, the JCS, the OSD, and the president have limited impact on the actual operations of the services. . . ."[20]

The view, then, from the pragmatic and political arguments is of an overall military structure (the Pentagon) in which power is highly decentralized, but within which small groups of actors and agencies predominate over specific policy areas (specialization). Within each circle or system, however, is a hierarchy of authority that is unique to the decision area. On matters of military procurement, for example, the distribution of power conforms more to an inverted pyramid, with the military services predominating at the preliminary stages of the procurement process, but subsequently dependent upon the consent of actors up the line of authority.

To institutionalize both their preeminent position in the procurement process and enhance the chances that their preferred systems will garner the support they need to be developed and deployed, the military services have embraced a number of management tools and procedures. One commonly employed tool is a concurrent management strategy (to guide military hardware development) that foreshortens the Milestone process by allowing weapons to be placed in production before development, testing, and evaluation have been completed. Although concurrency can expedite fielding of needed weapons and avoid technology obsolescence, the process also "forces decisionmakers to act without adequate information about a weapon's demonstrated operational effectiveness, reliability, logistic supportability, and readiness for production," with flawed systems being one important consequence.[21] This high-risk strategy also works to the advantage of a military service by insulating a weapon from critical evaluation until the production stage, when it is unlikely that a program will be terminated. More recently, the services have sought to further insulate preferred weapons from public scrutiny by designating them as classified, that is, placing them in the "black budget" category. Like a concurrent management strategy, black budget classifications serve an important function. Originally conceived to prevent America's enemies from gaining access to national security secrets, the practice is now widely exploited, according to members of Congress.

The military services gain greater discretion and autonomy from the fact that the mission of the Pentagon—to defend and protect the nation and its vital interests—is difficult to operationalize and, therefore, left ambiguous (see chapter 2). This allows the services to individually define what activities promote the public interest, with the result that national defense comes to be defined as an amalgamation of subinterests. Each service seeks to promote itself as indispensable to the security of the nation and defines its needs accordingly.[22] The bureaucratic reality of limited resources exacerbates the competition that goes on for shares of the budget that become surrogate measures for military importance—surrogate because it is difficult to reduce national security to quantifiable entities. Rather, weapons systems are assessed for their capacity to perform certain missions, and missions are assessed for their capacity to advance national security. These missions are what define the operational reality of a service, and they continue to be promoted independent of their military viability. Consider, for example, that the absence of a Soviet threat has raised questions about the two primary missions traditionally performed by the Air Force: strategic nuclear battle with the Soviets and

battle in the European theater. During the Cold War, these missions provided the rationale for land-based ICBMs, strategic bombers, advanced
fighter planes, and additional specialized hardware, accounting for the
disproportionate share of the procurement budget that the Air Force received. Already, ICBMs have been the target of arms control agreements,
and the demise of the Soviet Union has eliminated the opponent against
which much of this weaponry was to be used. In response, the Air Force
has tried to redefine the capabilities of its costly weapons, most notably
strategic bombers, which now perform a conventional mission. The B-2
bomber, conceived as part of the strategic nuclear deterrent, has been redesigned to provide tactical air support. The Navy too is struggling to redefine its existence in light of the absence of its major naval challenge, the
Soviet Union. According to Snow, "the absence of a viable opponent
raises questions about the continuing need for large numbers of vessels
[such as hunter-killer submarines and ballistic missile launching subma-
rines]."[23]

Further contributing to the disproportionate power (and autonomy)
of the military services and the highly decentralized nature of weapons
procurement, is the limited capacity of either the JCS or the OSD to provide the coordination and guidance requisite to rational decision-making, despite recent changes authorized (but not completely implemented)
under the Goldwater-Nichols Defense Reorganization Act of 1986. Even
today, the JCS continues to be influenced by the control that the military
services wield over promotions and assignments, including the selection
of its own members (with the recent exception of the chairman). The accountability that the promotion and assignment processes insure means
that the members of the JCS represent the interests of their individual
services. The services, then, collude in resolving competing interests in
order to present a unified military position that their civilian superiors
find hard to challenge.[24] In this way, the services have been able to
strengthen their hand in civilian-military relations. By subscribing to the
standard of fair shares (in making budgetary decisions), the services have
been able to prevent the possibility that intra- and interservice rivalry will
be used against them ("divide and conquer"). According to General
David C. Jones, former chairman of the JCS, "He who controls dollars,
promotions, and assignments controls the organization—the services so
control, especially with regard to personnel actions."[25]

Only recently have budgetary and structural changes been made that
are likely to alter the dynamic among and within the military services.
These changes derive from multiple sources; legislation mandating

changes in the way pay and promotion decisions are made (Federal Acquisition Streamlining Act of 1994, National Defense Authorization Act of FY 1994), a shrinking procurement budget following a 1985 peak (reversed again with the 1996 defense plan),[26] and a JCS chairman empowered to veto the votes of his colleagues without fear of reprisal[27] have all spurred renewed intra- and interservice rivalry. *Los Angeles Times* reporter Melissa Healy gives the examples of the fight between the Army and Marine Corps over who will control the low-intensity conflict mission, and between the Air Force and Navy over the long-range strategic force mission.[28]

Unlike the JCS, the defense secretary since the 1950s has had considerable legal (formal) authority to control and coordinate the services. In actuality, most defense secretaries have found their powers significantly circumscribed by the countervailing powers of the military services; i.e., they have lacked political power. Many defense secretaries, such as Reagan appointee Casper Weinberger, have conceded authority to the services. Others, such as Robert McNamara (Kennedy, Johnson) and James Schlesinger (Nixon), have found themselves on the losing end of a power struggle. The classic case is the TFX/F-111 fighter-bomber program controversy during the Kennedy administration.[29] The primary reasons for the defense secretary's limited influence relate to the political nature of the defense secretary's position and role and the structure and functions of the OSD. Most important is that the secretary of defense is a political appointee who serves the tenure of his president (in contrast with military personnel whose service is extensive), and whose loyalties must straddle two sets of constituencies, one in the Pentagon and the other in the executive office of the president. As an illustration, the dynamic between the Pentagon, Defense Secretary Harold Brown, and President Jimmy Carter over the cancellation of production funds for the B-1 bomber was resolved when Congress retained research and development (R&D) funding, and the Air Force arbitrarily transferred additional monies to keep the strategic bomber in development until the presidential election.[30] As concerns the institutional constraints on the OSD's power, defense analysts point out that (until recently) the OSD has been structured along functional or input lines (such as manpower and research and development) rather than output lines (such as force requirements and weapons programs). In fact, it wasn't until 1986 that a separate undersecretary of defense for procurement was appointed, although creation of this position was the cornerstone of the Packard Commission recommendations.[31] Even then, the first appointee, Richard Godwin, lasted only a year before he gave up trying to reform the military acquisition process, frustrated by the Pentagon bureaucracy that "refused to accept his leadership and blocked many of his policies."[32] In sum, the inability of the JCS or the OSD to coordinate activities effectively allows "each service to pursue its own mission and strategies largely independent of the others."[33]

Although disproportionately powerful, the military services are not fully autonomous given their placement in the military bureaucracy and subsequent reliance upon other actors and agencies. While the services conceive and initiate weapons systems, they must build a coalition of allies from within and outside the Pentagon in order to gain the support requisite to move a military program through to development and deployment. The military services first must resolve the competition from within their service (intraservice rivalry) and then from other services (interservice rivalry) as well, during the preliminary stages of the Milestone process.[34] The fragmentation of power characteristic of the Pentagon extends down to the subunits of the military services, which not only have organizational autonomy from each other, but are internally divided as well. Each service not only distinguishes between its combat and noncombat (or support) units, but among these units. The four services also differ in how they view what forces are necessary to secure the defense of the country, how military power should be organized, which weapons should be built, what strategies should be employed, and which services and missions should prevail. The command view from the Commanders-in-Chief (CINCs) differs from the administrative view of the services, despite the fact that military personnel rotate between combat and noncombat units. As noted earlier, for much of the post–Cold War era, the military services have found it expedient to collude as a strategy for compensating for the intense competition over budget shares that could doom their preferred weapons.

According to advocates of the political argument, reciprocity (if not collusion) is an important tool that the services use to overcome competition and opposition from actors outside the services. The cozy relationship between a service command, a congressional subcommittee, and a defense industry has led some to see a military subsystem. By building a stable set of relations with allies within the defense industry and Congress, the services have been able to guarantee support for their preferred programs.

The military services have come to depend upon defense contractors for research and development, and particularly for production. While most of the basic research is conducted by military laboratories, major defense companies maintain their own R&D operations. According to one insider, "The day is past when the military requirement for a major weapons system is set up by the military and passed on to industry to build the hardware. Today it is more likely that the military requirement is the result of joint participation of military and industrial personnel, and it is not unusual for industry's contribution to be a key factor."[35] When a defense company provides the impetus for a program, it generally serves both the mission needs of the service and the profit concerns of the company. More often, a defense manufacturer offers the assurances of technical feasibility that a service needs to pursue a potentially risky weapons system. In either case, the concerns that the defense industry has about its economic viability may be in conflict with military need, deflecting weapons development quite early from its intended rational course.

By entering into the process early, weapons developers enhance their chances of winning development and production contracts. The Pentagon has erected an elaborate, ostensibly open and competitive process for making contract decisions. Although competition is intense, only a few firms are sufficiently experienced and tooled to manufacture a major weapons system. For example, only two firms, the Electric Boat Division of the General Dynamics Corporation and the Newport News (Va.) Shipbuilding and Drydock Company of the Tenneco Corporation, are capable of building a nuclear submarine. Moreover, the lucrative and long-term rewards that a defense contract represents provide strong incentives for defense companies to engage in several questionable practices (such as the buy-in phenomenon), few of which carry punitive consequences. (The role of the defense industry is discussed again in chapters 4, 5, and 6.)

In short, the military services dominate, but do not control, the weapons procurement process, exercising power disproportionate to their status in the military bureaucracy, for organizational reasons. The result is a weapons procurement process that conforms more to an inverted pyramid, with decision-making proceeding in a bottom-top manner.

Cultural

The military culture that distinguishes and pervades the Pentagon serves to reinforce the structural patterns that promote parochialism and reciprocity. The survival of a military service, and that of its separate commands, is dependent upon shares of the budget, the acquisition of new weapons systems, and a service's projected role in a future military conflict. The success and therefore the survival of individuals within the military depends on achieving program outcomes. In neither case are agencies or actors rewarded for improving the decision-making processes (e.g., reducing costs, increasing efficiency) or achieving better or less costly weapons systems. The incentives, then, are strong for a service and its program managers to be optimistic (even unrealistic) in projecting the capabilities, cost, and time frame of a military program, and to act to expedite military hardware development, irrespective of quality and cost issues.[36]

As a cultural phenomenon, interservice rivalry is a by-product of the "pride" that military personnel have in their "mission, its doctrine and its customs, and discipline."[37] Moreover, interservice rivalry has contributed to an "ethos of change" in the military, a spur to innovativeness in weapons development.[38] On the negative side, interservice rivalry is faulted for promoting duplication and waste in military matters. In either case, the internecine battles being played out in the Pentagon foreshadow a more demanding bureaucratic war in the future as resources continue to shrink. In order to secure the capabilities to fight military wars, the services must first win the bureaucratic and political (or budgetary) wars. It thus becomes more rational for individuals to fight to secure their narrow organizational needs as a prerequisite to securing the broader security needs of the nation, absent an imminent military threat.

The prevailing incentive structure in the Pentagon is reinforced by a culture that equates parochial and public interests. "The belief structure of military men tends to reinforce their sense of professional importance and to justify their career to themselves."[39] Even when the military services use strategic arguments to further their organizational goals, then, these arguments may be in good faith. From the perspective of the military services, the two are indistinguishable because each service views its organizational perspective as compatible with and its organizational existence as indispensable to the public interest (national defense).[40] Accordingly, critics of the rational process model concede that the influence of nonmilitary factors in weapons development does not ipso facto evidence malfeasance or professional impropriety, although the consequences can be disastrous.[41]

The informal norms and standard operating procedures (SOPs) that are part of the military culture equip military personnel with the means to compensate for the risks and uncertainties associated with the development of major weapons systems. As noted earlier, the conditions for making rational decisions, such as perfect information and sufficient resources, are nonexistent even under the best of circumstances.[42] The challenges are even greater in the national security area. Here the problems for which solutions must be developed are extremely complex and ambiguous, the information necessary to make informed decisions is inherently uncertain and difficult to obtain, and the decisions to be made are responses to estimated "enemy" threats and military capabilities that are predicted to exist at some as-yet-undetermined future point in history. And since policy-making does not occur in a laboratory situation, other forces that cannot be controlled or compensated for influence military hardware decisions, such as the labor disputes that stalled the construction and timely completion of the Trident submarine and the political opposition in Utah and Nevada that doomed the deployment of the MX missile system in the Multiple Protective Shelter (MPS) basing mode. In short, the entire process is beset by uncertainties and ambiguities that are sure to impact weapons decisions themselves.

Consequences

From the perspective of the political and pragmatic critique, the quasi-bureaucratic structure and the military's culture for weapons development make it difficult to conceive, develop, and procure optimal military hardware, that is, the weapons best equipped to perform military missions. The foremost impediment to this is the autonomy of and competition among the services that contribute to unnecessary duplication and redundancy. As an illustration, critics of the nuclear triad note that during the Cold War the United States provided not one but three ways to deliver nuclear warheads to the Soviet Union—intercontinental ballistic missiles (ICBMs), submarine-launched ballistic missiles (SLBMs), and bombers. Moreover, the failed attempt to rescue the hostages in Iran, the muddled but ultimately successful invasion of Grenada, and the errors committed in Panama raise questions about the advisability of interservice logrolling and intraservice conflict. While some duplication is important to compensate for the uncertainties and risks of conducting foreign relations in a volatile and dangerous world, much of it is a wasteful residue of service rivalry. Rosati goes so far as to fault interservice rivalry for an out-of-control arms race that proved destabilizing during the Cold War.[43]

Another residue of the Pentagon's structure and culture are "wasteful practices" that result in wasteful spending. According to the General Accounting Office (GAO), the Pentagon continues to demand technical capabilities for their weapons that are "questionable" and have cost, schedule, and performance expectations that are "unrealistic"; use concurrency in military hardware development; and promote military hardware that is gold-plated. As recent scandals have demonstrated, gold-plating is not only evident in major weapons systems such as the F-15 fighter aircraft ($50 million apiece) and Aegis guided-missile cruiser ($1.25 billion apiece), but in simple spare parts such as hammers ($450), standard washers ($2,043), and coffee makers for warplanes ($3,046). The results of these wasteful practices are weapons that are not the most cost-effective solution to a mission need and, now, are even "questionable" given the collapse of the Soviet Union.[44]

A third consequence of current Pentagon practices is to exacerbate the delay that already is manifest in the development of highly sophisticated and complex weapons. Delay contributes to the fielding of weapons whose need is no longer pressing, although the weapons themselves are quite workable; or of weapons with capabilities that are then counteracted by advances in "enemy" technology. For example, consider concerns during the 1980s about advances in detecting stealth planes. Most seriously, though, delay can mean vulnerability during a critical period when existing weapons are no longer viable. Ronald Reagan, for example, justified his ambitious strategic modernization program (MX, B-1, Trident) by embracing the window of vulnerability argument during the 1980s. Importantly, even after the Scowcroft Commission officially discredited the window in their 1983 report, the program continued in production.

In sum, from the pragmatic and political perspectives, the weapons procurement process is a political one in which multiple actors—who hold conflicting values and perceptions and are motivated by organizational and personal concerns—engage in consensus-building that ultimately results in compromise weapons decisions. Intranational, intra-bureaucratic factors, in addition to foreign policy or national security forces, dictate military hardware decisions. Foreign and national security policy establish boundaries of permissible action, but these policy goals and objectives are insufficiently precise to bound the uncertainties that prevail in making military hardware decisions.[45] This does not mean that actors ignore foreign and national security objectives and goals. On the contrary, their organizational position and intellectual predispositions influence how they interpret these goals and objectives, and they respond accordingly. Decisions are made by individuals and organizations in the Pentagon who seek to maximize their professional interests and objectives. Weapons decisions are the results of bargaining, negotiation, and compromise among several agencies and actors. This explains why America's military hardware decisions too often reflect the internal structure and function of the military bureaucracy, rather than the public interest. In support of this portrait, analysts cite weapons whose mission capabilities are redundant (such as the D-5 Trident and MX missiles), that are nice to have but unnecessary from a broader strategic perspective (such as the Stealth bomber, the V-22 Osprey, and F-111 tactical aircraft), that are destabilizing (such as Multiple Independently-targetable Reentry Vehicles [MIRVs] and cruise missiles), that are hybrid systems (such as the M2 or Bradley personnel carrier), and that have been incomplete during critical periods of vulnerability (such as the MX missile system during the period referred to by the Reagan administration as the "window of vulnerability" before "Peacekeeper" was canceled). Rosati also cites the examples of the F-16 and F-18 fighter planes that can travel at Mach 2 (1,200 miles per hour), but that cannot sustain these speeds in an actual combat situation because they run out of gas too quickly.

A Clash of Models: An Empirical Test

The pragmatic, political, and rational process models offer contrasting descriptions of the organizational structure of the military bureaucracy and the process for making weapons decisions. Determining which analytical approach has the most descriptive and perhaps even explanatory value means answering three sets of questions. One question is whether the actual process of weapons procurement occurs in a top-bottom or bottom-top manner. A second concern is whether those involved in making weapons decisions are motivated by military or nonmilitary (i.e., organizational/personal/political) concerns. Third, are weapons decisions, as the outputs of the process, politically expedient or optimally viable?

Top-Down/Bottom-Up

On the basis of the cases of weapons procurement examined in this study, the process for making military hardware decisions conforms more to a bottom-top than top-bottom pattern. In every case examined, while the broad range of actors and agencies formally identified did play a role in the procurement process, the military services were dominant, creating a de facto centralized decision-making process at the bottom. Data calibrating the scope of participation for major weapons decisions found that in 58 percent of the cases, decision-making indeed included those policy arenas and agencies within each arena formally empowered to participate. Notwithstanding the breadth of the scope of bureaucratic in-

volvement, the military services were clearly predominant. This finding is
first supported by data indicating that a military service was the entity
that originated a major weapons system in 68 percent of the cases (see
Table 3.1). Moreover, the services prevailed in all but four cases in which
the secretary of defense and the president tried to challenge a military
recommendation. These four cases include President John Kennedy's decision to cancel the Skybolt missile program, President Jimmy Carter's
decision to cancel production of the B-1 bomber, Carter's decision to accelerate production of cruise missiles (President Reagan also supported
cruise missile production, but by that time the Air Force had come
onboard) and Reagan's decision to cancel DIVAD. In two of these cases,
however, the military service appears to have triumphed in the end.
Carter's B-1 bomber decision was effectively forestalled by the Air Force
and reversed by Reagan; the Air Force was compensated for the Skybolt
cancellation first with additional ICBMs and then with a new strategic
bomber program. In sum, the data seem to confirm both the autonomy
of the military services and the reluctance or inability of the secretary of
defense or president to effectively counter that autonomy. The military
services are clearly the preeminent actors in military hardware decisions.

TABLE 3.1

Structure of the Pentagon: Who Rules?

	Criteria		
Name	Originating Agency[1]	Concessions? y/n[2]	Administration Position[3]
Skybolt[4]	Service	no	opposed
Thor-Jupiter	Service	no	supported
TFX	OSD	yes	supported
Polaris	Service	no	supported
MX	Service	minor	supported
B-1	Service	minor	supported (Carter-opposed)
Cheyenne[4]	Service	yes	supported
C-5A	Service	no	supported
M16	Sub-Group[5]	yes	supported
Trident	Service	yes	supported
Bradley	Service	yes	opposed
A-10	Service	no	supported

(continued)

TABLE 3.1 *(continued)*

Name	Originating Agency[1]	Concessions? y/n[2]	Administration Position[3]
F-16	OSD	yes	supported
M-1	Service	yes	supported
Aegis	Service	minor	supported
Cruise	OSD	no	supported
DIVAD[4]	Service	no	supported
F/A-18	DDR&E	yes	supported (Carter-OSD opposed)
Skipper	Sub-Group[5]	no	supported

[1]Refers to the department or agency in which the weapon originated.

[2]Refers to the extent to which the originating agency found it expedient or necessary to compromise its original design and performance expectations in order to secure support from other groups and actors within the Pentagon.

[3]Refers to the position of the presidential administration.

[4]Indicates weapons that were canceled.

[5]In both cases, the weapon originated outside the normal service channels for initiating major weapons systems. Engineers at the China Lake Weapons Center developed the Skipper. The M-16 was the product of the Army Infantry Board and the defense industry.

Does Where You Sit Determine Where You Stand?

A second major point of contention between adherents to the different analytical approaches is what motivates actors to make decisions. Are policymakers rational actors who respond to military needs in developing weapons decisions? Or do defense planners and analysts in the Pentagon make decisions guided by their organizational position or affiliation—does "where you stand (on a policy issue) depend upon where you sit (in the bureaucracy)"? Any effort to measure motivations will be flawed given the difficulty of calibrating the cognitive process that precedes policy action. Even interview data (which were collected on weapons systems for which a completed case study was not available) are subject to contextual factors that cannot be effectively controlled for. Since establishing motivations is central to resolving the debate between the analytical approaches, surrogate measures were established as described below.

The rational process model assumes that weapons decisions are objective responses to clearly identified military problems (threats), on which there is a consensus of opinion. Therefore, it is first necessary to establish that there was a clear military need for a particular weapons system. To control for the subjectivity of the researcher, military need was gauged by assessing the *amount of agreement* among military analysts and defense analysts over the need for a particular weapons system. According to Reed, "[r]ational decision making, by definition, requires consensus on goals and objectives. . . ."[46]

In order to test the second presumption, that nonmilitary (i.e., bureaucratic/organizational and political) concerns prevail, the positions of key actors (for or against a weapons system) were compared with what their organizational role would predict. By combining the data and setting the position of the military service (for or against a weapon) in the context of the broader debate (if one exists) within the defense community over the military need for the weapon, it is possible to address both concerns. It is also possible to disentangle organizational from strategic issues and establish which of the two sets of influences predominant in any given weapons decision.

The nature of the military debate was assessed at the time the weapon was conceived (during Milestone 0-I). The measure was determined by consulting academic studies and government sources, most notably reports by the GAO, Congressional Budget Office (CBO), Congressional Research Service (CRS), and the *Congressional Record*. The position of the military service under whose jurisdiction the weapon would be developed was compared with the measure of military need. For example, the Air Force was (initially) opposed to the development of cruise missiles, which they viewed as jeopardizing the procurement of the B-1 bomber (organizational factor). In contrast, civilian personnel in the Pentagon and President Carter were enthusiastically supportive because they saw unmanned drones as safer, as accurate as missiles fired from bombers, and cheaper to produce than the B-1 (military factor). The assumption is that if a consensus exists that there is a strong military need for a particular weapons system, and the service opposes it, then some evidence supports the conclusion that organizational concerns have prevailed or been decisive. Conversely, if a service supports a weapon that others oppose for military reasons, organizational concerns are no doubt operating. Thus, the data in Table 3.2 should be read as follows. Column 2 cites the position of the military service (pro or con) and column 3 indicates whether there is (yes) or is not (no) evidence of a well-established military need for a weapon. Beginning with Skybolt, and continuing in the same pattern, although the Air Force supported the missile program, the president and important groups in the Pentagon opposed it because of the availability of cheaper and more effective alternatives such as ICBMs and SLBMs. The table concludes with Skipper, which the Navy opposed, although there was a clear military need for such a weapon (yes). In fact, the Navy, until Skipper and despite advances in aircraft (F-14 and F/A-18), had not upgraded its munitions since the late 1960s.

TABLE 3.2

Does Military Need or Organizational Position Prevail?

Weapon	Position-Service	Military Need
	(Pro/Con)	(Yes/No)
Skybolt	Pro	No
Thor-Jupiter	Pro	Yes
TFX	Con	Yes
Polaris	Pro	Yes
MX	Pro	No
B-1	Pro	No
Cheyenne	Pro	No
C-5A	Pro	Yes
M16	Con	Yes
Trident	Pro	Yes
Bradley	Pro	Yes
A-10	Pro	Yes
F-16	Pro	Yes
M-1	Pro	Yes
Aegis	Pro	Yes
Cruise	Con	Yes
DIVAD	Pro	Yes
F/A-18	Con	Yes
Skipper	Con	Yes

Table 3.2 summarizes a composite measure of both issues raised by the second theoretical concern. What can be concluded? In the bare majority of cases (53 percent), the position of the services is compatible with the military need for a weapons system. This is not definitive proof that the service is motivated by military, as opposed to organizational, concerns in the majority of cases. But it is heartening that, whatever the services' motivations, a well-established military need still exists for the majority of weapons, or

at least agreement on the need. Viewed differently, the data also suggest that in 47 percent of the cases, the military services are promoting (or opposing) weapons that are viewed as unnecessary (or necessary) from a military perspective. Given the closeness of the figures, it can either be concluded that the data challenge the view that the services are conceiving weapons for which there is no military rationale or reaffirm the assumption that the services are too often motivated by organizational concerns. Since the measure was taken at the initial stages of the procurement process, the data also do not rule out the possibility that weapons, once conceived, are transformed by the military service in ways that invalidate their original justification. This possibility is addressed below.

The same data can be read as evidence of considerable conflict between the military services and other groups in the Pentagon over the military need for a weapon in 47 percent of the cases. The existence of conflict is central to the pragmatic and political explanations, because it creates the incentive (in some cases, the requirement) for the bargaining and negotiation that is said to occur on major weapons systems. In sum, the evidence is inconclusive, although it is disconcerting that 47 percent of the weapons systems procured raise questions in the defense community about their military value.

Optimal or Politically Expedient?

A third point of contention concerns the nature of the outputs of the policy-making process: whether the weapons that result are the most optimal solutions to particular military problems or are compromise decisions on which agreement has been reached by the largest number of actors with a stake in the policies.[47] According to the political argument, in addition to being compromise decisions, policy outputs are often "unintended," resulting as they do from a process of bargaining and negotiation among key actors.

One important way to document bargaining is to determine the extent to which an original weapons idea, wholly supported by the originating agency, is modified as it passes through the various procurement stages. That is, to what extent were concessions made to subsequent actors in moving a military program through the bureaucracy? This chronology can also illuminate whether the final weapon conforms to the preferences of the originating agency, thus providing evidence of an "unintended resultant." If there is little evidence of compromise, and the final weapon fulfills the expectations of the originating agency (usually a military service), then the assumption of an "unintended resultant" is invalid. In establishing whether a weapons system is a compromise, the capabilities of the completed weapon are compared with the mission requirements previously established. Once again, government documents and scholarly case studies are the sources of data.

It has already been shown that in the majority of cases in this study, the military services initiated a weapons decision. The questions that remain are to what extent the originating service was compelled to compromise with other actors to advance its preferred weapon through the procurement process, whether the final weapon was modified significantly in the process of any bargaining and negotiation that is uncovered, and whether the final decision was a compromise one.

Table 3.1 summarizes data from a chronology of each weapons decision that identifies within which agency or office a weapons system originated and whether concessions were made by the originating agency to other key actors during the development and production stages. Other actors considered include another unit within the service (to partially capture intraservice rivalry), another military service (to partially capture interservice rivalry), the OSD, the JCS, a government research group, Congress, the president, and/or a defense contractor. The table also includes data that respond to the question of whether the original design of the weapon was modified because of concessions made to offices or individuals other than the originating agency. Since a number of the weapons in this study span several presidential administrations and the tenure of several defense secretaries, weapons systems on which administrative positions varied are cited more than once in the table.

First, consider in how few cases (30 percent) the military services made concessions in the design of a weapon (other than minor ones) to other groups within the Pentagon in order to win support for their preferred weapon. (This figure considers only cases in which a military service was the originating agency.) Even in the one of the two cases in which a subgroup within the military service bucked tradition and originated a rival weapon, the military service triumphed in the end. In the case of the M-16 rifle, which was conceived by the Army Infantry Board ("maverick" group), the Army Ordinance Department ("mainstream" group) was allowed to reformulate the performance specifications and redesign the rifle so that it would conform to traditional Army standards. As a result, the first series of M-16 rifles sent to Vietnam malfunctioned at such a rate that soldiers wrote home about them to their parents, and the Vietcong did not bother to retrieve the jammed rifles after successful battles with the Americans. In the other case, the Skipper bomb survived (remarkably) despite not only resistance from the majority of the Navy leadership, but the Air Force as well, which was supporting the development of a rival weapon. What literally saved the Skipper, which was conceived by "renegade" engineers at the Naval Weapons Center at China Lake ("mavericks"), was pressure from Anthony R. Battista, senior staff member of the House Armed Services Committee, the intervention of Navy Secretary John F. Lehman Jr., and the fact that the Skipper was an inexpensive and low-priority item for the Navy.

Similar results occurred when the OSD tried to "force" a weapon on a military service. In the majority of these cases, in the end, the OSD was compelled to concede ultimate decision-making authority to an originally reluctant military service in order to secure the support necessary to propel the weapon through the procurement process. The extreme example is the F-111, which was foiled by the Air Force and Navy. Another example is the F-16 fighter plane, which the Air Force originally resisted because of concerns that it would compete with the twin engine F-15, which they preferred. In the latter case, the Air Force was allowed to redesign the new fighter plane to incorporate features considered indispensable to performing air-to-air combat missions. In the process the plane was changed from a simple, light, maneuverable aircraft to one considerably heavier, more expensive, and more complex. In the case of the F-111 (TFX), the Air Force and Navy were successful in bifurcating the program so that each service could build the plane according to its organizational needs. The Navy version was canceled, although the Air Force version eventually matured (after major failed missions in Vietnam) into a competent fighter plane. Ultimately, the Air Force and Navy got funding for the planes they really wanted (the F-15 and F-14, respectively) despite McNamara's mandate for a joint service endeavor. The OSD did prevail in one important case involving the air-launched cruise missile (ALCM) program, which the Air Force eventually embraced after it realized it would otherwise lose its manned strategic bomber program.

Implicit in the political argument is the assumption that conflict breeds bargaining and negotiation, which produce compromise decisions that are not the best solution to a particular military problem. To a large extent, all governmental decisions are compromise ones, given the limits on rational decision-making and the dictates of the democratic process (pragmatic argument). The important question, then, is not whether America's military arsenal is full of weapons whose performance parameters and capabilities are the product of compromise, but whether in reaching a compromise, the viability of a weapon has been eroded. In other words, it doesn't really matter whether the M-1 tank reflects extensive bargaining and negotiation as long as it is a weapon that can perform its mission reliably in an actual combat situation. In fact, in the case of the M-1, the tank actually benefited from the process of negotiation that preceded its deployment. To what extent can the same be said of the other weapons in this study?

To capture the effects of compromise on weapons systems, earlier data ascribing to each weapons system a performance classification (sound/flawed) were correlated with the evidence in Table 3.1 identifying whether concessions were made in the bargaining over a particular weapons system. (This time, the entire sample was considered.) Table 3.3 contains the results. The cases are dispersed fairly equally throughout the cells, suggesting that the relationship is not a significant one. In other words, no evidence suggests that compromise is inevitably pernicious. In some important cases, including the Trident submarine and M-1 tank, the effects of compromise were valuable ones. In contrast, in some equally important cases, the effects of compromise were debilitating to the development of the weapon, most notably the Cheyenne helicopter and the Bradley personnel carrier. In short, while compromise can adversely affect weapons development, it doesn't always do so, suggesting that other forces also contribute to design and performance flaws.

TABLE 3.3

Compromise (Concessions) by Performance Problems

	Compromise?	
	Yes	No
Performance Problems?		
Yes	50%	45%
No	50%	55%
(N)	(8)	(11)

It is apparent that on most weapons systems, the military services are able to push through their preferred programs with few concessions to other actors and agencies in the Pentagon. In other words, if the services are engaged in compromise and negotiation with other actors in order to win support for their preferred program (as the political argument suggests), this has only minor effects on the performance capabilities of the weapons, with some important exceptions such as the Bradley personnel carrier. More importantly, the effects of bargaining and negotiation are not necessarily negative ones.

The evidence in this chapter fully supports neither the rational process nor the competing explanations. Rather, the pattern for making weapons procurement decisions validates elements of all three perspectives. More precisely, the military services are the defense planners most in control of weapons procurement, but they are also the actors best equipped to assess their military needs. Rarely do the services find themselves compelled to make serious compromises on the weapons they prefer, but this is not necessarily due to an absence of internal checks and balances on military service authority. In addition to their control, the military services appear too often (47 percent of the cases in this study) to be motivated by nonmilitary or organizational concerns. But in the bare majority of cases (53 percent), there is a clear consensus that a proposed weapons system is militarily needed.

Conclusion

What has been described in this chapter is the standard pattern for making procurement decisions in the Cold War period. The obvious question is whether this pattern is and will continue to be appropriate in the post–Cold War era. In other words, how relevant is the organizational structure and culture of the military establishment and the weapons procurement process for making the difficult decisions that are mandated by the easing of tensions between the United States and its former enemies? To what extent is the Pentagon in a position to incorporate or even resist efforts to downsize the military and reorient the force structure that the United States needs to meet future threats (mostly contingency and low-intensity)? What sorts of reforms are likely to be useful for preparing the military services for the changes in missions and norms that are prerequisites to confronting the problems facing national security policy in the future?

While these questions are difficult ones, several insights can be drawn from the analysis in this chapter and from past reform efforts. The most important of these is that the autonomy that the military services have exercised in the past will not work in the future. Organizational change is inevitable, and, to be effective, it must come from the top, not the bottom, of the military bureaucracy. The pattern of reforms during the past forty years has been toward more centralization at the top (through the JCS and the OSD) to balance the disproportionate power being exercised at the bottom by the military services. There have been two lines of reform. One has focused on strengthening the ability of the JCS and the OSD (in addition to the president and the NSC) at the preliminary stages to more carefully circumscribe the discretion of the services (through the NIE, defense planning guidance, and so on). The second line of reform has focused on improving the oversight that is exercised after preliminary decisions are made. The most obvious example is the institutionalization of extraservice approval through the Milestone process.

What the evidence from this study suggests is that those reforms directed at installing a viable system of checks and balances, one that recognizes the important expertise of the military services, but submits their decisions to oversight, are the most likely to work. To be successful, though, these reforms must alter the current incentive structure and release civilian and military personnel from the bondage of organizational affiliation.[48] This suggests needed changes in both the structure and the culture of the Pentagon. Of those structural changes made recently, the most notable are (1) releasing the Chairman of the JCS and the defense secretary from parochial ties and increasing their authority to make and enforce independent judgments, (2) restoring power to the CINCs and giving them a direct line to the JROC, (3) shifting to a biennial budget cycle, to allow more time for planning, (4) creating an under secretary of defense for acquisition and technology to provide more centralized control and supervision over the weapons acquisition process by OSD, and (5) establishing a deputy under secretary of defense for acquisition reform to initiate and guide acquisition reform efforts.[49]

Yet to be completed are Clinton administration efforts to further streamline and simplify the acquisition process by eliminating some regulations and requirements. The GAO, which is monitoring these changes, warned the Pentagon to be attentive to the delicate balance "between the cost of oversight and controls [and] the risk of making inadequately informed program decisions."[50] In other words, by removing layers of oversight, the advantages of this most democratic of procedures could be compromised, that is, decisions that benefit from the broad debate that several actors bring to an issue. As McNaugher notes, defense procurement is "a political process and must remain so, since it uses public money to buy a public good called defense."[51] In addition to instituting measures to streamline the agency, the Pentagon has taken the initiative to eliminate redundancy at the requirements stage; improve its means of estimating the cost, performance, and schedules of military hardware; and reduce the use of concurrency in high-risk weapons programs. (The Pentagon currently is using a concurrent management strategy in the F-22 program, however.) Another encouraging sign is the attention being paid to equalizing the painful process of cutting back the force structure, so that the sacrifice is shared by all four services, to preempt the collusion that might occur.

Congress has mandated further changes in the acquisition process with its passage of the Federal Acquisition Streamlining Act of 1994 and the National Defense Authorization Act for FY 1994. In the first act, the defense secretary is required to make personnel decisions (pay/promotions) on the basis of whether individuals achieve the projected cost, schedule, and performance goals for each phase of the acquisition cycle, rather than for the completed system. The Pentagon is also required to report to Congress on whether it is "achieving on average 90 percent of its cost, schedule, and performance goals" for military hardware. The act also eliminates some of the bureaucratic barriers to the military's buying of commercial components and streamlines the procurement process by reducing paperwork and some oversight provisions, such as strict testing and auditing requirements. The second act establishes the Commission on Roles and Missions of the Armed Forces. The primary mandate of the commission is to "examine the division of labor and responsibility among and within the military services [and determine] the most cost-effective mix of weapons to accomplish those missions and the services' responsibilities."[52] If successful, the commission's findings could offset interservice and intraservice rivalry. In addition to reevaluating the roles and missions of the services, the commission is empowered to examine the weapons acquisition process for evidence of duplication.

More than a decade has passed since the Packard Commission issued its recommendations (*A Quest for Excellence,* June 1986) and Congress passed the 1986 Department of Defense Reorganization Act mandating that the Pentagon reform its procedures and restructure its department. While these recommendations for the most part have been implemented and institutionalized, the military culture remains relatively impervious to change. As such, current reform efforts need to be directed toward altering those common practices in the Pentagon that promote parochialism. The plethora of reform activity notwithstanding, one dynamic of the Pentagon's structure, while altered, is unlikely to be eliminated—the division of authority along civilian-military, administrative-military, and command lines. The continuing existence of four separate and distinct military services, a civilian–military distinction, and a command and administration division set up adversarial relationships that cut across any organizational hierarchy. The four services continue to differ in how they view what forces are necessary to secure the defense of the country, the command view from the CINCs differs from the administrative view of the services,[53] and military and civilian actors respond to varying incentives best captured by Allison's statement that "where you stand depends upon where you sit." According to President Clinton's first term defense secretary, William Perry, resistance to reform from the Pentagon (as well as Congress and the defense industry) is still significant. Even labor and veterans' groups have joined the fray to protect special preferences that they receive under current acquisition laws.[54]

Even if the Pentagon was successfully reorganized, these changes would not automatically insure that the best decisions concerning weapons systems would result. Unless these organizational changes are complemented by major changes in the other sectors of the defense process, the results are likely to be disappointing.[55] Even the best weapons decision can be modified or counteracted by subsequent actions taken by the White House and Congress. And all weapons decisions are affected by the availability and reliability of technology. To what extent technology is capable of actually interfering with organizational and structural changes, and dictating weapons decisions, is the topic of the next chapter.

Notes

1. The following description is a composite account drawn from the defense and foreign policy literature. It has been corroborated with interviews in the Pentagon.

2. Samuel Huntington, "Organization and Strategy," in *Reorganizing America's Defense: Leadership in War and Peace*, eds. Robert J. Art, et al. (Washington, D.C.: Pergamon-Brassey's, 1985), 235.

3. During the planning stage (of PPBS), a number of different strategies are examined, a threat assessment made, and technology evaluated in terms of conceivable alternatives. During the programming stage, the hardware choices are made after an analysis is conducted of the alternatives to and consequences of weapons decisions. The budgeting stage links the process to the congressional authorizations and appropriations processes.

   Each weapon originates within a military service as a response to a military problem or need that is revealed by the threat assessment conducted annually. In advance of a Milestone O decision, the service defines the mission (MENs) that justifies a new or upgraded weapon system, and the operational requirements of the weapon if it is to perform its mission. (Prior to 1976 [Circular A-109], mission need was expressed in terms of performance specifications or system characteristics rather than operational requirements.) At this point JROC compares and ranks all of the major weapons being sought by the four services against each other. Once the mission and weapon idea are approved (Milestone 0), the project moves to the demonstration and validation stage of the Milestone process. It is during this second stage that the weapon idea takes on more form, and the operational requirements are fully assessed against the full range of alternatives. With Milestone I approval, the weapon proceeds into the next phase when a prototype of the weapon actually undergoes limited production for operational testing and evaluation. (The design for the weapons system and its support components also proceed.) With approval (Milestone II), the weapon enters the final procurement stage, which extends from production approval to the actual deployment of the weapons system to active forces. In theory, a weapon can still be terminated at this stage for performance failure or excessive cost overruns (Milestone III). Once a weapon has been in service for awhile, reviews are conducted one or two (Milestone IV) and then five to ten years later (Milestone V) to determine whether the system is operational. The DAB was created to examine each military service's acquisition wish-list to determine the necessity of items relative to strategic requirements. See Fen Hampson, *Unguided Missiles* (New York: W.W. Norton, 1989), chapter 2, for a fuller discussion of the PPBS and Milestone processes.

4. The CIA and DIA are assisted by several additional groups including the National Security Association (NSA), the National Reconnaissance Office, the State Department's Bureau of Intelligence and Research, and the intelligence divisions in the separate military services. Since the Goldwater-Nichols (or DoD Reorganization) Act 1986, the field command units (CINCs) have played a greater role in gathering intelligence data and threat assessment. The CINCs also have formal access to the JCS, and exercise more power in weapons decisions than in the past, when the administrative arms of the military services prevailed. This has resulted in the reduction of the power and autonomy of the services. This is the case because the 1986 act created an operational line running from the president and defense secretary to the CINCs to assist in the development of strategy, operational plans, weapons, and force level requirements; and an administrative line running from the president and defense secretary to the services to provide the forces needed by the combatant commands. The act also insures that the needs of the CINCs are included in the services' POMs through the integrated priorities list (IPLs), which requires the Pentagon to undergo a major reorganization and restructuring of their roles and missions, and modifies the *Annual Report of the Secretary of Defense*.

5. The NSC is the principal national security planning agency. It is linked directly to the PPBS and JSP systems, which make defense policy and force development decisions. It is input from NSC that composes the presidential decisions that set out our current military policy.

6. The secretary of defense prepares the defense planning guidance report that establishes military priorities, sets precise goals, and delineates military strategy. The defense guidance report is the "official statement outlining the strategy the department of defense should pursue to meet that threat." The annual consolidated guidance report was intended to both promote policy guidance in budgeting and reduce the power of the military services. Since 1982 DoD requires that the defense guidance consider fiscal constraints in an effort to produce more realistic goals and direction, and to strengthen the links between the planning, and programming and budgeting phases of the PPBS process.

7. The Bush administration replaced the DRB with the downsized Defense Planning and Resources Board (DPRB). See Colonel John M. Dorger, "Resource Allocation Planning in the Department of Defense: Putting the First 'P' Into PPBS," 1990 (unpublished manuscript), DoD, The Pentagon.

8. JROC was created during the 1980s to evaluate weapons programs at the Milestone 0 and I decision points.

9. In 1986 the Packard Commission released its recommendations for creating a more centralized and disciplined military policy-making process capable of matching strategy with force structure. Congress responded with statutory authorization. A number of the recommendations are directed toward the improvement of the performance of weapons systems, and some have been implemented with the Goldwater-Nichols Act of 1986 (DoD Reorganization Act of 1986), the Military Retirement Reform Act of 1986, the Defense Acquisition Improvement Act of 1986, and the 1987 Defense Authorization Bill. In 1989 Defense Secretary Dick Cheney released his own set of recommendations in the defense management report. His recommendations, many of which have been implemented, sought to streamline the decision-making process (through the elimination of some regulations and requirements), clarify the lines of authority (especially those of the chairman of the JCS, the defense secretary, and the CINCs), revitalize the planning part of the PPBS, make the defense guidance document a viable one that matches resources to needs or strategy, and rework the military services' mission assignments, strategies, and doctrines.

10. President's Blue Ribbon Commission on Defense Management, *A Quest for Excellence: Final Report to the President*, June 1986, 5. Herein referred to as the Packard Commission.

11. The conditions for making rational decisions, such as perfect information and sufficient resources, are nonexistent even under the best of circumstances. See Herbert Simon, *Administrative Behavior: A Study of Decision-Making Processes in Administrative Organization* (New York: The Free Press, 1976). As was noted in the last chapter, the challenges are even greater in the national security area. Here the problems for which solutions must be developed are extremely complex and ambiguous, the information necessary to make informed decisions is inherently uncertain and difficult to obtain, and the decisions to be made are responses to estimated "enemy" threats and military capabilities that are predicted to exist at some as yet determined future point in history. In short, the entire process is beset by uncertainties and ambiguities that are sure to impact weapons decisions themselves. This means that planners and decision makers, to some extent, must rely upon projection and estimation. This may lead to a situation where a weapon, conceived to perform a certain mission in anticipation of a defense need, is deployed at a time when the need is no longer pressing, although the weapon may be quite workable. Or, the result might be that a weapon's capabilities are counteracted by advances in "enemy" technology by the time it is deployed. Since weapons take on average five to fifteen years to be deployed, and can be in the inventory for as many as thirty years, military planners must anticipate a threat well in advance. Finally, whether the United States has miscalculated an "enemy" reaction may not become evident until engagement in an actual conflict.

12. *Unguided Missiles*, 19.

13. *IEEE Spectrum*, November 1988: 41.

14. *New York Times*, 24 April 1990, A23.

15. Until 1982 this was the case because the services actually issued POMs before the defense guidance was completed. This sequence has been reversed so that now guidance is suppose to drive the POMs.

16. More often, an agreement is reached between industry and the military to modify performance expectations or redefine the mission. According to J. Ronald Fox, while in theory "if a weapon system developed by a contractor is not satisfactory in terms of performance or cost, it will not enter production, [in practice] when a weapon system performs unsatisfactorily, DoD normally arranges an accommodation with the company already under contract." Examples include the F-111, C-5A, MK-48 torpedo, and TACFIRE battlefield electronic control system. Ronald J. Fox, *The Defense Management Challenge: Weapons Acquisition* (Boston.: Harvard Business School Press, 1988), 27.

17. According to one defense analyst, it is the public belief that those in the Pentagon are "a bunch of cheaters" that in turn contributed to the web of regulations that the current reform efforts are just beginning to untangle. Interview with author, notes, Pentagon, 11 April 1990.

18. David C. Jones, "What's Wrong with Our Defense Establishment?" *New York Times Magazine*, 7 November 1982: 38.

19. Jerel A. Rosati, *The Politics of United States Foreign Policy* (New York: Harcourt Brace Jovanovich, 1993), 145.

20. Ibid., 144.

21. U.S. General Accounting Office, *Defense Weapons Systems Acquisition* (Washington, D.C.: Government Printing Office, February 1995), 16–17.

22. U.S. Congress, *Defense Organization: The Need for Change*, Committee Print, Senate Committee on Armed Services, 99 Cong. 1 sess. (Government Printing Office, 1985), 623.

23. Donald Snow, *National Security: Defense Policy for a New International Order*, 3rd. ed. (New York: St. Martin's Press, 1995).

24. Ibid., 144. Since the McNamara era, the services have found it expedient not to engage in rivalry per se but logrolling. Initially, this was a reaction to the implementation of PPBS, which placed the military services in the position of competing for scarce resources to support favored weapons systems. Once it became clear to the services that a defense secretary could exploit interservice rivalry to advance his own defense goals, the services agreed "to submerge divergent views on the important issues for mutual parochial gain." Also, Center for International Studies (CIS), *Defense Organization: The Need for Change*, 619. Rivalry continues at lower levels of organizational activity. See Morton Mintz, *America Inc.: Who Owns and Operates the U.S.* (New York: Dial Press, 1971), 26. General David C. Jones describes the interaction among the services resulting in "negotiated treaties." According to Jones, the services avoid challenges to their interest with the result that gaps and unwarranted duplications in our defense capabilities are not removed through professional oversight. "What is lacking is a counterbalancing system, one that involves officers not so beholden to their services, who can objectively examine strategy, roles, missions, weapons systems, war planning, and other contentious issues to offset the influence of the individual services." See Jones, "What's Wrong with the Defense Establishment?" in *Defense Reform Debate*, eds. Asa A. Clark IV et al. (Baltimore: The Johns Hopkins University Press, 1984), 272–286. For a more positive perspective on interservice rivalry as a spurt to innovation see Thomas L. McNaugher, *New Weapons Old Politics* (Washington, D.C.: The Brookings Institution, 1989) and Lawrence Korb, *The Fall and Rise of the Pentagon: American Defense Policies in the 1970s* (Westport, Conn.: Greenwood Press, 1979).

25. Jones, "What's Wrong with Our Defense Establishment?" *New York Times Magazine,* 7 November 1982, 38.

26. Defense spending reached a peak level for procurement in 1985. Since that time, procurement spending has declined by approximately 65 percent. The number of tanks, strategic missiles, aircraft, and ships purchased have declined by 100 percent, 95 percent, 86 percent, and 80 percent, respectively. *Defense News,* 14 February 1994–20 February 1994, p. 1.

27. The legislation passed that year and affecting reorganization and reform includes the Military Retirement Reform Act of 1986, the Defense Acquisition Improvement Act of 1986, and the Department of Defense Reorganization Act of 1986. While it is still too early to assess the full impact of the legislation passed in 1986 on defense policy (since it authorizes the Pentagon to engage in a reorganization of the institution), it is interesting to mention the initial reaction to the newly created position of under secretary of defense, acquisitions, established by the Military Retirement Act of 1986. The first acquisitions chief resigned in frustration after only five months, citing the resistance of the military services to his power. Efforts at reorganization begun by the Bush administration were continued under the Clinton administration.

28. National Security Studies Panel, discussion, International Studies Association Meeting, Washington, D.C., 12 April 1990.

29. When McNamara found that both the Air Force and the Navy were developing new tactical fighters, he proposed a joint effort, one plane that would meet the needs of both services, but with enough commonality to save the expense of two separate programs. The services were successful in resisting this effort. Although McNamara did have some notable successes in the strategic area, none of the programs canceled during the Kennedy administration succeeded without some concessions to the military services on the part of the OSD. Here, the classic examples are the Skybolt and Minuteman missile compromises.

30. Evangelista would attribute the success of the military to the lack of legal formalism and the existence of organizational slack in the Pentagon. The first concept is defined as "the extent to which an organization imposes set rules and procedures for its members to follow," and the second as "the degree to which uncommitted resources are available to an organization." See Matthew Evangelista, *Innovation and the Arms Race: How the United States and the Soviet Union Develop New Military Technologies* (Ithaca: Cornell University Press, 1988), 38, 45.

31. Barry M. Blechman and William J. Lynn, eds., *Toward a More Effective Defense: Report of the Defense Reorganization Project* (Cambridge, Mass.: Ballinger, 1985), 2, 17.

32. *Defense News,* 22 November 1993–28 November 1993, p. 1.

33. Rosati, *The Politics of United States Foreign Policy,* 151.

34. See James Fallows, *National Defense* (New York: Random House, 1981), 20.

35. Quoted in Hampson, *Unguided Missiles,* 7.

36. Rosati, *The Politics of United States Foreign Policy,* 147.

37. Stubbing, *Defense Game,* 33.

38. Evangelista, *Innovation and the Arms Race,* 60.

39. Ted Greenwood, *Making the MIRV: A Study of Defense Decision Making* (Cambridge, Mass.: Ballinger, 1975), 52–57.

40. According to Greenwood, "There is no doubt that for the military, strategic preference blends with organizational interest until it is difficult to distinguish between them. Strategic arguments are employed in order to advance the

programs that the technical organizations need in order to remain active, to maintain their technological and organizational independence and to expand or protect their roles and missions. But strategic preferences also form part of the belief structure of military personnel and are thereby influential in their own right." Greenwood, *Making the MIRV*, 80.

41. See Alexander L. George, "Adapting to Constraints on Rational Decisionmaking," in *International Politics: Anarchy, Force, Political Economy, and Decision-Making*, eds. Robert J. Art and Robert Jervis (New York: Harper Collins, 1985), 491–509.

42. See Herbert Simon, *Administrative Behavior: A Study of Decision-Making Processes in Administrative Organization* (New York: The Free Press, 1976).

43. Rosati, *Politics of United States Foreign Policy*, 155.

44. GAO, *Defense Weapons Systems Acquisition*, 10.

45. The PPBS and the Milestone Review Process were intended to bound these uncertainties. Because these processes define structure and functions, they cannot dictate and, thus, limit behavior, however.

46. In Clark et al., *Defense Reform Debate*, 237.

47. Roger Hilsman, *The Politics of Policy Making in Defense and Foreign Affairs: Conceptual Models and Bureaucratic Politics*, 3rd ed. (Englewood Cliffs, N.J.: Prentice-Hall, 1993), 72.

48. A number of people believe that the Pentagon already has sufficient means to produce better weapons decisions, and that what prevents the defense process from working more efficiently and effectively is the incentive structure that is built into the process. The relationship between structure and incentives is an age-old dilemma. Will reorganization modify the motivations causing people to act in parochial ways, or are systemic changes evidence that the culture and values of members of the Pentagon are in the process of reorientation? Personal interview, notes, International Studies Association Meeting, Washington, D.C., 12 April 1990. Personal interview, notes, Pentagon, 11 April 1990. For additional attention to this question see Robert F. Coulam, *Illusions of Choice: The F-111 and the Problem of Weapons Acquisition Reform* (Princeton: Princeton University Press,1977), 390. Also, *New York Times*, 15 July 1987 and Fallows, *National Defense*, 63.

49. GAO, *Defense Weapons Systems Acquisition*, 19.

50. Ibid.

51. Thomas L. McNaugher, "Break a Few Rules," *International Defense Review* 1 (February 1994): 3.

52. GAO, *Defense Weapons Systems Acquisition*, 23.

53. According to Stubbing, "[w]hile the developers are interested in advanced weaponry to counter the theoretical threats of the twenty-first century, field commanders are interested in modern, effective reliable weapons which can be deployed in adequate numbers to counter the immediate threat. At times the two distinct goals can be fused in a successful weapon-development effort." *Defense Game*, 156.

54. *Defense News*, 22 November 1993–28 November 1993, p. 1.

55. Robert F. Coulam, *Illusions of Choice: The F-111 and the Problem of Weapons Acquisition Reform* (Princeton: Princeton University Press, 1977), 390.

HIGHLIGHT

Cheyenne
When Everything Goes Wrong

The Cheyenne helicopter was conceived to fill a widely recognized gap in close air support and was canceled because it was an operational failure, the victim of interservice rivalry, excessive technical expectations, and contract irregularities.

The Kennedy administration gave birth to the idea of an aircraft (to replace the UH-1B) capable of performing close air support (in 1961) consistent with its policy of flexible response and its objective to build an unconventional warfare (counterinsurgency) capability. The confusion created by the Key West Agreement of 1948 (which designated service missions and roles) was the incentive for the Air Force and Army to fight over control of the new program. The Army pushed a helicopter to give itself a role in the close air support mission dominated by the Air Force. The reluctance of the Air Force to take more seriously its (unglamorous) mission to protect Army ground forces fueled the battle. The Air Force sought to protect its role by attacking helicopters (to which the Army was limited) as inept. McNamara intervened and contrived for the Army to win the competition through the source selection decisions, a feat made possible by the changes he brought to the Pentagon (PPBS and systems analysis, e.g.) and the close ties of the assistant secretary of research and development to Lockheed (where he had been vice president).

Victory was short-lived, however, as the Army found its program mired in technical problems (three prototype crashes with one death), cost overruns (seven times the estimated costs), and schedule delays. The convergence of demanding technology, contractor malfeasance, an inappropriate contract scheme, organizational constraints, and bureaucratic politics explains the Cheyenne's demise. Since it was the first helicopter designed specifically as a combat vehicle, the technological demands of the Cheyenne were tremendous (even revolutionary). Working under the constraints of a fixed force structure and with no funding ceiling, the Army mandated that the helicopter perform many missions (including fire support, reconnaissance, and escorting) and sport all sorts of "bells

(continued)

Cheyenne (continued)

and whistles" (gold-plated). The contractor (Lockheed), which made exaggerated claims in order to get the contract (such as cost, speed, and weight estimates), was selected over two more-seasoned companies and committed to a fixed-price contract (total program procurement). The problems with technology eventually resulted in the downgrading of Cheyenne's performance standards and the narrowing of its mission capabilities, effectively orphaning the weapon.

Primary Sources: Craig Liske and Barry Rundquist, *The Politics of Weapons Procurement: The Role of Congress* (Denver, Colo.: University of Denver, 1974); G. Michael Mullen, *Choppers Grounded: The Supply-Demand Problem* (Washington, D.C.: National Defense University Press, 1988); *Aviation Week and Space Technology* (several issues).

HIGHLIGHT

Skipper
Beating the Odds

An "anomaly," a weapon that was designed to fulfill a well-established need (increase the survivability of Navy attack pilots), was produced "quickly and inexpensively," and "works as advertised," is how *The Washington Post*[1] once described the aircraft-launched Skipper (AGM-123A) air-to-surface missile.

The development of the Skipper is the story of perseverance, commitment, and competence. Despite a clear need for new munitions for the Navy's F-14 and F/A-18 fighter planes (particularly a "stand-off" bomb), the service expressed little interest in this low-visibility item until the Soviet invasion of Afghanistan and competition from an Air Force rival, the Low-Level Laser Guided Bomb or LLLGB (Triple L). The Skipper originated under the direction of technical advisor Burrell Hays and the guidance of Navy Captain John Jude Lahr at the China Lake Naval Weapons Center and was designed by "renegade" engineers who fashioned a cheap, effective missile from existing (off-the-shelf) weapons components. The Pentagon and Congress threw their support behind the Texas Instruments sleek, complex, and expensive Triple L. The "homely" weapon survived through the intervention of Navy Secretary John F. Lehman Jr., who experienced first-hand the performance of the missile while serving an annual reserve duty as a naval bombardier. Despite an organized effort by Texas Instruments, the Senate Armed Services Committee chair, Senator John Tower (a Republican from Texas), and the Air Force, Lehman and Lahr were successful in convincing senior House Armed Services Committee staff member Anthony R. Battista to pressure the defense committee to mandate a competitive testing of the Skipper and Triple L missiles. While the Skipper survived and is still carried on naval aircraft, Captain Lahr retired early under pressure from the Pentagon, which condemned him for having violated conventional norms, first by going outside the chain of command in support of Skipper, and then by manipulating discretionary funds to keep the missile program alive.

(continued)

Skipper (*continued*)

[1]Fred Hiatt and Rick Atkinson, "Navy Renegades Engineer a Real Bomb-shell," *Washington Post* (21 May 1985), p. 1.

Primary Sources: Hiatt and Atkinson, "Navy Renegades Engineer a Real Bombshell"; Richard A. Stubbing, *The Defense Game* (New York: Harper and Row, 1986); confidential interviews, Washington, D.C., summer 1991.

HIGHLIGHT

Bradley
The Quintessential Hybrid

"The proverbial camel . . . that does nothing very well," is how Thomas McNaugher once described the Bradley (M2) personnel carrier. How the Bradley evolved from a straightforward, simple, lightweight, affordable motorized infantry combat vehicle (MICV) to an overly complex, weighty, expensive, slow-moving multimission armored personnel carrier (to transport troops onto the battlefield) and infantry fighting vehicle (IFV), is the story of bureaucratic conflict, negotiation, and consensus-building. Today the Bradley is the quintessential hybrid, a combination of incompatible missions and performance requirements, and thus capabilities, that have not only compromised its survivability, but forced the Army to reconsider mechanized infantry doctrine as well. The M2 is expected to transport troops onto the battlefield; perform scouting, reconnaissance, and security missions; and fire its 25 mm automatic cannon and/or TOW antitank guided missiles when necessary.

The M2 was conceived in 1963 to fulfill a valid military need for both an IFV (to replace the M113) and a mobile missile-carrying tank killer, and to close a perceived IFV gap between the United States and Soviet Union (which had the BMP). The Infantry Center at Fort Benning, Georgia, wanted a personnel transport vehicle from which troops could also fight; the U.S. Army Armor Center at Fort Knox wanted a heavy tank killer; and the light cavalry unit wanted a three-man armored scout vehicle. There was also the expectation that the IFV would be fast enough to keep up with the M-1 tank.[1] While the military was engaged in intraservice rivalry, the National Security Council was recommending that the U.S. buy the Marder, a West German MICV. The Army organized a high-level study group to discredit the Marder, and proceeded to accelerate efforts to build their own gold-plated vehicle. Despite early evidence of performance failures and recommendations from the Office of Management and Budget (OMB) (during the Carter administration) that funding be cut, the Bradley went into production in the summer of 1980, helped along by the coordinated efforts of its contractor, FMC Corporation, and the Army, which colluded in hiding fraudulent testing and reporting

(continued)

Bradley *(continued)*

(NYT), and successfully lobbied Congress, mobilizing critical support from key members of the House and Senate Armed Services Committees. During the production phase, some of the most intense bureaucratic disagreements occurred primarily over issues of survivability and testing, between OSD and the Army. Much later, President Ronald Reagan sought to accelerate and expand the program in line with his military buildup, requesting 150 more vehicles than the Army wanted, a request rejected by Congress.

[1]John Fialka, "The Bradley: Bells and Whistles," *The Washington Monthly* (April 1982): 22–35.

Primary Sources: Fialka, "The Bradley"; William Rosenau, *Live Fire: Testing of the U.S. Army's Bradley Fighting Vehicle* (Cambridge, Mass.: John F. Kennedy School of Government, Harvard University, 1988); Richard Simpkin, "The Infantry Fighting Vehicle," *Military Technology* 9 (1985): 55–62.

F-16
The Air Force Prevails in the End

The evolution of the F-16 illustrates how difficult it is to initiate a new weapons system outside the formally established acquisition bureaucracies, and the advantages that accrue from foreshortening (streamlining) the military hardware procurement process in some cases. During the Nixon administration, a clear need for a cheap, lightweight, maneuverable plane was established. The initial design and development of just such an aircraft, the F-16, was swift and dramatic, originating with the so-called Air Force "Fighter Mafia" (a group of maverick weapons designers operating with minimal bureaucratic constraints, including loose but succinct performance requirements). To complement the innovative process, competing contractors were given a lot of discretion and autonomy in designing and testing their prototypes. Once conceived, however, the simple, austere plane encountered resistance from the Air Force, which saw the single-engine plane as a competitor for their preferred (and more costly) two-engine F-15.

The F-16 found protectors in the defense secretary, James Schlesinger, and the deputy secretary of state, David Packard (OSD), both of whom supported simple, inexpensive weapons, and intervened to override the Air Force. With support from the OSD, competition from the Navy that was also working on a new lightweight fighter plane, Congressional concerns over the costs of the F-15, and glowing reports from the pilots who flew the F-16 prototypes, the Air Force changed strategy. The Air Force embraced the F-16 (which the OSD funded as an additional incentive), and turned it over to its Air Force Systems Command for full-scale development . There, the manager applied standard procedures, and the F-16 was redesigned to be another highly sophisticated plane (which the Air Force sold to Congress as a light-weight complement to its F-15). The plane's mission needs also were adjusted, despite stability in the military threat, to justify the technical complexity of a multimission plane. Thomas McNaugher concludes that despite "a new, more detailed, and more demanding set of requirements"

(continued)

F-16 *(continued)*

that were "leveled at the project" by the Air Force, "the number of changes was relatively small and the planes emerged as the recognizable progeny of their prototypes."[1]

[1]Thomas L. McNaugher, *New Weapons Old Politics* (Washington, D.C.: The Brookings Institution, 1989).

Primary Sources: McNaugher, *New Weapons Old Politics*; Jacob Goodwin, *Brotherhood of Arms* ((New York: Times Books, 1986); Jerauld R. Gentry, *Evolution of the F-16 Multinational Fighter* (Washington, D.C.: Industrial College of the Armed Forces, 1976).

CHAPTER 4

Prometheus Unbound

Technology and Weapons Development

The evidence in the last chapter reaffirms the predominant role that the Pentagon (particularly the military services) plays in weapons acquisition decisions. The data also point to both military and organizational concerns as important forces motivating military hardware decisions. However, much of the defense policy literature suggests that the dynamic relationships that guide weapons decisions *in* the Pentagon are formed with groups *outside* the Pentagon, that is, with the scientific and technological community, the defense industry, and members of Congress.

This chapter considers the role of the scientific community in the decisions to build and deploy major weapons. According to the technical perspective, technology can either provide the original impetus for the procurement of a military project (technological determinism), or it can influence the subsequent development of weapons conceived for military or political reasons (technological influence). The first or extreme position is a reaction to the assumption of the rational perspective that military forces are predictive in hardware decisions. "In an ideal world, doctrine would be developed first and inform all other decisions, dictating what kinds of military forces need to be deployed and what equipment they require."[1] Instead, technology is posited as determinant both as the initial impetus for weapons procurement and as the primary force driving the design and performance requirements of military hardware. "Instead of building weapons that permit pursuit of previously determined interests, the military has capabilities searching for missions, weapons and forces in need of justification."[2] Since technology is a force "impervious to political regulation," America's military arsenal is filled with unnecessary weapons whose only advantage is their technical sophistication, according to this position. The second or moderate perspective responds to the rational claim that the military decision-making process is a sequential, objective search for the best weapon capable of responding to a military threat. According to this view, technical considerations must compete with military and bureaucratic claims when weapons decisions are made. Weapons specialists too must compromise in order to attract allies from within the Pentagon and Congress to build a coalition in support of their preferred ideas for weapons. From this perspective, technology is important but not determinant. The consequences of this process for the performance of weapons systems can be either positive or negative. While the performance of some weapons has been literally compromised, other systems have benefited from the spur to innovation that competition, bargaining, and negotiation promote, contributing to the most sophisticated military arsenal in the world.

Both positions are first analyzed theoretically, and then tested empirically in this chapter, relying upon the data provided in the nineteen case studies of weapons acquisition decisions. A concluding section considers the future role of technology in military hardware development.

The Role of Technology:
A Theoretical Consideration

The Radical View:
Technological Determinism and Its Consequences

Proponents of technological determinism believe that technology has become a substitute for military concerns in the conception and development of military hardware. Advocates of this position contend that technology has a momentum of its own, that it drives weapons development independent of any other logic, even a military one. This momentum is particularly present in the development of strategic systems, but can also be a factor in the development of major conventional weapons.

As technology becomes a driving force throughout the procurement process, the initial design of a weapon is modified. Unfortunately, the technically motivated improvements may not be militarily necessary. Rather than matching "weapons with our opponents; we seek to acquire whatever Nature proffers," asserts Ralph Lapp, one of the original spokes-persons for the extreme view. And elsewhere: "The unremitting buildup of the atomic arsenal represents just another example of the technological imperative—when technology beckons, men are helpless."[3]

Those who embrace the extreme view contend that military scientists and technicians constitute an elite group whose actions are driven solely by scientific and technical questions. Motivated by the thrill of scientific discovery and the excitement of applying technical advances to military hardware, these elites have lost sight of the larger public interest—na-tional security. These are not "evil men" consumed by "malice, greed, and lust for power," asserts Herbert York, but men with "a religious faith in technology."[4] Nonetheless, President Eisenhower was sufficiently con-cerned to warn the nation of the dangers of a technical elite in his farewell speech of 17 January 1961: "Yet in holding scientific research and discov-ery in respect, as we should, we must also be alert to the equal and oppo-site danger that public policy could itself become the captive of a scien-tific-technological elite."

Advocates of the radical perspective generally view scientifically in-spired weapons development as being ultimately of negative value, the more so because of the absence of political constraints on the scientific-technological elite. In other words, it is not technology itself, but technol-ogy unrestrained that is the evil. Robert Dahl has expressed the concern that society wrongly concedes to scientists unparalleled moral and ethical judgment, and even common sense. David Tarr asserts that the nonscien-tific community inappropriately assumes that scientists have a "special claim to infallibility."[5] York challenges the "widely held myth: that techni-cal experts—generals, scientists, strategic analysts—have some special knowledge making it possible for them, and only them, to arrive at sound political judgments about the arms race." This belief is held by "much" of the general public and "many experts."[6] All of these scholars extol the vir-tues of political supervision as corrective and balancing. In the first case, political oversight can correct judgments of error committed below. In the second, a broader perspective on weapons procurement can insure the correct combination of design parameters.[7]

The deference paid to science in the United States partially explains the facility with which top-level policymakers are "duped" into support-ing the application of innovative scientific principles that promise to pro-vide more national security. Once committed to a new idea, scientists, military analysts, and policymakers build a momentum in support of a weapon that is difficult to reverse later when political forces are more likely to come into play. For this reason, the technical-scientific elite seek to build support as early as possible. They also make claims to secrecy in an effort to shield from public view and participation new technical developments in military hardware.[8]

To advance their ideas, the scientific-technical elite forge a coalition of support with members of the defense industry, military services, and eventually Congress. The coalition builds upon the organizational and professional benefits that can be derived from supporting highly advanced and sophisticated military hardware.[9] For the military services, the benefits are monetary (larger shares of the budget) and practical (advanced weaponry). Sophisticated weaponry is expensive. It also promises greater and more varied performance capabilities that can compensate for the uncertainties in the strategic environment, most notably the capabilities and intentions of our adversaries (see chapter 2). Members of the military services also share the "wonder-weapon mentality."[10] The military services are thus vulnerable to the purveyors of advanced technology that promise to produce weapons systems that are reliable, workable, manageable, and safe to their users.

Once sucked in, the services themselves become advocates "of the newest technology for that purpose."[11] They seek the plane with the highest top speed, the ballistic missile with the largest payload, and the armored battle tank with the longest range. The military consequences of top performance in one area are overlooked. For example, in order to achieve performance in one area, such as speed, other performance characteristics may be sacrificed, leading to reliability and maintainability problems. Harold Brown, defense secretary during the Carter administration, gives the example of fleet air-defense missiles that were "given ranges considerably beyond those at which the radar associated with them could provide reliable target information." In the case of the Aegis fleet air-defense system, "the radar outperforms the missile. Almost always, these unnecessary increments of performance have been paid for in unreliability, demonstrated in either more frequent equipment failure or more frequent maintenance requirements."[12]

The defense industry also benefits from the pursuit of the "magic weapon," since in some important cases their scientists have been the source of the discovery. The obvious advantage is profits. Defense is big business. Spending on defense constitutes close to 7 percent of the gross national product (GNP) and as much as 30 percent of the total federal spending.[13] "The Defense Department is the largest single purchaser of goods and services in the nation."[14]

Completing the traditional subsystem dynamic are select legislators, who realize benefits in constituent service and, therefore, enhanced electability. Defense constitutes an enormous source of public-works spending and jobs. "Counting the military, DoD civilians, and industrial employees directly and indirectly working in the defense sector, 10–15 percent of the U.S. labor force were involved in the defense sector in 1983. These 12 to 14 million workers included one fourth the physicists, one fifth the mathematicians, and one sixth the machinists in the U.S."[15] Even today, the Pentagon is the employer of 30 percent of all federal civil servants.[16]

A situation in which military hardware can provide for the multiple needs of so many different actors and agencies serves to bind these groups into a cozy and reciprocal relationship. The relationship constitutes the subsystem that is said to be operating in the defense policy area, and against which Eisenhower also warned in his farewell speech.

In addition to the mutual benefits to be gained and the pervasive fascination with advanced technology, what other forces bind the defense industry, military services, and weapons specialists together into a symbiotic relationship? (The role of Congress in the acquisition of major weapons systems will be explored more fully in the next chapter.) A third force is the location of scientists, technicians, and weapons specialists, who form the scientific-technical elite, in private industry and government research teams within each of the military services. Each of the military services also maintains its own research and development (R&D) groups.[17]

Working together, the defense industry, professional soldiers, scientists, and select legislators, "driven by technical and scientific developments," are strong enough to outweigh the countervailing forces of a pluralist society.[18] "The Congressman who seeks a new defense establishment in his district; the company in Los Angeles, Denver, or Baltimore that wants an order for more airplanes; the services which want them; the armies of scientists who want so terribly to test their newest views; put all of these together and you have a lobby," asserted Eisenhower. "We must never let the weight of this combination endanger our liberties or democratic processes. We should take nothing for granted. Only an alert and knowledgeable citizenry can compel the proper meshing of the huge industrial and military machinery of defense with our peaceful methods and goals so that security and liberty may prosper together." Otherwise, policies will reflect parochial, rather than national interests, and weapons systems will represent the influence of special interests rather than the national interest.[19]

Inevitably, the results of making weapons decisions for technical and scientific reasons rather than military ones are grave. One important consequence is that the technological imperative reverses the formal process in which needs, missions, and doctrine guide requirements. Rather than making decisions about the technical capabilities of military hardware on the basis of preceding decisions about military tactics and doctrine, technical decisions come to influence or even dictate tactics, strategy, and ultimately politics.[20] "Weapons grow out of the impetus of what is technically possible—especially major or 'strategic' weapons systems—and their military and political values tend to be defined after the fact. Weapons tend to search for strategies rather than strategies for weapons."[21] In many cases, a weapon's development is well advanced before a strategy or policy is found to justify its existence.[22] For example, the scientific discoveries that made possible the development of ballistic missiles, in particular Intercontinental Ballistic Missiles (ICBMs) and missile-launching submarines, subsequently "influenced the strategy of deterrence and a variety of supporting operational policies (targeting policy, a launch condition policy, and deployment policy). . . ."[23] More precisely, scientific advances made nuclear weapons so destructive and the accuracy and speed of ballistic missiles so great that defense was impossible. The only way to avoid war, then, was through deterrence and/or arms control. Technological improvements also meant that the United States could move to a counterforce strategy (that would target military installations) and transformed second-strike weapons into first-strike ones.

The most dangerous situations are those in which technology has spawned weapons that have altered the balance of power, and subsequently proved to be militarily devitalizing.[24] Milton Leitenberg gives the examples of solid-fuel missiles, the Polaris ballistic submarine system, satellite reconnaissance and surveillance, and antisubmarine warfare (ASW) systems, all of which, he claims, accelerated the arms race.[25] A profound consequence of technological development, particularly unrestrained by political supervision, then, is the arms race.[26] Multiple Independently-targetable Reentry Vehicles (MIRVs) and cruise missiles are examples of weapons systems that were allowed to develop for technical reasons, but with little forethought for their subsequent strategic consequences.[27] By concentrating warheads at a single aim point, a missile's accuracy is increased, providing a greater incentive for the "enemy" to strike first in a situation where war is imminent. Similar claims were initially made about possible deployment of a national Anti-Ballistic Missile (ABM) system, which, it was asserted, would encourage the Soviets to offset America's defense with improvements in their offensive capabilities.[28] Increasing improvements in reliability and guidance accuracy had similar effects on Soviet-American relations. Importantly, not all scientific advances bear fruit, especially when they proceed in tandem with their antidote, as was the case with "parallel advances" in the Polaris missile and submarine program and in ASW systems between 1960 and 1972. The more sophisticated antisubmarine warfare became, the more vulnerable submarines became, jeopardizing their deterrence value. A more recent example is the B-1B, whose mission was challenged initially by advances in Soviet air capabilities (and now changes in Russian-American relations). "Advances in military technology may be so uniquely powerful and unpredictable, that, even if we succeed in preserving technological superiority, we may create a world still more dangerous for ourselves than the one we now inhabit."[29]

A second consequence of the technological imperative is its effect on the quality of major weapons systems, most notably the production of weapons with capabilities that are viewed as militarily excessive, redundant, insufficient, or unnecessary. The most common result is the production of gold-plated systems that sport many impressive capabilities that are only vaguely related to real military needs. Unfortunately, many of these exotic weapons are too complicated or difficult for military personnel to operate, or the sophisticated equipment is unreliable. The F-16 fighter plane is an example of a competent fighter plane with so much advanced technology in the tracking equipment that many pilots choose not to use it. According to one study, the United States loses as much as a quarter of the potential performance that is designed into a weapons system because military personnel find highly sophisticated weaponry difficult to operate and maintain.[30] Martin Binkin gives the example of the Stinger (shoulder-fired, infrared-guided missile). The Stinger's mission is to counter attacks by low-altitude enemy aircraft. It incorporates a number of technological advances, including an improved infrared guidance system, airframe and propulsion, and an identification-friend-or-foe system. All of these enhancements, however, have added to the complexity of the weapon, making it difficult for personnel to use.[31] According to one senior Army officer: "The gunner has to complete an 18-step sequence, some of which is quite complex, and he must make many crucial decisions along the way. First, he has to decide whether or not the aircraft is hostile, then he has to run through a complicated set of inbound and outbound range rings to determine the correct distance, and remember the sequence order. We worried that under the pressures of combat, he would forget some and miss."[32]

Weaponry that depends upon advanced technology is also risky since there is no way to predict with certainty the likely results of the application of new scientific principles to military hardware development. Rarely does weapons development go according to plan. Projections are always exaggerated, and high-tech weapons are inclined to fall below initial performance and reliability estimates and above cost estimates. In most cases, the system that emerges from the development process is "quite different from the one initially conceived. . . ."[33] Klein supports this assertion with a study of six fighter-plane development projects. "In order to make them satisfactory flying machines, five of the airframes had to be extensively modified; three of the fighters came out of development essentially different airplanes. Of the six planes, three ended up by having quite different operational roles from what was originally planned for them. Only one of the planes possessed the same technological ingredients and had the same kind of operational role that had been initially planned for it."[34] One government study attributed a third of the cost overruns and "much" of the performance failure in weapons systems to the uncertainties associated with advanced technology.[35] More recently, Dan Goure has noted how inept scientists, policymakers, and military leaders have been in the past in "assessing the military implications of revolutionary technology and forecasting their effects on future battlefields."[36]

High-tech hardware is also difficult and in some cases too expensive to test adequately. Since there was no way other than simulation to actually determine the likelihood that an American ICBM would clear gravitational and polar forces in its programmed route to Soviet targets, uncertainty prevailed for much of the Cold War. At $571 million per aircraft (1990 figures), genuine testing of the B-2 (Stealth) bomber in a realistic combat situation is unlikely (and at this point unnecessary). Concerns are now being raised about future plans to use computer technology to simulate the combat situations in which weapons will be used as a way to test their viability.

The problem of inadequate testing is most apparent in weapons systems being built under a concurrent management strategy, which is the most common approach. When this strategy is used in combination with advanced technology, the risks and uncertainties associated with building exotic weapons are enhanced.[37] Concurrency allows a weapon to be rushed into production before adequate testing has been completed to demonstrate that a prototype does or does not work. Inadequate testing means that problems may arise during the production phase, when error correction is even more costly. Naturally, production is stalled as well. Michael Brown gives the example of the B-1B, "one of the most concurrent weapon acquisition programs in history," and also a program that was "deceptively ambitious technologically."[38] What proved to be the most challenging was the bomber's defensive avionics system. Brown concludes that "it is not surprising that the program had its most serious cost, schedule, and performance problems where technological ambitiousness intersected with unbridled concurrency."[39]

A related problem with similar consequences is the inclination of the military services to modify a weapon in production as high-tech components are developed. Again, the case of the F-16 fighter plane illustrates this problem. Designed as a highly maneuverable, lightweight air combat aircraft, the F-16 evolved into a considerably heavier, multimission plane with a great deal of electronic equipment. Jacob Goodwin describes the original F-16 as a "technological marvel." It had increased fuel and equipment capacity, and a cockpit that provided excellent visibility; it maneuvered better than the older planes, used less fuel than the F-14 Phantom, and generated little visible smoke.[40] Since the plane originated outside the normal weapons channels in the Air Force, the service allowed their engineers to "redesign" the plane to meet their specifications. The redesign permission became "an open invitation to add an extensive electronics system to the aircraft."[41] Many of the changes that the Air Force made were warranted given the pace of changing technology. Some of them (such as top speed and heavy electronic equipment) were unnecessary, from a tactical perspective.

Exotic or high-performance weapons are expensive weapons, so expensive in some cases that the military may end up procuring fewer units. High cost, then, can have important strategic consequences, if it precludes the purchase of a number of units sufficient to make the weapon workable as a system. Pierre Sprey validates this argument in an historical and contemporary comparison of the battlefield effectiveness of "cheap" and "expensive" weapons. With respect to the F-16 and F-15, Sprey notes that "two F-16s [can be purchased] for the same cost as one F-15. In addition, each F-16 can fly about 50 percent more sorties per day than an F-15, due to its considerably lower failure rates and maintenance requirements."[42]

The problem is exacerbated when the investment is in a few high-tech and exotic systems at the expense of a larger number of moderate projects. According to Richard Head, there is a preference in the United States for the development of whole new systems rather than for "incremental growth or cumulative product improvement."[43] To prove their point, critics of high-tech systems cite two exceptions, the B-52 and F-4, both of which have been in the inventory since the early 1950s. The enormous buildup during the Reagan administration is cited as an example of how large amounts of money spent on exotic weaponry can do little to enhance citizens' sense of national security.

Highly sophisticated or overly complex weapons systems are also more prone to reliability and maintainability problems. The Defense Department defines reliability as "the duration or probability of failure-free performance under stated conditions."[44] Maintainability has been defined as "the probability that an item will be retained in or restored to a specified condition within a given period of time." Maintainability is "measured by 'mean time to repair', or the average time required to restore the system when it malfunctions."[45] The inverse relationship between reliability and complexity in tactical aircraft is well established.[46] According to one aircraft engineer, the Air Force has not had any better luck with the B-1B than with its predecessors, although it is equipped with a built-in computerized test bench. "Like every computerized test bench before, it's an unbelievable pain. You've got to constantly reprogram it and they can never get rid of the software bugs. And it never winds up giving diagnoses more accurate than 60 percent or 70 percent, which is pretty bad."[47] Avionics in general have been found to suffer reliability and maintainability problems.

Reliability and maintainability problems are not confined to the Air Force. The M-1 tank, a highly complex system with a lot of advanced technology equipment, has experienced reliability, availability, and maintainability problems in part because of its automated test equipment.[48] The Army has also experienced problems with integrating complex electronics into their tactical weapons ("fix-forward" concept) and Patriot surface-to-air missile.[49] In 1983, Frans Nauta concluded that the Patriot's "improved built-in diagnostics and off-line, computer-based troubleshooting aides have not achieved required performance levels."[50] In 1991, the air-defense weapon was tested in combat. Original official assessments of the Patriot as determined by the number of Scuds destroyed during Operation Desert Storm were 100 percent. This figure dropped to 70 percent in postwar congressional testimony. The House Government Operations Subcommittee on Legislation and National Security, in an unpublished staff report completed in October 1992, determined that Patriot missiles had destroyed only 52 percent of the Iraqi Scuds. A General Accounting Office (GAO) report released in Sep-

tember 1992 dropped the figure to 9 percent.[51] Officials from Raytheon
Co., the maker of Patriot, assert a 90 percent success rate.[52]

Repair time is influenced by a number of factors, but generally "it
takes longer to diagnose failures in complex systems and often takes
longer to remove and replace components that are not readily accessible."
It is for this reason that complex systems are less maintainable.[53] A Rand
report, after studying military programs during the 1950s and 1960s,
concluded that it is becoming increasingly difficult to maintain "the combat readiness of our air crews and their equipment" because of the growing complexity of tactical aircraft.[54] Complex hardware requires increasingly "higher support costs and increased maintenance manpower
requirements."[55] Similar conclusions have been made about weapons in
the 1970s, 1980s, and 1990s.[56]

The ultimate danger of the technological imperative is that the United
States, by becoming dependent upon technology to solve what are essentially political problems, abandons political judgment. This danger has
been widely noted by a diverse range of analysts. "Star Wars is only the latest effort to harness technology to escape a nuclear predicament that at
heart is political in nature and subject only to political resolution."[57] The
risk is that life-and-death decisions come to be made by technicians and
machines. "In the United States the power to decide whether or not dooms-
day has arrived is in the process of passing from statesmen and politicians
to lower level officers and technicians and, eventually, to machines."[58] "Ours
is a world of nuclear giants and ethical infants. We know more about war
than we know about peace, more about killing than we know about living.
If we continue to develop our technology without wisdom or prudence our
servant may prove to be our executioner."[59] "Since technology and war operate on a logic which is not only different but actually opposed, nothing is
less conducive to victory in war than to wage it on technical principles, an
approach which . . . treats war merely as an extension of technology. . . .
[T]he successful use of technology in war very often means that there is a
price to be paid in terms of deliberately diminished efficiency."[60]

For these critics, the national security of the country would be better
served with the production of less expensive and less complex weapons
equally capable of performing the same missions. Sprey gives several examples in ten different missions areas including armor (M60A1 versus
the M-1), air defense (the Oerlikon 35-mm versus the DIVAD), antitank
(the 106 recoilless rifle versus the TOW), ASW escort (the Kortenaer versus the Spruance), submarine (the 210 diesel versus the SSN-688), air-
to-air (the F-16A versus the F-15 A/C), tank hunting (the A-10 versus the

F-15E), close support (the A-4M versus the AV-8B), interdiction (the A-7 versus the F-18), and antitank ammo (the 30-mm versus the I² Maverick).[61] Judith Reppy makes the same point. "Weapons designed to exploit a lower level of technology may be as effective as more sophisticated weapons when produced in quantity and integrated with an appropriate military doctrine."[62] A military reform group has coalesced around support for the government procurement of "a larger number of proven, less sophisticated (and cheaper) weapons."[63] The changed and changing global situation make these recommendations eminently reasonable.

The Moderate View: Technological Influence

Most students of defense policy recognize the central importance of technology in weapons development, but have adopted a more moderate position on its influence. The moderate view differs from the radical position on several claims. For one, there is the view that technology, while sometimes decisive, is not always determinant. Dr. John S. Foster Jr., director of research and engineering in the Pentagon during the 1960s, expressed this position when he told the Senate that research and development activity in the United States was "driven" by "two forces." "Either we see from the field of science and technology some new possibilities, which we think we ought to explore, or we see threats on the horizon, possible threats usually not something the enemy has done but something we have thought ourselves that he might do, we must therefore be prepared for."[64] Even during the later stages of development, technology, while significant, is not viewed as determinant.

Since technology is not determinant, the culprit is not technology per se, but technology in combination with other forces. For Michael Brown, the other force is the management strategies employed by the military services. Problems arise when advanced technology is combined with an inappropriate management strategy. "Unfortunately, for most of the postwar period, American weapons acquisition programs have typically been based on one of the least appropriate combinations of objectives and strategies: concurrency coupled with great technological adventure. . . ." For this reason, American weapons acquisition programs have consistently experienced cost overruns, schedule delays, and performance problems.[65]

Although Brown has tested this theory only in the case of manned strategic bombers, it has a great deal of intuitive validity. Why, then, is concurrency still the preferred style of managing major weapons systems?

Concurrency is attractive and therefore widely used because it works to the advantage of the military services and defense industries; it expedites the fielding of weapons by collapsing procurement stages. According to Brown, the cases in which concurrency is most viable are those in which the technology demanded by the weapon is modest or moderate in nature. Unfortunately, it is also used in cases of advanced technology, where rushing into production weapons that have not been adequately tested or in which the bugs have not been adequately corrected can prove disastrous and expensive. Design changes made to a weapon while it is in production increase its costs and subject the program to schedule delays. Moreover, such changes can cause the fielding of a weapon with performance capabilities inadequate for performing its missions. Nonetheless, the defense industry prefers this approach as well. Collapsing procurement stages allows the contractor to disguise the total costs of a weapon system and provides for stability in funding. As funds are sunk into a weapon system, a momentum builds that is difficult to reverse.

Since technology is not the culprit, highly sophisticated weaponry has value that can be enhanced when the appropriate management approach is adopted. According to Brown, the appropriate strategy is a sequential one in cases of sophisticated technology. "Sequential strategies are based on the assumption that research and development programs are laced with technological uncertainties that are best resolved by proceeding in an orderly, sequential manner."[66] "Sequential strategies are particularly appropriate, even essential, for programs with ambitious development objectives."[67] By definition, programs with ambitious technology are risky, and development is uncertain. A sequential strategy requires that a system meet its program requirements before moving through the various stages of procurement—research, design, full-scale development, production, and deployment. "Programs that rely on major technological advances need extensive prototype testing to ensure that all major technological questions are resolved before system designs are frozen and production decisions are made."[68] This makes it "possible to build technologically ambitious weapons without incurring cost overruns, schedule slippages, and performance shortfalls."[69]

For advocates of a military technology revolution in the United States, advanced technology also has value when it is appropriately combined with changes in military doctrine and organizational structure. Together, changes in military organization, operations, capabilities, and new technologies can result in revolutionary (not just evolutionary) increases in combat performance.[70] (The implications of a military technology revolution will be discussed more fully in the concluding chapter.) Most recently, advances in technology have spurred plans to digitize, robotize, and computerize the battlefield in ways that will change the way we fight wars. With rifles that shoot around corners (individual combat weapons), thermal eyes that see in the dark, digitized battlefields, computers that can be carried in backpacks, and laser-guided smart weapons, troops will not have to expose themselves to the enemy by massing close in, thus avoiding the risks of combat. Instead, troops will be able to move around in small units to pinpoint the enemy, and then call in massive firepower to complete the job.[71] The danger, according to Carol Fitzgerald, civilian manager of the Army's 21st Century Land Warrior Program, is that technology will come to substitute for, rather than augment, basic soldiering skills. Thus far, the dramatic improvements in military capabilities brought on by advanced technologies have resulted in changes in strategy that have augmented rather than replaced more conventional approaches to warfare. Frank Kendall gives the example of the Joint Precision Interdiction (JPI), which has come to replace the Follow-on-Forces Attack (FOFA) with the elimination of the Warsaw Pact threat.[72] The most important organizational change that has resulted from the military technology revolution is the emphasis on shared roles and missions.

The GAO, a persistent critic of weapons acquisition in the Pentagon, has echoed the refrain that technology alone is not the culprit. However, in combination with "high performance demands, inadequate testing of systems, design deficiencies, supply issues, maintenance issues, logistics concepts, management, and training," highly sophisticated weapons can lead to "budget problems, inventory shortfalls, and a low state of readiness for certain combat categories." Sophisticated, complex weapons systems alone do not cause these problems, but they do provide the basis for the other factors to be influential.[73] The GAO gives the example of the Navy's F-14 (Tomcat) fighter plane, in which sophistication has led to reliability problems, which in turn have led to inadequate supply support, which has led to low readiness rates.[74]

A second but related challenge to the radical perspective is the claim that technical decisions are concentrated in the hands of a scientific-technical elite. On the contrary, the democratic and pluralistic nature of the military procurement process precludes a single force dictating public policy. Political guidance is inevitable in a democratic country such as the United States, where several different groups have both the power and incentive to be involved. Moreover, political officials in the executive branch and Congress are formally linked to the Pentagon, and the Joint Chiefs of

Staff (JCS) and the Office of the Secretary of Defense (OSD) are formally linked to the scientific community through the Planning, Programming, and Budgeting System (PPBS) and Milestone review processes. Political guidance is provided at the beginning of the process in the form of national security directives, and throughout in the form of executive (OMB, NSC), legislative, and military (DAB/DSARC, JROC, OSD, JCS) oversight, regulation, and approval. On nuclear weapons, the Atomic Energy Commission is also involved. More importantly, scientists themselves are sensitive and responsive to military concerns.[75]

The democratic and pluralistic process has institutionalized bargaining and negotiation as ways to reach decisions even on technical issues such as weapons systems. Because scientists and technicians do not have sufficient formal power to push through their ideas without allies, all sides make concessions during a process of bargaining and negotiation. Nontechnical actors and agencies, including the services, the OSD, and Congress, have their own sets of concerns independent of scientific and technical ones that they must be sensitive to for organizational and professional reasons, and that may not be capable of being realized through a new and exotic weapons system, making them less vulnerable to the argument in favor of glitzy hardware.[76] In short, while technology may be a necessary condition for weapons development, it is not a sufficient one.[77]

The argument for democracy cites the defense industry as an autonomous and, therefore, countervailing force, and not a dependent force subject to the dictates of a scientific-technical elite. In most cases the defense industry does not see new and exotic weaponry as an advantage. Rather, their preferences are for upgrades and follow-on systems, which carry fewer risks and more certainty regarding contracts and profits. Complex, sophisticated designs are viewed as risky during research and development and during production. It becomes particularly costly and time-consuming to the contractor to incorporate technological changes to a weapon mandated by a military service as discoveries are made during the latter stages of the weapons acquisition process.[78] Daniel Kaufman has found that "companies with large capital and personnel investments prefer R&D approaches that emphasize relatively low-risk, tradition-oriented lines."[79] James Kurth has substantiated this claim with a study of major production lines in the military aerospace industry from 1960 to 1990, in which he documents the follow-on imperative.[80]

A somewhat different line of argument challenges the claim that there are advantages to be gained from a democratic weapons development process. On the contrary, it is not the absence of political constraints but their presence that distorts the procurement process. Weapons development "has become increasingly enmeshed in American political procedures that are glaringly at odds with what is required to develop advanced technology."[81] The best weapons projects are produced in situations of unified and concentrated authority and power. Such situations allow the uncertainties that invariably plague advanced technology to be worked out without the nagging interference from political actors, who are reluctant to concede the time and additional funding to allow for the natural progression of problem-solving. Instead, weapons decisions are made in a process of bargaining and negotiation that invariably leads to compromise decisions that burden a weapon with so many superfluous and redundant capabilities as to compromise its performance. It is the consensus-building process that drives "the requirements for a new system to higher levels of technical risk [more] than any single participant in the requirements process would alone have sought."[82]

The Bradley armored personnel carrier is cited as the classic example. In order to win the support needed to go into production, the Bradley was redesigned several times, ultimately transforming an originally straightforward design into a complex one. The numerous design changes also created weight and cost problems. According to John Fialka, the conflicts among the many actors involved in designing and developing an MICV (Mechanized Infantry Combat Vehicle) account for the hybrid nature of the Bradley. "There was the Infantry Center at Fort Benning, Georgia, which wanted something to haul infantry into battle in a way that would allow them to fight from the vehicle. There was the U.S. Army Armor Center at Fort Knox, which wanted a heavy vehicle that could kill tanks. Then there was the light cavalry which was in the process of developing a light, three-man armored scout vehicle." In addition, the MICV had to have sufficient speed to keep up with the M-1 tank. When during the mid-1970s the NSC expressed an interest in purchasing the Marder (a West German MICV), the Army released a report recommending that the MICV (now referred to as an IFV—Infantry Fighting Vehicle) carry wire-guided TOW antitank missiles and a new 25 mm cannon, in order to increase its firepower. It was this increase in fire power that resulted in the name change from MICV to the IFV. Controversy, conflict, and compromise have continued to plague the Bradley during R&D, production, and deployment. In fact, the bureaucratic stakes increased as more resources were committed to the program. In short, "political pressures thus encourage consensus-building where technical circumstances might benefit from decisiveness."[83]

In a parallel vein, Thomas McNaugher argues that the defense industry is overregulated and burdened by political pressures that force them to compromise their judgment, eventually compromising the quality of military hardware as well. The defense industry is wrongly blamed for the performance problems and cost overruns that weapons encounter, which too often are the result of design changes dictated by the military services and policymakers. The American method of defense contracting encourages defense industrialists to lie (underbid on the development contract as a way to buy into a production contract), exaggerate (the performance capabilities in a weapon design to win a contract), and deceive (rush a weapon into production in order to disguise performance problems) in order to stay in business. Moreover, there are no rewards for producing quality weapons at cost and on schedule. Few procurement funds are awarded through competitive bidding, and contractors have consistently been "cushioned from the impact of their inefficiency" with grants and contracts intended to bail them out of trouble.[84] To reverse the situation, McNaugher recommends more competition across projects and among the services and more extensive testing at the earliest stages possible, before production.[85] In short, there are political pressures to produce advanced weaponry. It is not technology that pushes politics, but politics that pushes technology, and pushes it to absurd levels of sophistication and complexity. "Powerful bureaucratic and organizational forces . . . push American acquisition efforts in the direction . . . of technological ambitiousness. . . ."[86]

A third line of argument counters the radical claim that all technological developments have been negative. In fact, a number of important military advances owe their existence to "technology push," including radar, jet engines, and the atomic bomb.[87] In addition, a number of highly complex weapons are in fact easier to maintain than their less sophisticated equivalents. Martin Binkin gives the examples of the F-16 and F/A-18 fighter planes, and the M-1 tank as weapons that are both more sophisticated and easier to maintain than their equivalents, the V-4, F-4 Phantom, and M-60, respectively.[88] On the other hand, Binkin underscores that these cases are clearly exceptions to the general rule of the inverse relationship between complexity and maintainability. Also, despite the improved maintainability of the M-1 over the M-60, the Abrams tank has nonetheless encountered serious reliability, availability, and even maintainability problems.[89]

Moderates also add that the technological sophistication of American weaponry was important in sustaining parity with the Soviets. More precisely, American weapons are high value and multipurpose, compensating for the quantitative edge that the Soviets held during the latter part of the

Cold War. The quick and clean military encounter in Desert Storm is invoked in further defense of the benefits of highly complex weapons systems. For many, Desert Storm, in which the application of advanced technology (such as precision munitions) and new doctrines and organizational structures (such as the Army's Air Land Battle doctrine) proved decisive, epitomizes the advantages of a much-debated military technical revolution.[90] Advocates of this revolution assert that American advances in guided weapons (electronics); computer-based command, control, and communications systems; and space technology are likely to keep the United States at the forefront of military power for some time.[91]

Desert Storm illustrates yet other advantages of advanced American weaponry: its flexibility and adaptability, both consequences of sophistication. The majority of the military hardware used in Kuwait was conceived and produced for use primarily (although not exclusively) against the Soviet Union and the Warsaw Pact in the European theater. Yet the weapons (such as the Apache helicopter and M-1A1 tank) proved adaptable to the desert climate of the Middle East.

The claim that advanced technology unconstrained by politics has fueled the arms race and destabilized Soviet-American relations is also challenged by citing counterexamples such as Star Wars. The threat of Star Wars technology in combination with the enormous defense buildup of the Reagan administration is largely credited by moderates and conservatives with pushing the Soviets to make important concessions in arms control to forestall economic disaster. According to Jonathan Stein, political forces rather than technology dictate and shape the decisions to develop advanced weapons technology, most notably the hydrogen bomb and Star Wars. "Politics provides the determining and sustaining impetus to genuinely new weapons development and acquisition processes."[92] For Stein, then, the arms race is a political, not a technological, race: "technology becomes either a convenient tool to further organizational or personal ends or an invaluable aid in promoting a professed doctrine or strategy."[93]

Testing the Claims of the Technology Argument

It is evident from the literature that considerable controversy exists over the exact nature and impact of technology in weapons development. Advocates of both the radical and the moderate views readily cite—albeit in a piecemeal and anecdotal manner—convincing examples to support their relative perspectives. Can the explanatory value of the moderate and radical views be demonstrated more systematically? Although the entire arguments are not subject to empirical examination, at least three assertions lend themselves to analysis: (1) technology is determinant; (2) political controls over technological development are lacking; and (3) complex, sophisticated weapons are fundamentally flawed systems.

Technology Is Determinant

A primary claim dividing the two perspectives is that technology is the impetus for the development of new weapons ("technology push"). In this case, a technological advance emerges first, which then provides the impetus for the development of a weapon in which the technology can be used. Scientists in private industry and the government, who have developed the new or advanced technology for which there is no existing military need, must thus convince potential users that it is expedient to exploit the new technology. The counterclaim is that weapons develop in response to "user pull." In this second case, a military service (the "user"), during the military requirements stage, determines that existing weapons systems are inadequate for meeting military needs and that new weapons with different requirements and levels of performance are necessary.[94] According to Daniel Kaufman, user pull can be the product of three trends: changes in battlefield conditions that challenge existing weaponry; changes in doctrine or tactics; and an interest in performing tasks previously considered infeasible. The development of the tank during World War I, the Bradley IFV, and SDI, respectively, illustrate the three trends. As a general pattern in the post–World War II period, new weapons systems have been the result of "technology push." These have included the first generation of such systems as the ICBM and the main battlefield tank. In the majority of cases, however, weapons have been follow-on systems, owing their origin to the military service that already had and wanted to retain a mission, but with a weapon that incorporated more advanced capabilities. Even in these cases, however, it still needs to be determined whether the military service was the source of the planned performance improvements or whether weapons scientists in private industry or the government were involved in convincing the service of the indispensable nature of a change.

What percentage of the weapons in this study were the product of user pull as opposed to technology push? The process used to identify the initial impetus for the weapons systems in this study relied upon primary and secondary sources, such as government documents (particularly Congressional Research Service issue briefs) and analytical case studies, respectively. Since there are several sources available for every weapons system, the data can be cross-validated.

Table 4.1 includes the findings from this analysis. Not unexpectedly, the vast majority of weapons (84 percent) in this study are the product of user pull, rather than technology push, challenging the assumption that technology is determinant. In fact, only cruise missiles can trace their origin solely to technology push. Both technology push and user pull together explain the conception of the Thor-Jupiter and MX missile systems. These findings reaffirm the key role that the military services play during the preliminary stages of the weapons acquisition process, a phenomenon that the President's Blue Ribbon Commission on Defense Management found disconcerting. The commission rejects both technology push and user pull as methods for establishing the military need for a new system because they result in gold-plating: technology push because it promotes scientific advances for their own sake, and user pull because it ignores the political, fiscal, and even scientific implications in establishing military requirements.[95]

TABLE 4.1

Impetus for Weapons Systems

Weapon	Impetus: Technology Push or User Pull
Skybolt	User Pull
Thor-Jupiter	Both
TFX	User Pull
Polaris	User Pull
MX	Both
B-1	User Pull
Cheyenne	User Pull
C-5A	User Pull
M16	User Pull
Trident	User Pull
Bradley	User Pull
A-10	User Pull
F-16	User Pull
M-1	User Pull
Aegis	User Pull
Cruise	Technology Push
DIVAD	User Pull
F/A-18	User Pull
Skipper	User Pull

Political Controls Are Lacking

A second central claim on which students of defense policy diverge is that technicians and scientists constitute an elite. Developing operational measures for an elite and verifying the existence of such a group is a highly subjective and inexact process. As an alternative, this study addresses the related claim that scientists and technicians are allowed to operate with limited political guidance, by examining the scope of participation in weapons procurement. The implicit assumption in this relationship is that the broader the scope of participation, the more political guidance there has been.

The scope of participation is used to refer to the number of policy arenas and agencies within each arena actively involved in an acquisition decision. The scope is broad when actors in addition to those formally empowered to participate are involved in a particular weapons procurement decision. The most obvious cases of narrow participation include programs that have been classified for purposes of secrecy. The number of weapons programs for which spending is classified is increasing. According to the Department of Defense, 47 percent of spending on Research, Development, Testing and Evaluation (RDT&E) was classified in 1989.[96] At the other extreme are projects that for reasons of controversy have incited to action groups and agencies normally only peripherally involved. (For a review of the formal actors and agencies, see chapters two and three). In what percentage of the weapons in this study was the scope of participation broad? Narrow? The results are presented in Table 4.2.

TABLE 4.2

Weapons Systems by Scope of Participation

	Criteria	
Name	Service	Scope of Participation
Skybolt	AF	Narrow
Thor-Jupiter	AF/Army	Narrow
TFX	AF/Navy	Narrow
Polaris	Navy	Narrow
MX	AF	Broad
B-1	AF	Broad
Cheyenne	Army	Narrow

(continued)

TABLE 4.2 *(continued)*

| | Criteria | |
Name	Service	Scope of Participation
C-5A	AF	Broad
M16	Army	Narrow
Trident	Navy	Broad
Bradley	Army	Narrow
A-10	AF	Narrow
F-16	AF	Narrow
M-1	Army	Broad
Aegis	Navy	Narrow
Cruise	AF	Broad
DIVAD	Army	Broad
F/A-18	Navy	Broad
Skipper	Navy	Narrow

Of the weapons systems analyzed in this study, the majority (58 percent) were decided in a policy-making process characterized by a narrow range of actors and agencies formally empowered to participate in weapons procurement decisions. (This finding is consistent with that of the last chapter, which indicated that conflict within the Pentagon over a weapons system was evidenced in only 47 percent of the cases.) In 42 percent of the cases, the scope of participation was broad, including actors and agencies traditionally uninvolved or only marginally involved with military hardware matters. The findings are not necessarily definitive, given the close range of figures. What can be concluded, however, is that if there is a scientific-technical elite, in the majority of cases it acts relatively unimpeded. Another dimension of the question, one that if examined might provide more useful findings, is the extent to which the scope of participation matters. Recall that advocates of the radical approach claim that the lack of oversight distorts the process by allowing technology to dictate military decisions. Even some advocates of the moderate perspective find the broad scope of participation (challenged by the findings in Table 4.2) bad for policy reasons. Since there are already data characterizing the various weapons systems as being either flawed or sound, a correlation between the two conditions might be revealing. As seen in

TABLE 4.3

Scope of Participation by Performance

	Scope of Participation	
	Limited	Inclusive
Performs Well	73%	50%
Performs Poorly	27%	50%
(N)	(11)	(8)

chapter 1, of the nineteen cases studied, 53 percent were classified as performing well, and 47 percent were classified as performing poorly. (Again, of the latter, one-third of the systems were eventually canceled.)

Table 4.3 contains the results from a cross-tabulation between the scope of involvement and performance. In 73 percent of the cases in which involvement was limited, the weapons selected were sound ones. On the other hand, the impact of a large number of individuals actively participating in the defense process on weapons performance is inconclusive. In exactly 50 percent of the cases in which involvement was broad, the ultimate policy outcome was a weapons system with serious performance problems.

Sophisticated Weapons Are Fundamentally Flawed

A third point of contention is that technologically ambitious weapons are also flawed ones. In order to determine the validity of this assertion, each weapon system was classified by the amount of challenge demanded by its technical requirements. Technological sophistication was then correlated with the performance status of each system. The assumption is that the more ambitious and less certain the technology required by the newly conceived weapon, the greater the likelihood that the completed weapon will perform poorly. Conversely, the more modest and more certain the technological requirements, the more likely it is that the system will perform well.

How was the technological sophistication of the weapons determined? According to a number of sources interviewed in the Pentagon, such technical judgments are instinctive and intuitive.[97] Other sources were more informative, however. One approach suggests that a distinction can be made between systems that represent major innovative leaps, such as the first ICBMs or cruise missiles, and those that require evolutionary steps, such as Minuteman II and III.[98] An early Rand Institute study developed a scheme for rating the technical advance of individual weapons along a continuum, relying upon several criteria associated with the innovation of the technology and design required by the new system.[99] The GAO states that since "there is no precise way to define sophistication, complexity, or high performance . . . a good indicator is development and procurement cost. Operating cost is also a good indicator. High-performance systems usually cost more to develop, test, produce, and operate."[100] More recently, the CBO recommended that the Pentagon consider the technological risk posed by a major weapons system. Two factors are cited as important in assessing the risk posed by technical elements, the "level of technology being attempted" and the "feasibility of implementing system design concepts."[101]

Drawing upon previous research, weapons in this study were classified as ambitious, moderate, or modest. "Ambitious" programs are those in which the production of the weapon system depends on (a) the development of new technology; and/or (b) the completion of new designs in either the system or several of its subcomponents. "Moderate" programs are those for which the technology is already available, but successful weapon production requires (a) that major improvements be made; and/or (b) that this technology be integrated in ambitious ways. "Modest" programs are generally follow-on systems that might require (a) some limited improvements; and/or (b) the integration of existing technology in simple ways. In some cases (c) neither new technology nor new knowledge is required. In sum, ambitious programs are those that challenge scientists and technicians to discover new principles or applications. Moderate programs generally involve the less demanding challenge of combining familiar principles or applications in new and complex ways. Demands are modest when scientists are required merely to apply and build upon known principles.[102]

Producing data to assess the impact of the technical facet of the procurement issue was challenging, but proved feasible. For the most part, previously published studies characterize the technical components of the nineteen weapons systems in terms and meanings identical to those developed in this research. For example, McNaugher refers to the Cheyenne helicopter as "technically ambitious," Harvey Sapolsky contends that the technical risks or uncertainties associated with Polaris lay in the "integration" of the component subsystems, and Rand refers to TFX technology as "ambitious." In the remaining cases there was sufficient technical information to determine whether the weapons system required innovative technology, challenging subsystem integration, or only modest changes to an existing system. One of the most useful sources of technical information outside of published case studies is a weapon's military requirements—also referred to as performance requirements, military

characteristics, and system specifications. The statements of these requirements specify the performance capabilities of a proposed weapon.[103]

The assumption is that the uncertainties associated with developing
and applying innovative technological principles are likely to subvert
the original design of a weapon. The more uncertain the technology,
the more likely it is that the weapon's performance will fall short of the
original expectations. The data do support this relationship.[104] (See
Table 4.4.) The more challenging the technology posed by a weapons
system, the more likely the project is to be flawed in its performance. In
only 29 percent of the cases confronting technicians with challenging
technology were the problems worked out sufficiently to produce weapons that performed well. In contrast, in all of the cases in which the
technical requirements were modest ones, the systems performed as expected.[105] Of particular prescriptive significance is the finding that
moderate technological challenges are less likely to result in weapons
with performance problems. The budget deficit in combination with
changes in Russian-American relations recommends a reconsideration
of the current force structure away from overly ambitious (or highly
risky) technology. Weapons posing moderate technological challenges
(such as upgrades) are less operationally risky, but still technically sophisticated enough to sustain scientific progress. As Jonathan Klein
noted years ago, the "initial estimates of a system's performance, reliability, and cost are subject to very large errors—errors that can be substantially eliminated only by developing systems that incorporate more
modest advances than have typified military development projects."[106]
"If the advances sought are relatively modest (e.g., as in developing a
transport plane), the uncertainties are ordinarily much more easily resolved than if the advances sought are relatively ambitious (e.g., as in
developing a new kind of missile)."[107]

TABLE 4.4

Technological Sophistication by Performance Problems

	Technological Sophistication		
	Ambitious	Moderate	Modest
Performance Problems			
Yes	71%	56%	0%
No	29%	44%	100%
(N)	(7)	(9)	(3)

Conclusion

The evidence in this chapter challenges the position that technology plays a determinant role in the conception of major weapons systems. Consistent with the findings in the last chapter, the evidence in this one shows the role of the military services to be preeminent and relatively autonomous, with few exceptions, at least during the preliminary stages. These findings do not necessarily mean, however, that the services themselves do not promote technically sophisticated weaponry for its own sake. In fact, the contrary may be the case. The impact of a fixed (and declining) force structure and limits on military spending may cause the services in many cases to pursue highly advanced systems that reaffirm their organizational stature. Therefore, while technology is not determinant (the first cause), it is a critical factor in the establishment of military requirements. In many cases, the services establish military requirements that anticipate rather than build upon existing technical capabilities. Technocratic theory as the impetus for weapons development, then, does have some explanatory value during the research and development and production stages. Moreover, technology continues to influence decisions throughout the weapons acquisition process, during development and production. While not determinant, often it becomes a tool to promote other political, organizational, or personal interests.

A second important finding is that technologically ambitious weapons are not necessarily inherently sound ones. While not significant, the data suggest that technologically ambitious weapons are more likely to encounter performance problems, schedule delays, and cost overruns. The policy implications of this finding are significant and suggest that defense planners seek to procure military hardware with modest or moderate technical demands. According to Martin Binkin, procuring less technically demanding hardware can be accomplished by eliminating subsystems and requirements that are not essential to performing the mission. This suggestion reaffirms the importance of the initial decisions establishing and then linking foreign, defense, and military policy objectives (see chapter 2). It is important to keep these findings in mind, coming as they do at a time when the United States is said to be "in the midst of, or standing poised on the brink of [a military-technical revolution]. . . ."[108] The Army and Marine Corps in particular are investing heavily in high-tech hardware to "transform their forces into video-displaying, real time transmitting, new age cybergrunts." Already there are plans for rifles that will shoot around corners, thermal eyes that can see in the dark, digitized battlefields that do not expose soldiers to the risks of combat, computers that can be carried in backpacks, and increasing use of laser-guided smart weapons.[109] The challenge is to utilize the technical advantages in ways that create not only an enhanced military capability, but one that is more certain. This means coordinating technical innovation with changes in the way war is planned and conducted. The danger is that the rapid technical innovation that is in evidence today will spin out of control.

Third, concerns about the lack of political controls in the procurement process appear to be unfounded, at least if the measure is the workability of major weapons systems. According to the findings in this study, the democratic ideal of an open decision-making process is not necessarily corrective. Rather, the findings that associate flawed systems with broad participation suggest that weapons systems are best procured by a small group of actors. (Importantly, this is consistent with the finding in chapter 3 that the absence of conflict within the Pentagon, and control by a service, are conducive to workable weapons.) Given the implications for democratic theory, any suggestion that the defense decision-making process be attenuated is controversial. (This issue will be explored more fully in chapter 6.) Of more immediate concern is how to reconcile the role of Congress with evidence that weapons development benefits from an abridged policy-making process, a dilemma that is addressed in the next chapter.

Notes

1. Center for Strategic and International Studies (CSIS), *Military Technology Revolution: A Structural Framework* (Washington, D.C.: Georgetown University, 1993).

2. Thomas H. Etzold, *Defense or Delusion? America's Military in the 1980s* (New York: Harper and Row, 1982), 121–122.

3. Ralph E. Lapp, *Arms Beyond Doubt: The Tyranny of Weapons Technology* (New York: Cowles, 1970), 4.

4. Herbert York, *Race to Oblivion: A Participant's View of the Arms Race* (New York: Simon and Schuster, 1970).

5. David Tarr, "Military Technology and the Policy Process," *Western Political Quarterly* 18 (March 1965): 143.

6. York, *Race to Oblivion*, 237.

7. Lapp, *Arms Beyond Doubt.*

8. Tarr, "Military Technology," 135.

9. Sam Marullo, *Ending the Cold War at Home: From Militarism to a More Peaceful World Order* (New York: Lexington Books, 1993), chapter 7.

10. James Fallows, *National Defense* (New York: Random House, 1981), 29, 35.

11. Harold Brown, *Thinking About Security: Defense and Foreign Policy in a Dangerous World* (Boulder, Colo.: Westview Press, 1983).

12. Ibid., 238.

13. Jerel A. Rosati, *The Politics of United States Foreign Policy* (New York: Harcourt Brace Jovanovich, 1993), 136–137. Also, Asa A. Clark IV, "The Role of Technology in U.S. National Security: An Introduction," in *Defense Technology*, eds. Asa A. Clark IV and John F. Lilley (New York: Praeger, 1989), 8.

14. Michael Weisskopf, "Profit, Patriotism Produce a Ubiquitous Alliance," in *Bureaucratic Politics and National Security: Theory and Practice*, eds. David C. Kozak and James M. Keagle (Boulder, Colo.: Rienner, 1988), 283.

15. Asa A. Clark IV, "The Role of Technology in U.S. National Security," 8.

16. Rosati, *Politics of United States Foreign Policy*, 137.

17. Daniel J. Kaufman, "The Defense Technology Community: Players and Roles," in Clark and Lilley, *Defense Technology*, 190.

18. M. Weisskopf, "Profit, Patriotism," 283.

19. Steven Rosen, ed., *Testing the Theory of the Military-Industrial Complex* (Lexington, Mass.: Lexington Books, 1973), 278.

20. Solly Zuckerman, *Scientists and War: The Impact of Science on Military and Civil Affairs* (New York: Harper and Row, 1966).

21. Tarr, "Military Technology," 140.

22. Ibid., 147.

23. Asa A. Clark IV, "The Role of Technology," 14.

24. Not all technological advances are revolutionary. A number of incremental changes can add up to a revolutionary capacity.

25. Milton Leitenberg, "The Dynamics of Military Technology Today," *International Social Science Journal* 25 (1973): 341.

26. See, for example, B.T. Feld et al., *Impact of New Technologies on the Arms Race* (Cambridge, Mass.: MIT Press, 1970). Also, Evangelista, *Innovation and the Arms Race*, and Harvey Brooks, "The Military Innovation System." More frightening is the claim that those responsible for advances in weaponry are not evil men, but dedicated scientists who fail to comprehend the grave possibilities of their discoveries. "Dealing with errors committed by sincere men acting in good faith is extremely difficult, if not impossible." York, *Race to Oblivion*, 234.

27. Richard Head, "Technology and the Military Balance," *Foreign Affairs* 56 (April 1978): 544–563.

28. George W. Rathjens, "Introduction: Technology and the Arms Race—Where We Stand," in B.T. Feld et al., *Impact of New Technologies on the Arms Race*, 8.

29. Judith Reppy, "Research and Development of Arms: Military R&D. Institutions, Output, and Arms Control." *Policy Studies Journal* 8 (Autumn 1979): 84–91.

30. J.W. Kehoe and K.S. Brower, "U.S. and Soviet Weapon System Design Practices," *International Defense Review* 15 (1982).

31. Martin Binkin, *Military Technology and Defense Manpower* (Washington, D.C.: The Brookings Institution, 1986), 65–68.

32. Colonel John Little quoted in ibid., 65.

33. Burton H. Klein, "The Decision Making Problem in Development," in National Bureau Committee for Economic Research, *The Rate and Direction of Inventive Activity* (Princeton, N.J.: Princeton University Press, 1962), 478.

34. Ibid., 478–479.

35. U.S. General Accounting Office (GAO), *Implications of Highly Sophisticated Weapon Systems on Military Capabilities*, Report, PSAD-80-61 (Washington, D.C.: Government Printing Office, 1980). Also, Robert Perry et al., *System Acquisition Strategies* (Santa Monica, Calif.: Rand, 1972), 16.

36. Dan Goure, "Is There a Military Technology Revolution In America's Future? *Washington Quarterly* 16 (Fall 1993): 175–196.

37. See Michael E. Brown, *Flying Blind: The Politics of the U.S. Strategic Bomber Program* (Ithaca: Cornell University Press, 1992).

38. Ibid., 303.

39. Ibid., 304.

40. Jacob Goodwin, *Brotherhood of Arms: General Dynamics and the Business of Defending America* (New York: Times Books, 1986), 11.

41. Ibid., 13.

42. Pierre Sprey, "The Case for Better and Cheaper Weapons," in *The Defense Reform Debate*, eds. Asa A. Clark IV et al., 199–200.

43. Head, "Technology and the Military Balance," 555.

44. Department of Defense Directive 5000.40, "Reliability and Maintainability," 8 July 1980.

45. Binkin, *Military Technology and Defense Manpower*, 7.

46. *Armed Forces Journal International* (May 1980): 10. Harold Brown provides a chart showing an inverse relationship between weapon complexity (or the number of components a system has) and system reliability (how often a system fails).

47. Anonymous aircraft engineer quoted in Binkin, *Military Technology and Defense Manpower*, 62.

48. Binkin, *Military Technology and Defense Manpower*. Also see F.M. Scherer, *The Weapons Acquisition Process: Economic Incentives* (Cambridge: Harvard University Press, 1964).

49. See Binkin, *Military Technology and Defense Manpower*; Stubbing, *The Defense Game*.

50. Frans Nauta, *Fix-Forward: A Comparison of the Army's Requirements and Capabilities for Forward Support Maintenance*, prepared for the Office of the Assistant Secretary of Defense for Manpower, Reserve Affairs, and Logistics (Bethesda, Md.: Logistics Management Institute, 1983), 3–9.

51. See *Defense News*, 8 February 1993–14 February 1993: 4, 52.

52. See a letter by Robert Skelly, vice president for public and financial relations for Raytheon Co., Lexington, Mass., published in *Defense News*, 13 May 1991: 33.

53. *Defense News,* 13 May 1991: 65.

54. Perry et al., *System Acquisition Strategies,* 1972.

55. Head, "Technology and Military Balance," 559.

56. Binkin, *Military Technology and Defense Manpower*. Also, GAO, *Weapons Acquisition: A Rare Opportunity for Lasting Change* (Washington, D.C.: Government Printing Office, December 1992), and GAO, *Defense Weapons Systems Acquisition* (Washington, D.C.: Government Printing Office, February 1995).

57. Robert E. Hunter, quoted in Jonathan B. Stein, *From H-Bomb to Star Wars* (Lexington, Mass.: Lexington Books, 1984), xi.

58. York, *Race to Oblivion*.

59. General Omar Bradley. Quoted in Clark, "The Role of Technology in U. S. National Security," 4.

60. Martin Van Creveld, *Technology and War* (New York: The Free Press, 1989), 319.

61. Sprey, "The Case for Better and Cheaper Weapons," 198f.

62. Reppy, "Research and Development of Arms: Military R&D," 85.

63. Clark, *The Defense Reform Debate*, xi.

64. Quoted in ibid.

65. Michael E. Brown, "The Organizational Sources of Weapon Acquisition Policy." Paper delivered at the 1987 Annual Meeting of the American Political Science Association, Chicago, Ill., 1987, 19.

66. Brown, *Flying Blind*, 17.

67. Ibid., 19.

68. Ibid., 20.

69. Ibid., 21.

70. Goure, "Is There a Military Technology Revolution in America's Future?" 178–179.

71. *Salt Lake Tribune*, 28 August 1995, 1, A4.

72. Frank Kendall, "Exploiting the Military Technical Revolution: A Concept for Joint Warfare," *Strategic Review* 20 (Spring 1992): 23–30.

73. GAO, *Implications of Highly Sophisticated Weapon Systems on Military Capabilities*, 1980, 1.

74. Ibid., 17.

75. Solly Zuckerman, *Nuclear Illusion and Reality* (New York: Viking Press, 1982), 103.

76. Thomas McNaugher, "Weapons Procurement: The Futility of Reform," *International Security* 12 (Fall 1987): 91.

77. But even Lapp, who subscribes to an extreme view of the technological imperative, does not contend that technology is the *only* force. Notice that he uses the word "dominated," rather than dictated or determined. Lapp, *Arms Beyond Doubt*.

78. James R. Kurth, "The Military-Industrial Complex Revisited," in *American Defense Annual: 1989–1990*, ed. Joseph Kruzel (Lexington, Mass.: Lexington Books, 1989), 195–288.

79. In Clark and Lilley, *Defense Technology*, 196.

80. See James R. Kurth, "The Military-Industrial Complex Revisited."

81. McNaugher, *New Weapons*: 102. Also see Tarr, "Military Technology."

82. McNaugher, "Weapons Procurement: The Futility of Reform," 92.

83. John J. Fialka, "Army Fighting Vehicle," *Washington Monthly*, 14 (April 1982), 1, 2.

84. McNaugher, "Weapons Procurement: The Futility of Reform," 91.

85. McNaugher, *New Weapons Old Politics*, 103–104.

86. Brown, "The Organizational Sources of Weapons Acquisition Policy."

87. Kaufman, "The Defense Technology Community: Players and Roles," 185–186. Also, President's Blue Ribbon Commission on Defense Management, *A Quest for Excellence: Final Report to the President*, June 1986, 45.

88. Binkin, *Military Technology and Defense Manpower*, 52, 55.

89. Ibid., 63.

90. See, for example, U.S. Department of Defense, *Conduct of the Persian Gulf War, Final Report to Congress* (Washington, D.C.: Government Printing Office, April 1992), xx–xxiii), Mary C. Fitzgerald, "The Soviet Image of Future War: 'Through

the Prism of the Persian Gulf.'" HI-4145 (The Hudson Institute, Washington, D.C., May 1991), and Frank Kendall, "Exploiting the Military Technical Revolution: A Concept for Joint Warfare," *Strategic Review* 20 (Spring 1992), 28–29.

91. Ibid., 5.

92. From Stein, *From H-Bomb to Star Wars*, 1.

93. Ibid., 2.

94. *A Quest for Excellence,* 45.

95. Ibid.

96. See Table 8-1, James M. Lindsay, *Congress and Nuclear Weapons* (Baltimore: The Johns Hopkins University Press, 1991), 155.

97. Several individuals in the Pentagon were contacted by telephone to find out how a particular weapons system came to be classified as technically ambitious or modest. The author was told consistently that there was no formal procedure, and that individuals working in procurement understand the technical demands of the systems.

98. Jonathan B. Stein, *From H-Bomb to Star Wars: The Politics of Strategic Decision Making* (Lexington, Mass.: D.C. Heath, 1984).

99. Robert L. Perry et al., *System Acquisition Strategies* (Santa Monica, Calif.: RAND, 1971).

100. From GAO, *Implications of Highly Sophisticated Weapon Systems on Military Capabilities,* 1980, 20.

101. U.S. Congress, Congressional Budget Office, *Concurrent Weapons Development and Production* (Washington, D.C.: Government Printing Office, 1988), 33. Also see Brown, *Flying Blind,* 21–22.

102. A technical description of each weapons system was compiled drawing upon the case study data and government publications. The CRS Issue Briefs and GAO reports were particularly useful.

103. Brown, "The Organizational Sources of Weapon Acquisition Policy," 9.

104. Collapsing the moderate and modest categories did not significantly alter the findings.

105. The relationships between technological sophistication, and cost overruns and schedule delays were also tabulated. The results were similar to those found between technology and performance. Therefore, the data are not reproduced in tables. The results of the cross-tabulations for the relationship between technology and cost, and technology and delays were identical, although in some cases different weapons systems were found to have encountered cost overruns and schedule delays. The results for both correlations were as follows: 71 percent of the weapons with "ambitious" technology, 56 percent of the systems with "moderate" technology, and 33 percent of those with "modest" technology encountered both cost overruns and schedule delays.

106. Burton H. Klein, "Policy Issues Involved in the Conduct of Military Development Programs," in *Problems of the Modern Economy: Defense, Science, and Public Policy,* ed. Edwin Mansfield (New York: W.W. Norton, 1968), 105.

107. Klein, "The Decision Making Problem in Development," 487.

108. Goure, "Is There A Military Technology Revolution in America's Future?"

109. *Salt Lake Tribune,* 28 August 1995, A1, A4.

HIGHLIGHT

Aegis
Too Sophisticated to Identify the Enemy?

From its conception, critics of the Aegis air defense (radar and fire control) system have attacked the weapon for its technological complexity, which, they have asserted, would confound naval personnel in an actual combat situation; the Pentagon for inadequate and improper testing procedures; and the Navy for unrealistic performance expectations. On 3 July 1988, the cruiser USS Vincennes, relying upon an Aegis system, shot down an Iranian passenger airplane, killing all 300 individuals, having mistaken it for an enemy military jet. According to analysts, the Aegis performed as expected, providing a lot of comprehensive (but in some cases conflicting) information that the crew could not process efficiently under the strain of combat. Most important (in light of testing) was the inability of the crew using Aegis to discriminate between enemy missiles and friendly aircraft.

Aegis was conceived and designed as an anti-air warfare weapon to protect the Navy's carrier battle groups from Soviet air- and sea-launched missiles. During its two decades of procurement, the military capabilities of the Aegis have been consistently compromised by its technical features (advanced technology), which subsequently have affected its development, testing, and combat performance. The system was designed to track more than 200 attacking missiles and planes simultaneously while also guiding U.S. missiles to enemy targets, demanding a capacity to display large amounts of instant and accurate data. The performance requirements of the Aegis challenged the contractor, RCA Missile and Surface Radar. To insure continued support for Aegis and neutralize opponents (particularly those who attacked Aegis for being an unnecessarily costly alternative to diversifying the fleet), tests were conducted under unrealistic and favorable conditions, guaranteeing success. According to one GAO report, the Navy went so far as to fake the tests of Aegis, providing ships' crews with crucial information beforehand to minimize the challenge of discriminating between targets. The absence of comprehensive and realistic testing (particularly in simulated combat situations) meant that it was not possible to anticipate the problems that the crew actually would have under the stress of an imminent threat. Ironically, the highly sophisticated computer and strong radar systems that compose Aegis also make an Aegis carrying ship an easily recognizable target, according to critics.

Primary Sources: Joseph E. Rousseau, "The Ticonderoga Class 'Aegis' Guided Missile Cruiser." White Paper, Center for Defense Information, August 1989; Eric J. Lerner, "Lessons of Flight 655: Special Report," 27 *Aerospace America* (April 1989): 18–26; *Aviation Week and Space Technology* (7 May 1984; 20 February 1984; 13 February 1984; 29 July 1985).

Thor-Jupiter
The Technical Rush to Obsolescence

While two nearly identical, ostensibly revolutionary, and competitive missile development projects seemed a rational response to the developments in Soviet missile technology during the 1950s, in the hands of the military services Thor and Jupiter became organizational tools for resolving disputes over budget and mission shares between the Army and Air Force. The Army saw an IRBM (Jupiter) as a way to regain a larger share of the defense budget and acquire a nuclear role. The Air Force sought to beat out the Army and gain a monopoly over strategic missions with its Thor IRBM program. What encouraged the interservice rivalry that doomed Thor-Jupiter was the devolution of authority over funding and weapons decisions to the services and the ambiguity concerning missions in the New Look policy.

Under pressure to meet an urgent national strategic need for a deployable nuclear missile (the core of President Eisenhower's New Look policy), a crash program of parallel intermediate-range ballistic missile (IRBM) development projects was inaugurated. The assumption was that dual projects (particularly the innovation that competition breeds) would expedite the development, production, and deployment of a new and novel nuclear missile and provide a fall-back if one program failed. The reverse occurred, with each service actually avoiding technical risks to ensure program survival. According to Michael Armacost, the urgency of the perceived military need for a new missile combined with interservice rivalry encouraged risk reduction to ensure technical success. At the time, the secretary of defense and other civilian leaders in the Pentagon lacked the resources, budgetary control, and bold leadership to intervene and redirect, or even coordinate, the programs. As a consequence, development was protracted, few technical advances were made, and the IRBM program became prematurely obsolete with the development of an ICBM.

While Thor-Jupiter was an unmitigated military disaster, it was politically and bureaucratically important. First, the controversy was a crucial catalyst for the organizational reforms that strengthened the OSD and the power of the secretary of defense, installed

greater extra-service oversight in weapons procurement, and reduced the power and autonomy of the military services. Second, it
served to promote a critical political debate over missile development and broaden the scope and arena of debate over military procurement matters, an unintended by-product of the efforts of each
service to build a coalition of support among allies in industry and
Congress and discredit their competitors.

Primary Sources: Michael H. Armacost, *The Politics of Weapons Innovation: The Thor-Jupiter Controversy* (New York: Columbia University Press,
1969); Thomas L. McNaugher, *New Weapons Old Politics: America's
Military Procurement Middle* (Washington, D.C.: The Brookings Institution, 1989).

ALCM
A Weapon Looking for a Mission

A weapon looking for a mission is how Richard K. Betts describes the air-launched cruise missile (ALCM) during the early stages of its research and development. After twenty years (beginning in the 1950s) of evolutionary progress in cruise missile technology, a technical breakthrough (during the 1970s) provided the basis for the distinctively new and modern long-range missiles that are used today. What spurred and propelled the cruise missile program (in all three services), despite resistance from the professional military (for bureaucratic reasons), was the convergence of scientific discovery, civilian (OSD) interest, and the timely intervention of Henry Kissinger (who ordered the Air Force to build ALCMs in the aftermath of the SALT I agreement), Defense Secretary Melvin Laird (who mandated a joint Air Force-Navy cruise missile program) and Presidents Gerald Ford and Jimmy Carter (who canceled production funds for the B-1 bomber in lieu of cruise missiles). The reluctance of the Air Force to embrace cruise missiles, seeing them as a threat to their preferred manned strategic bomber program, was short-lived when they realized that under President Ronald Reagan they would be funded for both programs.

Thus, despite preliminary service resistance and the initial absence of a clear and concise military need, cruise missiles have developed into one of the most effective and usable weapons systems that the United States owns, with technology that continues to be at the cutting edge of the military technical revolution. Since the late 1980s, the advanced cruise missile (ACM) program has taken advantage of advances in guidance capabilities, warhead technology, accuracy, range, reliability, and engine design. Cruise missiles are versatile, cheap, effective, elegant, user friendly, and conducive to survivability. Their potentially devastating effect on the nuclear arms race during the Cold War was addressed in both the SALT II and START agreements. The small, robotic, jet-powered planes can carry nuclear warheads thousands of miles. They reach their target by reading the contours of the terrain beneath them (as they fly low) and comparing it to maps stored in their computers. Despite its original mission to hit Soviet targets from points outside Soviet airspace, cruise missiles were used in both Operation Just Cause and Operation Desert Storm.

Primary Sources: Kenneth P. Werrell, *The Evolution of the Cruise Missile* (Washington, D.C.: Government Printing Office, 1985); Richard K. Betts, ed., *Cruise Missiles: Technology, Strategy, Politics* (Washington, D.C.: The Brookings Institution, 1981); Charles A. Sorrels, *U.S. Cruise Missile Programs: Development, Deployment and Implications for Arms Control* (New York: McGraw-Hill, 1983).

CHAPTER 5

The Role of Congress in Weapons Acquisition Decisions

Process and Policy Considerations

The "ideas" for new weapons systems may germinate in the minds of scientists, engineers, or defense analysts, but only Congress can provide the material support which insures that such ideas become workable systems. With the constitutional power of the purse as its tool, the national legislature can vote to sustain, divert, or cancel a weapons system at several points in the procurement process. No matter how well established the military and doctrinal need for a weapon, the imminence of the military threat that the weapon is intended to meet, or the amount of resources committed to a project, Congress can decide to reverse its fate. It can do so on an annual basis and for reasons that have little or nothing to do with the national security of the country.

While students of Congress dispute whether the national legislature's involvement promotes or retards the procurement of viable and affordable weapons systems, it is clear that Congress plays a significant role in military hardware development. From the rational perspective, the parochial concerns that motivate members of Congress mean that their participation is disruptive to efforts to match military hardware to national security needs. Proponents of the political argument counter with evidence that supports both a prevailing policy concern among legislators and the independent benefits of a democratic policy-making process.

The discussion of Congress in this chapter proceeds as follows. The chapter first examines the nature of congressional powers to establish the parameters of potential legislative influence. Congress's actual role in

145

military procurement matters is then assessed, drawing upon past studies, a set of interviews in the Pentagon and on Capitol Hill, and data collected on the nineteen weapons acquisition cases. These same data sources are used to determine whether manifest legislative *involvement* means *influence* over military hardware decisions. The normative implications of the findings are then considered particularly as the discussion informs the debate between advocates of the rational and political perspectives over the value of legislative involvement in national security matters. The chapter concludes with a consideration of the future role of Congress in light of the end of the Cold War.

Congressional Powers: Vast or Limited?

Regarding the first concern, the national security powers of Congress, there is little debate. The legal basis for Congress's role in weapons acquisition issues is a broad and substantial one. Drawing upon its war powers,[1] Congress is recognized as having the legal authority to determine a wide range of military issues, including the nature of the armed forces, the types and numbers of weapons procured, and the rationale underlying procurement decisions. The taxing and spending powers that Congress holds generally serve to reaffirm with predictable regularity its role in defense policy. Today, every weapon and piece of military hardware developed must be preceded by a specific authorization from the Armed Services Committees (now the National Security Committee in the House of Representatives).[2] Finally, Congress has a responsibility to oversee federal practices, including those involved in weapons acquisition (oversight powers). In this way, Congress can provide a forum in which public criticism can be voiced directly or reflected, which can then lead to legislative counsel.[3]

Congress also has substantial statutory authority and plentiful resources (staff and assistance from special-interest groups and research organizations), giving it extensive practical means to control defense policy.[4] The proof is widespread. Congress now requires that the Pentagon provide regular arms control statements and quarterly weapons systems progress reports. Congress's investigatory powers are vast, supported by the capacities of its research organizations—the General Accounting Office (GAO), the Congressional Research Service (CRS), the Congressional Budget Office (CBO), and, until recently, the Office of Technology Assessment (OTA). Congress has been singularly ingenious in applying domestic policy to the defense policy arena. As illustrated by the cases of the MX missile and Trident submarine programs, Congress will invoke nonmilitary legislation (in this case, the National Environmental Policy Act [NEPA] of 1969 or the Federal Land Policy and Management Act [FLPMA] of 1976) to try to exert influence over defense matters.[5] The democratization of the institution of Congress during the 1970s, which fragmented power and increased access to committee and floor debate, has widened the scope of legislative participation on defense matters. The result is that more committees and subcommittees can now claim some jurisdiction over defense issues. Since the 1970s, several major weapons systems have been of legislative interest to a number of members, including those serving on the Armed Services, Appropriations, Budget, Foreign Relations, Small Business, Veteran Affairs, Governmental Affairs, Banking, Commerce, Intelligence, and House Energy Committees. In short, Congress has plentiful mechanisms available by which it can influence military policy.[6]

Congressional Involvement: Potential or Actual?

Congress has been using its defense powers with increasing enthusiasm and intensity since the late 1960s, and especially the mid-1970s when congressional hearings and markup sessions first were opened to the public.[7] The scope of legislative participation is one indication of such enhanced activity. In 1989 alone, one-quarter of the membership of Congress sat as conferees to resolve the National Defense Authorization Act.[8] In the majority (58 percent) of the nineteen cases analyzed for this study, the scope of participation was also broad, bringing in members not formally empowered to participate.[9] In contrast, in only 42 percent of the cases was legislative involvement confined primarily (although not exclusively) to the House and Senate Armed Services and Defense Appropriations Subcommittees. Importantly, this figure held true even when controlling for fiscal year.[10]

    As further evidence of the increased scope and vigor of legislative involvement in defense (as in other policy areas), there is the exponential increase in the staff assigned to defense policy, in hearings held on the defense budget, in floor amendment activity, and in congressionally mandated reports, studies, and investigations,[11] trends only recently (1994) challenged. Since 1970, for example, the number of reports and studies requested of the Pentagon by Congress has increased by a factor of twelve.[12] Since the 1960s, the number of floor amendments being offered in the House and Senate has increased by a factor of thirty. The 1989 defense authorization bill came to the House floor with 240 amendments waiting to be considered.[13] According to James Lindsay, the length of a hearing, measured in terms of the numbers of pages devoted to defense policy, increased from an average of 1,700 pages in the 1960s to close to 6,000 pages in the 1980s and early 1990s.[14] During this same period, the defense committees increased their staff resources fourfold.[15] Beginning in 1994, House Speaker Newt Gingrich (R-Ga.) initiated efforts to reduce staff and resources and centralize decision-making. The convergence of concerns over deficit spending, hostility to Democratic president Bill Clinton's foreign and defense policy agenda and activities, and congressional leadership efforts to relocate legislative power portend possible changes in the nature and scope of legislative participation, but not, importantly, interest, in military procurement matters.

Despite the broadening of the power base and interest in military affairs, most legislative work continues to be conducted in the defense committees. The Senate and House Armed Services (authorizations) Committees (SASC and HASC) consider fundamental policy decisions such as whether a particular program should be funded. The House and Senate Appropriations Defense Subcommittees (HADS and SADS) address resource allocation questions, such as how much to fund a program.[16] Since each line item corresponds to an individual weapons system or ammunition program in a particular budgetary account, legislative influence can be selective and precise. Congress regularly changes the procurement accounts in the defense budget. In 1984, the House and Senate Armed Services Committees "changed 440, or 23.3 percent, of the procurement line entries and 317, or 35.3 percent, of all R&D programs," in the FY 1985 Defense Authorization budget.[17] In March of 1986 Congress mandated that the Pentagon make a 4.9 percent across-the-board reduction in the defense budget.[18] An examination of the FY 1987 and FY 1988 DoD authorizations bills is also telling. In those fiscal years, Congress acted on procurement and/or research and development funding requests from the Pentagon for nine of the weapons systems in this study. In 18 percent of the study cases, Congressional funding was identical to the requested amounts. In 9 percent of these cases Congress approved more and in 73 percent less than the Pentagon had requested. Moreover, in 85 percent of these cases, funding changes were in excess of the 5 percent designated by fiscal analysts as being substantively significant.[19]

The breadth of legislative influence is even more apparent when the defense budgets are disaggregated, and individual weapons programs are examined.[20] During the 1980s, Congress consistently cut funds for the Strategic Defense Initiative (SDI). After once again trimming SDI funding (by 9 percent) in the FY 1990 defense budget, Congress sought to restore those funds in the FY 1996 budget in line with the National Security Restoration Act (that Republicans passed to implement promises contained in the "Contract with America"). In spring of 1996 the Senate once again buried Star Wars. In 1980, Congress deleted funds for development of a cruise missile carrier airplane and prohibited the Pentagon from spending monies on fixed silo basing for the MX missile.[21] When President Carter canceled production funds for the B-1 bomber program in 1977, Congress appropriated enough money to keep the program in research and development, allowing the strategic bomber to be resurrected by President Reagan. Congress also successfully invoked its fiscal powers to compel the Air Force to embrace cruise missiles during the 1970s by deleting monies for air-launched cruise missiles (ALCM) and authorizing the Navy's cruise missile program. Legislative action on the FY 1992 and 1993 budget requests further demonstrates Congress's willingness to alter the funding of specific weapons programs in ways that impact American forces and defense policies.[22] During consideration of the 1996 FY DoD authorizations bills, the Senate added $1.3 billion to fund a helicopter carrier, and the House included $500 million for twenty additional B-2 bombers (eventual cost: $15 billion) that neither the Pentagon nor the president requested; and the House deleted $1.5 billion for a third Seawolf submarine, which the administration supported.

Congress also has sought to expand its role in weapons acquisition matters by dictating how decision-making should proceed in the Pentagon. Through statutory mandates intended to streamline military decision-making and to rationalize the industrial component in the procurement process, Congress has tried to improve the product that the Department of Defense submits for legislative consideration and to depoliticize military-industrial relations as well. The various reorganization acts that Congress has authorized in the post–World War II period are examples.[23] In 1982 Congress mandated that the post of assistant secretary for operational test and evaluation be created in the Pentagon. In 1983 Congress established an independent office "to prevent the services from rigging weapons tests." In 1984 it passed the Competition in Contracting Act. In 1986 the Goldwater-Nichols Act was voted into law, requiring the president to present Congress with a national security strategy report accompanying the annual budget request, that relates national security threats and objectives to defense spending, arms control, and related policies.[24] In 1986 Congress created the

post of under secretary of defense for acquisition.[25] Jacques Gansler notes
that "by the end of the 1980s . . . Congress was passing procurement reform
legislation at the rate of over 150 bills a year,"[26] a pattern that has continued
into the 1990s. The Federal Acquisition Streamlining Act of 1994 is one
prominent example.

The legislative hearings on the defense budget that Congress holds
annually are increasingly being used as a forum for a cross-examination
of the defense and foreign policy goals and objectives that guide military
decision-making. When sufficiently probing, legislators have been able to
disclose (although not necessarily successfully address) unsettled questions about strategic, doctrinal, and tactical issues, such as the continuing
utility of the nuclear triad, a warfighting doctrine, power projection, and
forward defense (policy oversight).[27] This is one way in which Congress
can discipline the military process.

Since the end of the Cold War, Congress has been particularly active in
forcing a reconsideration and forging a redefinition of American forces and
defense policies, filling a "policy vacuum" left by inaction during the Bush
and Clinton administrations.[28] The national legislature's willingness to step
into the policy void resulting from the dramatic changes in international
relations since the late 1980s challenges a criticism consistently leveled: that
Congress, while exercising fiscal and programmatic oversight, has been
negligent in exercising policy oversight. While it is true that Congress, until
recently, generally has avoided the process of linking up the strategic debate
with its examination of military hardware, even during the Cold War Congress was attentive to some strategic and doctrinal questions.[29] For example, Congress consistently expressed concerns over the destabilizing implications of the hard-target capability of the MX (now canceled) and
Trident II missiles. It also involved itself in the debate over the military viability of manned strategic bombers. Congress resisted funding the F-16,
despite its being a more austere compliment to the F-15 fighter plane, until
the Air Force made a convincing argument that there was a clear military
need (rationale) for another plane capable of performing the air-to-air
combat mission.[30] Since 1990 Congress has sponsored several hearings to
debate the military need for and technical merits of the V-22 Osprey, tilt-
rotor, transport aircraft, and sealift cargo ships.

Congress has also increasingly invoked its statutory power to try to
influence the management of individual weapons systems through legislative mandates directing the Pentagon to act. Over the twenty years spent
scrutinizing the MX missile program, Congress directed the Air Force to
abandon several basing modes including MPS and Dense Pack, consis-

tently tied its approval of defense bills to the fulfillment of specific legislative demands (such as producing an environmental impact statement), and invoked the legislative veto on several occasions.[31] Congress also directed the Navy to choose a derivative of the Air Force's F-16 for its new air combat fighter plane, made funding of DIVAD contingent upon Army willingness to incorporate proven technologies and components into the air defense system, and refused to release production funds until the Navy selected a final design for the Trident submarine. Congress also mandated live operational tests for the Bradley fighting vehicle and imposed stringent testing requirements on the B-2 bomber program to demonstrate its workability before it would agree to fund the project for full-scale development.

Data from the cases in this study provide systematic support for the argument that Congress has been and continues to be actively involved in weapons procurement matters in a variety of ways. Table 5.1 provides a listing of the various instruments that Congress invokes in its efforts to influence weapons acquisition decisions. The range includes use of the legislative veto (still in use despite being declared unconstitutional in *Immigration and Naturalization Service v. Chadha*, 1983), information requests, informal bargaining and negotiation, legislative directives (i.e., legislation mandating that the executive branch do something before receiving funding), investigations, public hearings (other than those used for funding purposes), and funding activities.

TABLE 5.1

Congressional-Executive Relations on Major Weapons Systems

Weapons	Disagreement	Nature of Influence	Outcome
Skybolt	low	funding, hearings	support
Thor-Jupiter	low	funding	support
TFX	moderate	hearings, funding	support AF version canceled Navy)
Polaris	low	funding	mutual accommodation/ more units, funds modified
MX	high	full range	mutual accommodation
B-1	high	funding, formal bargaining, directive	support/delayed
Cheyenne	low	funding, hearings	mutual accommodation

(continued)

TABLE 5.1 *(continued)*

Weapons	Disagreement	Nature of Influence	Outcome
C-5A	low	investigations, funding	support/cut funds
M16	low	investigations, hearings, funding	support/no change
Trident	high	funding, directive	support/delay (cut funds)
Bradley	moderate	funding, directive	support weapon/reversed Carter
A-10	low	funding	support/funds modified
F-16	low	funding	support/cut funds
M-1	high	funding, informal negotiation, directive	postpone, more units, mutual accommodation
Aegis	low	funding, directive	support/management changes
ALCM	low	funding	support/cut funds
DIVAD	moderate	funding, directive	cut funds, design and management changes, mutual accommodation
F/A-18	moderate	directive, funding, hearings	change number units, support plane (reversed Carter)
Skipper	low	funding, directive	mutual accommodation

Funding decisions are the most common form of involvement. However, funding was used *exclusively* in only 27 percent of the cases. More often, the legislature uses funding in conjunction with its other powers. Importantly, legislative activity is rarely directed toward altering the fate of a weapons system. Rather, Congress seeks to postpone, stretch out, reduce, or increase the number of units purchased or funds spent, or dictate certain program management changes (such as competitive contracting for the M-1 tank, live tests for the Skipper, and an improved Environmental Impact Statement [EIS] for MX/MPS). Seldom does Congress seek to influence the types of weapons systems being built by the Pentagon or their performance parameters. For example, while rejecting two prior proposals to build a new Army tank, Congress has never opposed battle tanks in principle, despite arguments about their "increasing obsolescence."[32] The same is true for helicopters and carrier groups. Although Congress has debated the merits of continuous improvements in the accuracy and firepower of Intercontinental Ballistic Missiles (ICBMs) and of strategic bombers, it has not interfered with their development. For example, while the MX missile system seems to be the exception to the rule, even here Congress confined itself to dictating basing mode decisions for the ten-warhead ICBM. Similarly, Congressional action has not been directed at altering the fate of the Trident submarine system, Bradley personnel carrier, B-2 strategic bomber (until recently), or division air defense (DIVAD) gun. In other words, legislative involvement fails to change the basic commitments made by the military services. This is not to suggest that Congress avoids these issues. Rather, its debate on military need is not consistently linked to the details of weapons systems acquisition.[33]

Does Activism Mean Influence?

Congress has the capabilities and the determination to influence military hardware decisions. Congress can and does designate the amount of money that will be spent on a weapons system (fiscal oversight); the nature and structure of the acquisition process in the Pentagon, and the management and design of individual weapons programs (programmatic oversight); and the rationale for and performance of the military hardware (policy oversight).[34] But to what effect? What have been the substantive results of legislative involvement? For example, what have been the consequences of funding changes on the status of individual weapons systems; and what effect has reorganization had on the conduct of the Pentagon? Have the legislative mandates resulted in the Pentagon acting in prescribed ways?

Initiation, Resurrection, or Cancellation?

Does legislative involvement in policy-making change the substance of policy?[35] If the measure of influence is the cancellation or origination of a weapon system, or the resurrection of a program terminated by the Pentagon, then the answer is, rarely (see Table 5.1). Congress seldom succeeds in canceling major weapons systems and even less often successfully initiates them. Its record in resurrecting programs, while more solid, is not significant. Overall, in most cases (63 percent) legislative action comports with executive action. Table 5.1 includes a brief description of the legislative response to executive recommendations for the nineteen cases in this study.

There are some notable exceptions to this pattern of executive-legislative consensus (in some instances deference), however, both from this study and generally. During the 1960s, for example, Congress refused to fund two main battle tank programs—the MBT-70 and the XM-803—because of the excessive costs and technical risks involved. Such legislative action had the effect of dictating the cost and technical parameters of the M-1 tank, which Congress ultimately approved. Legislative concerns over DIVAD also contributed to Secretary of Defense Casper Weinberger's decision to cancel that program, just as earlier congressional pressure had led to a previous decision to cancel the Cheyenne helicopter program during the 1970s. According to James Lindsay, "Congress forced Carter to abandon his cruise missile carrier proposal, pushed him to accept the MX missile and MPS basing, and generally pressured him to spend more on defense."[36]

In addition to the cases in this study, there are other important examples of Congress taking a position contrary to that of the executive branch. Congress strangled the Navy's tactical nuclear modernization program and restrained the Army Tactical Missile System (ATACMS) during research and development. Midgetman owes its brief life as a viable idea to Congress, which urged the Scowcroft Commission to endorse the Small Intercontinental Ballistic Missile (SICBM) concept, and then appropriated funds to initiate research and development by the Air Force, despite opposition from both the service and civilians in the Office of the Secretary of Defense (OSD). Congress also placed a weight limit on the missile and tied MX funding to Midgetman development to "prod" the White House to develop a mobile missile.[37] In the end, Midgetman was abandoned because of resistance from the OSD, members of the SASC, and the Air Force, and because of the costs of the program. Beginning in 1989, Congress voted annually to reverse the defense secretary's decision to terminate both the Navy's F-14 fighter plane and the Marine Corps's Osprey V-22.[38] During his first term, Clinton was plagued by Republican-led congressional efforts to alter America's force structure.

Modification?

While Congress is less inclined to initiate, cancel, or resurrect major weapons systems, it does not hesitate to change military hardware programs. If modification is the standard of influence, then Congress has been remarkably influential. Congress has forced (albeit mostly short-term) modifications in military hardware that have changed the properties (cost, scheduling, and performance parameters), procedure (management strategy), and purpose (mission capabilities) of major weapons systems.

Referring again to the data in Table 5.1, it is evident that the most common consequence of legislative activism has been the modification of the properties of major weapons systems, in particular cost and schedule. As noted earlier, Congress regularly invokes its fiscal power to modify requested funding by significant amounts (plus or minus 5 percent). Congress is also inclined to stretch out funding over a number of years, thus contributing to schedule delays. In 1984 alone, Congress voted to stretch out twenty-two weapons systems.[39] Delays can have significant consequences in terms of a weapons system's costs, performance, and military viability. Delays increase costs, which in turn often compromises performance. Delays can also jeopardize the military viability of a weapon.[40]

Congress has made a few attempts to influence the performance parameters and the management of military hardware. During the early 1970s, Congress cut army research and development funds for the DIVAD until the Army agreed to incorporate already proven technologies and components into the air defense gun. Congress also pressured the military to adopt a concurrent production and testing schedule.[41] According to the CBO, the combination of demands, reflecting Congress's concerns that cost and technical risks be minimized, distorted what might otherwise have been an effective system. The use of a concurrent management strategy in the development of DIVAD exacerbated the technical problems by moving the system into production before tests were completed and the bugs worked out of the weapon.[42]

Congress also sought influence over the F/A-18 (Hornet) program by asking the Navy to choose a derivative of the F-16 rather than develop a new fighter plane—a request the Navy ignored. Congress also compelled the Air Force to abandon several basing modes for the MX missile system, altering considerably the final design of the military program. Additional examples include the requirement in the 1987 authorization act that the Bradley undergo live operational tests, a legislative mandate that the Skipper and Triple L prototypes undergo a live competition, and the provision in the FY 1984 Defense Authorization Bill that the Army "not make a contract for the purpose of establishing a second source for the production of the engine for the M-1 tank."[43]

Assessing Congressional Involvement: Positive, Negative, or Neutral?

Congress commonly is chastised for interfering with the realization of America's national security and defense needs. These criticisms are divided into five major areas of concern. Congress is accused of (1) micro-

managing the procurement budget, (2) canceling necessary weapons and
restoring militarily superfluous ones, (3) forcing modifications in existing programs that cause performance problems, (4) distracting defense
analysts from the important work of national security policy-making,
and (5) acting to advance parochial interests rather than the public interest, which is the national security of the nation.

On the first point, if micromanagement means disaggregating the
defense budget and specifying amounts for individual weapons programs, then Congress stands guilty.[44] But of what? Despite the breadth of
the changes in the 1984 budget cited above, the conference committee ultimately authorized approximately 93 percent of the budget authority requested by the administration. Although the funding changes that Congress made to the FY 1987 and FY 1988 DoD authorization bills exceeded
the 5 percent standard in 85 percent of the cases in this study, in none of
the cases did the fiscal changes actually affect the procurement status of
the weapon itself, that is, its design and projected performance. The 4.9
percent across-the-board reduction in the 1986 defense budget did not
carry with it any analysis or management judgments about priorities or
the effects of these cuts on defense programs and forces.[45] Despite repeated funding decisions to reject suitable basing modes for the MX missiles, Congress ultimately approved interim silo basing (albeit on a temporary basis). Although they made regular cuts to SDI, Congress
maintained the controversial system in research and development and never challenged the viability of the program until
Clinton canceled it in 1993. Congress's efforts in 1996 to revive the anti-
ballistic missile defense program failed. In short, while Congress does
micromanage the procurement budget, the results carry minor policy implications.

Moreover, micromanagement can be useful if legislators use cost-ef-
fectiveness and affordability factors as an impetus for judging the value of
military hardware. The current debate over whether to support a new
light attack helicopter, continue producing existing ones (such as the AH-
64 Apache helicopter or an improved version of the OH-58D scout aircraft), or purchase a foreign helicopter (such as the Italian A-129
Mangusta) has been motivated by fiscal concerns.[46] Similarly, the debate
over the military viability of sealift cargo ships revolves around the question of whether they are cost-effective given changes in the nature of the
military threats in the post–Cold War period. During the Bush administration, Defense Secretary Cheney opposed fast transport ships as unnecessary in light of America's capacity to preposition weapons close to pro-

jected areas of conflict.[47] Congress retorted that the ships were crucial for providing the greater mobility that the new global situation demands. Third, by adding funds for the B-2 bomber and deleting them for the Seawolf submarine, Congress has positioned itself in the debate over the future utility of weapons conceived for use against the Soviet threat.

What about the second concern, that Congress cancels militarily necessary weapons while maintaining existing but unnecessary ones? Is there any validity to this claim? As the evidence from this study demonstrates, Congress rarely cancels major weapons systems. In those cases where Congress has canceled a program, little conclusive evidence suggests that the weapon was militarily essential. Of the nineteen weapons systems examined in this study, for example, the only system that Congress canceled was the Navy version of the TFX (F-111B) fighter-bomber plane, following Senate hearings documenting serious performance shortfalls and pressure from the Navy leadership.

On the other hand, there is evidence to suggest that Congress does maintain some existing but unnecessary systems. In fact, if Congress can be faulted for anything, it is its failure to cancel more systems—and cancel them earlier—when sufficient evidence exists to challenge their military or technical value or fiscal viability. The strength of this claim, however, hinges on the meaning of "unnecessary." The only weapons systems considered truly unnecessary from a strategic perspective were the Intermediate Range Ballistic Missile (IRBM) programs (Thor-Jupiter), procured during the 1960s. Not only were the two projects redundant, but, given advances in the development of solid-fuel missiles and changes in strategic doctrine (to stabilized deterrence and arms control away from nuclear retaliation), liquid-fuel IRBMs immediately became obsolete.

The other systems that Congress is faulted for not canceling, DIVAD and the C-5A jumbo transport plane, were problematical for technical or fiscal reasons and consequently for military reasons. Importantly, both DIVAD and the C-5A plane were initiated to respond to clearly defined and well-established military needs. While the technical and fiscal problems that they experienced compromised their military viability, this did not invalidate the need for improvements in our transport and combat protection capabilities. To many observers, it was more cost-effective to try and work out the technical bugs in the two existing programs than to initiate new ones.

There are three other programs (from this study) that Congress voted to sustain, despite presidential action to the contrary, the Bradley infantry carrier, F/A-18 fighter plane, and B-1 bomber programs. Here, again, for none of the programs was there a consensus that the weapons were unnecessary from a strategic perspective. Despite technical problems with the Bradley, there was a broad agreement on the military need for a new personnel carrier to replace the twenty-five-year-old M-113. Similarly, defense expert disagreement has existed over the military need for and value of the Navy's F/A-18 fighter plane. Some consider it redundant, while others tout it as critical given its dual mission capabilities. The debate over the military value of the B-1 program really was a debate over the future utility of manned strategic bombers in light of developments in cruise missile and ballistic missile technologies, and, eventually, changes in strategic needs given the end of the Cold War. By providing enough research and development funds to keep the B-1 bomber alive (after President Carter canceled production funds in 1977), Congress saw itself as providing an opportunity for the strategic debate to be resolved.

The case of the Osprey V-22 also illustrates this same ambiguity because it represents a weapons system that works as expected and contributes to maintaining highly mobile forces, which many argue are essential in the post–Cold War climate. Even Defense Secretary Dick Cheney, who canceled the Marine Corps program for fiscal reasons (not affordable in the current economic environment), admitted that a tilt-rotor aircraft had some military value.

Thirdly, does Congress mandate changes in weapons programs that ultimately cause them to exceed cost and schedule estimates and encounter performance problems? While considerable evidence supports the assertion that congressional involvement does contribute to cost overruns and schedule delays, little evidence suggests that, ultimately, weapons performance has been compromised. Similarly, there is little support for the assertion that legislative involvement directly compromises the military integrity of major weapons systems. For example, Congress's obsession with fiscal matters contributed to but did not cause the M-1 tank's performance problems.[48] As late as 1986, the capacity of the tank to achieve its design requirements for reliability, durability, maintainability, and availability (RAM-D) was still in doubt.[49] Congress's ceiling on unit costs may have encouraged (but certainly did not cause) the manufacturer to compromise and use inferior parts in order to stay within the lines of the contract agreement. Congressional action clearly delayed its procurement (it reached its initial operational capability in 1981), and, ironically, in so doing, contributed to increases in the costs. But the delays also meant that a number of the tank's technical problems would be corrected. While critics argue that the tank is unnecessarily sophisticated and thus more expensive than necessary, and that its value is made more ambiguous by advances in antitank technology, Congressional action is not at fault.

In the case of the Trident submarine, Congressional concerns over such issues as the environment (the enormous size of the submarine), arms control (the hard-target capability of the Trident II missile), and cost (the exorbitant costs tied to its size) resulted in statutory action altering the procurement practices of the military, rather than the design of the system. When Congress eventually confronted the construction problems that the Trident program was experiencing (1979–1982), its reaction again was to hold hearings and compel the Pentagon to consider alternatives to a weapon system that had entered full-scale development in 1971. The primary effects of congressional action on the Trident were to delay a program already subject to slow-downs because of contractor difficulties and problems in the design and performance parameters of the weapon system.

There are some (albeit again ambiguous) exceptions, however. The MX missile system is one. Despite concerns during the Reagan administration that the failure to complete the MX missile system exacerbated the window of vulnerability, there were many defense analysts (including members of the Scowcroft Commission) who challenged the very idea of such a window. Analysts also made the more serious argument that the placement of MX missiles in retrofitted Minuteman silos enhanced their use as first-strike weapons, elevating the risk of nuclear war. Ironically, the improvement in American-Russian relations, which Congress could not predict, invalidated the utility of highly accurate, multiple warhead ICBMs, contributing to the decision to cancel the program. In sum, while legislative action has postponed important decisions, these delays often have worked to the advantage of the United States, but sometimes in ways totally unanticipated by members of Congress (or anyone else, for that matter).

Another less ambiguous example is DIVAD. As noted earlier, evidence suggests that Congressional action on DIVAD did contribute to (but did not cause) its cancellation and performance problems. According to one account, the Army identified a "real" need in the early 1970s for a division air defense system that would have a longer range for battlefield use to replace the Vulcan system. Congress intervened and "cut successive army R&D requests until the Army agreed, reluctantly and despite serious misgivings, to develop an air defense system that incorporated technologies and components already proven in other areas. Concurrent production and testing were undertaken to satisfy congressional dictates."[50] Eventually, Defense Secretary Weinberger canceled the program, leaving frontline troops without an effective defense against enemy helicopters.

The fourth charge leveled at Congress is that it distracts members of the Pentagon and the national security policy-making apparatus, leaving them less time to attend to the important task of making defense decisions. Defense analysts in the Pentagon believe this to be the case.[51] However, evidence in chapter 3 combined with findings in this chapter suggest otherwise. Foremost is the finding in chapter 3 that members of the military, rather than being constrained, operate relatively unencumbered in making major weapons decisions. Second is the evidence that the military services are too often (47 percent of the cases in this study) motivated by nonmilitary or organizational concerns. As James Lindsay notes, there are "numerous examples of how non-objective factors led the services to develop (or not to develop) weapons."[52] One example is the Trident submarine, which owes its behemoth proportions not to military need but to the influence of Admiral Hyman Rickover, who wanted a suitable platform for his new nuclear reactor. Another example is continuous patrol aircraft basing for MX missiles, which was opposed by the Air Force not for technical or military reasons but because it jeopardized funding for other, faster planes preferred by the service. Third is the implicit assumption that the demands that Congress makes on the Pentagon are superfluous. Not unexpectedly, defense analysts in the Pentagon and senior staff members of the defense committees provide different (subjective) assessments on this question. One interviewee, however, working in the Legislative Liaison Office in the Pentagon, acknowledged that Congress cannot perform adequate oversight without the requisite information.

Finally, regardless of how many information demands Congress makes, the Pentagon regulates the flow of information. According to one observer, "the relevant PPBS documents are tightly controlled, [and] avenues for congressional influence in the Pentagon's budget-making process are opened largely at the discretion of the military services."[53] Moreover, the military services are increasingly hiding major weapons systems in "black boxes."[54] Representatives Les Aspin (D-Wis.) and William Dickinson (R-Ala.), formerly chair and ranking member of HASC, respectively, once estimated that "fully 70 percent of all the funds that are now obscured under the 'black' umbrella could be listed publicly in the budget without causing any harm to national security."[55]

A fifth charge is that members of Congress are singularly influenced by constituent and interest-group demands at the expense of the public good, the security of the nation. (The impact of constituent and interest-group influence on legislative voting behavior will be explored more fully in the context of a defense subsystem in the next chapter.) The impressionistic (or what Lindsay calls the anecdotal) evidence does point to a Congress whose strings are pulled by constituents and special-interest groups. Constituent concern over the environmental, social, cultural, and strategic implications of MX/MPS deployment in the Great Basin region of Utah and Nevada is largely credited with the changes in the congressional (and, importantly, presidential) positions on the ten-warhead missile program. Similarly, defense contractor Northrop's location in southern California is credited with defense "dove" and critic Senator Alan Cranston's (D-Calif.) consistently supportive votes on the B-1 bomber system.

The case of the Navy's F/A-18 (Hornet) strike fighter program also demonstrates that even legislators generally critical of the military will act to protect a program in which constituents' jobs are at stake. When President Carter threatened to cut the Hornet program in 1978, Representative Tip O'Neil (D-Mass.) and Senators Ted Kennedy (D-Mass.), Alan Cranston (D-Calif.), and Thomas Eagleton (D-Mo.) intervened. The planes are constructed by Northrop (California) and McDonnell-Douglas (Missouri), and the engines are built by General Electric (Massachusetts). In 1972, when Senators Lloyd Bentsen (D-Tex.) and Thomas McIntyre (D-N.H.) led the resistance to Defense Secretary Melvin Laird's request for production money for the Trident submarine until the military produced an approved design, Senator Henry Jackson (D-Wash.) organized congressional support and was rewarded with a Trident base in his state.

When the impact of constituent and interest-group influence is assessed more systematically, however, considerably different conclusions emerge (at least since the late 1960s). Most notably, empirical studies measuring the relative influence of parochialism versus ideology provide consistent evidence that the majority of members of Congress vote their conscience at least on strategic weapons systems. In other words, when the issue is manned strategic bombers, nuclear submarines, cruise missiles, or ICBMs, there is little conclusive evidence to support the assertion that legislative voting patterns are dictated by parochial concerns.[56]

A similar analysis of conventional systems produces analogous findings.[57] While there is evidence to suggest that parochialism is more common, its impact is relatively benign. In other words, Congress does not compromise the security of the country when its members rely upon parochialism as a cue in making conventional weapons decisions. Rather than dictating the decisions as to whether or not to build a certain weapon, parochial concerns more likely influence the amount of money to be committed to a system or, less often, its management and performance parameters. When the survival of a weapon is at stake, members of Congress vote their conscience, unless they face serious political risks in doing otherwise. Since few congressional districts benefit substantially from major weapons production, the majority being more dependent upon military base or installation spending, most legislators are not bound by constituent or interest-group ties. In short, while parochialism is less likely to influence the decision of whether or not to support a major weapons system, it may determine whether New Jersey, Massachusetts, Texas, or California continues to benefit from the production of the F-14, the F/A-18, HARMs (High Speed Anti-Radiation Missiles), or the B-1B, respectively. While a defense contract is not an insignificant consideration, it is not one that carries the life-and-death consequences imputed to legislative decision-making.

"Fire-Alarm" Oversight

In addition to challenging the major claims made against congressional involvement in military hardware decisions, a positive case can be made for Congress. Lindsay argues in support of legislative involvement from a theoretical perspective that invokes democratic principles.[58] But there is more concrete evidence that legislative involvement in weapons acquisition decisions is good, i.e., that clear substantive benefits result from Congress's concern with America's military arsenal. The most important benefit is the forum that Congress provides for a public examination of major weapons decisions.

Who provided the incentive for modifications to the M-16 rifle, which turned it into one of the finest pieces of combat equipment in the world? To whom do whistle-blowers turn when they detect evidence of malfeasance in the Pentagon? Which institution has proven itself responsive to claims that policymakers (whether the defense secretary, the President, or colleagues in Congress) have compromised the defense decision-making process in advance of their self-interests? Congress with increasing frequency has used its statutory power to create channels of influence; that is, to empower nonlegislative actors and its own members to scrutinize the activities of the military and bring cases of malfeasance or questionable practices to its attention. Recognizing the limited nature of its own institutional resources to compete with the Pentagon and executive branch on major weapons systems, Congress's role is more promotional. Congress may lack the expertise to challenge the military on matters of technology and strategy, the time to scrutinize each weapons program thoroughly, and the incentive to terminate or initiate military hardware programs, but it does have the statutory power and responsibility to insure that major concerns over military hardware decisions have an opportunity to be heard and debated. While Congress does not perform this role perfectly, a number of cases from this study illustrate the importance of this oversight function.

When maverick developers of the Navy's Skipper (AGM-123A) missile at China Lake Weapons Center found themselves stymied by supporters of the Pentagon rival (the Triple L) developed by Texas Instruments (located in the home state of the SASC chairman, John Tower), the HASC proved receptive to their concerns and mandated a live competition between the two missiles. The Skipper, a considerably cheaper and more efficient alternative, won, and is currently carried by Navy planes. When young soldiers in Vietnam were unable to seek redress for the deaths among their compatriots due to the high malfunction rate of the first series of M-16 rifles used, the same committee held an investigation and a series of public hearings and issued a stern condemnation of the Army's conduct during the procurement of the rifle. Subsequent technical changes, not necessarily in line with the committee report, did result in the production of a reliable rifle.[59] In the 1960s, evidence of military waste and industry malfeasance in the procurement of the C-5A transport plane was revealed during legislative hearings.[60]

Congress also made it possible for the public to influence the MX debate through its passage of statutory authority such as NEPA and FLPMA. Utah State Senator Frances Farley was able to obtain a sufficient amount of information through the Freedom of Information Act (FOIA) to file a lawsuit against the Air Force on NEPA and FLPMA grounds. Importantly, the public opposition to MX fueled a policy debate over the nuclear triad, MIRVed missiles, and America's unspoken "first strike" option. Shortly after coming to power, President Reagan abandoned the planned deployment of MX in MPS basing, in retrospect abandoning one of the only viable basing mode ideas.

Evidence of technical flaws in the armaments and air frame system, and auditing irregularities in the development and production of the F/A-18 (Hornet) fighter plane were revealed by the CBO. Congressional hearings were held, and several legislators vowed not to consider any further funding until a legal investigation was conducted.[61] DIVAD was exposed by Representative Denny Smith (R-Ore.) after he received incriminating information from confidential Pentagon sources. Public revelations of technical flaws and testing violations were significant in Defense Secretary Weinberger's decision to cancel the weapons system. Smith's ability to influence military policy, despite not holding a formal position on the House Armed Services Committee or Defense Appropriations Subcommittee, was made possible by legislatively mandated changes in the distribution of power in Congress.[62] Despite making it possible for evidence to come to light that DIVAD was seriously flawed, Congress did not act to cancel the antiaircraft gun and continued to support it through 1984, in deference to the military.

In short, Congress has made it possible for military hardware flaws, whether technical, economic, or military, to be brought to its attention. The broadening of the scope of participation both within and outside Congress has multiplied the number of people who can scrutinize military policy, and thus has increased the likelihood of "fire-alarms" being set off. Congress functions as a forum in which public criticism can be voiced directly or reflected.[63] On the other hand, Congress rarely responds to evidence of procurement difficulties with statutory action directed at the problem per se, once again underscoring the limited substantive consequences of legislative involvement. The case of the M-16 rifle and B-1B are two notable examples.

Congressional Influence: A Prospective

According to evidence in this chapter, legislators have broad and substantial national security powers and are enormously involved in procurement matters, with varying levels of influence. While Congress is actively involved in the funding, management, and design of major weapons systems, and the strategic debates over the rationale for and performance of military hardware, they act less often to reverse or seriously compromise a military or presidential position. It is more often the case (63 percent) that legislators outside the circle of defense experts choose not to be actively involved (see Table 5.1). While Congress less often places itself in an adversarial position on weapons procurement matters, when it does its actions can contribute to (although not necessarily cause) marginal projects being terminated (such as DIVAD, Cheyenne, and, ironically, Thor-Jupiter). In sum, Congress has the power and determination to influence military hardware decisions, but often fails to realize the full extent of its potential when the measure of influence is the cancellation or origination of a weapons system, or the resurrection of a program terminated by the Pentagon or the president. If the standard of influence is modification, then Congress has been quite influential. As noted earlier, Congress has forced changes in major weapons systems that have modified the cost, scheduling, and performance parameters, management strategy, and mission capabilities of major weapons systems. In short, Congress is an important, albeit junior, player in military hardware decisions.

Will Congress continue to play an important part in military policy? The (cynical) response from the rational perspective suggests that as long as there are electoral benefits to be gained, members of Congress will be motivated to review requests for weapons systems, tying the hands of experts whose responsibility it is to fashion a coherent force posture and structure. In other words, as long as Congress is a political institution, it will make weapons decisions in a decidedly parochial manner. The findings in this chapter have largely discredited this argument. Events since the fall of the Berlin Wall and breakup of the Soviet Union further challenge the idea that legislators are unable to transcend parochialism. As Paul N. Stockton argues convincingly, the policy vacuum left by the unwillingness of the Bush administration to fashion a replacement for the Cold War policies was filled by Congress, which first considered a new approach to defense policy and then began altering weapons systems accordingly.[64]

The response from the political perspective is that institutional and political changes will determine the nature and direction of Congress's future role and influence. In other words, while motives (parochial or policy concerns) are important, the institutional capacity for Congress to act also needs to be considered. What has constrained Congress in the past is a combination of a lack of incentive and the absence of the resources necessary and the capacity to challenge the executive branch on issues of military policy. Legislators are unlikely to abandon their interest in procurement matters. The reasons for their initial entrance into the fray of military hardware policy still remain valid. There is a strong incentive for Congress to continue to contribute to the national security debate that will define America's role in the world for decades, an incentive that is even greater now that Congress and the President have fundamental disagreements about America's future role in the New World Order. Moreover, weapons decisions still mean jobs for some members, a consideration that will become even more important as the budget is cut. Thus, the more immediate consideration is the extent to which institutional and political forces are conducive to legislative activism and influence.

Traditionally, Congress has been at a disadvantage in the debate with the president over military matters because of its highly decentralized and democratic institutional arrangement and relatively fewer resources (compared to those of the executive branch). While Congress has succeeded in expanding exponentially its resources during the past two decades, those of the executive branch are still superior. Moreover, to a large extent, Congress continues to be dependent upon the Pentagon, especially for information. With increasing success, the Pentagon has been able to withhold weapons systems from congressional scrutiny by designating them as "black box" programs. The Pentagon also has ways to circumvent Congress, such as through reprogramming, which in some cases can be done without congressional approval or prior notification. Ron Fox gives the example of the Navy successfully shifting funds from the Harpoon Missile program to the Phoenix Missile program.[65] More recently, Defense Secretary Cheney, in deference to the Navy, "approved the diversion of some of [the funds appropriated by Congress for transport ships] for other programs of interest to the Pentagon and simply refused to spend the rest."[66] A further consideration is how Congress's resource base will be affected by efforts of Republicans in Congress to decrease its operating budget by cutting staff and either reducing the size of or eliminating (e.g., the OTA) some of its research agencies.

Since 1992 there have been attempts to challenge the makeup of the institution. Efforts to reorganize Congress to reverse the decentralization and equalization of power that has been a trend since the 1970s invariably will affect the scope of legislative participation. If successful, plans to strengthen the party leadership, weaken the committee and subcommittees system, and related procedural changes, could more narrowly circumscribe the arena of debate on military hardware matters. On the other hand, a more centralized institution would be in a better position to fashion a legislative consensus sufficiently broad to successfully challenge the executive branch. While Congress has been quite adept at challenging military hardware recommendations in the past, it has been less competent at providing an alternative to the administration plan.[67]

One factor that has consistently operated to weaken Congress's ability to gain consensus, and that could be reasonably offset by a more centralized and autocratic institution, is the ideological composition of Congress. (Overcoming the constraints that a presidential veto poses is a more formidable problem.[68]) While "hawks" generally have prevailed during the 1970s and 1980s, their numbers have been adequately offset by the "doves" and "moderates" in Congress. Since the Vietnam War, Congress has found it difficult to overcome ideological disagreement and build a coalition large enough to challenge the executive branch.[69] For example, while a small group of congressional doves worked to discredit the highly sophisticated Aegis tracking system, they were unable to provoke the interest of a majority of their colleagues until the Vincennes disaster that claimed the lives of 300 Iranian civilian passengers at the hands of American sailors. Even during the 1990s, Republican efforts in Congress to dictate military procurement priorities have been stymied by the conflicts between conservative Republicans in the House and more moderate Republicans in the Senate. The ongoing battle between the two houses over funding for the Stealth bomber illustrates the divisive nature of ideology.

Conclusion

Over the past thirty years, a number of major weapons systems have experienced cost overruns, schedule slippages, and performance failures.[70] Congress's preference for stretching out the funding schedule for, rather than terminating or modifying the design of, a weapons system does contribute to (although does not necessarily cause) cost overruns. Its enthusiasm for micromanagement[71] directly contributes to (although does not necessarily cause) procurement delays. To implicate Congress in the performance failures that some systems have experienced is problematical, since its influence over the design or operational requirements of a weapons system has not been decisive in most cases. Congress can be accused of indirectly affecting the value or operational viability of military hardware through its contribution to scheduling delays and cost overruns. At worst, Congress can be faulted for inadequate oversight, even if we apply a fire-alarm standard.

If Congress is not the primary culprit in the problems that major weapons systems have encountered, then can it be a primary benefactor? Can Congress be faulted for not doing more to guard against the problems that befall military hardware procurement? Although Congress cannot be expected to compete with the Pentagon in the making of weapons procurement decisions, it can assist in improving the weapons selection process in the Pentagon, in both its technical and operational aspects. It has a constitutional responsibility to execute the sort of oversight that guards against malfeasance. Congress can continue to take legislative action to increase the opportunities for "fire-alarms" to be rung (something Republican legislators are likely to resist) and be more responsive to these alarms. It can also act to improve what is overseen—that is, the decisions that the Pentagon makes. It can do (and has done) this by legislating against interservice collusion. To counter the effects of military service logrolling, Congress should continue to legislate changes in the Pentagon.[72] Any efforts to reduce the autonomy and power of the defense secretary and chairman of the Joint Chiefs of Staff to make definitive selections from among several military preferences relying upon military need criteria should be resisted. The Senate should continue to engage in scrutiny of the professional qualifications of nominees for positions in the DoD, such as occurred in the case of the late Senator John Tower (R-Tex.).

It remains for Congress to legislate more competition at the preproduction as well as at the production stages through expanded financial support at the research and development stage, and for dual sourcing and prototype testing.[73] Moreover, Congress should continue its practice of multiyear budgeting (begun in FY 1988) and requiring votes on mission areas rather than on individual programs or projects.[74] These measures can strengthen Congress's capacity to engage in long-term planning and make funding trade-offs on the basis of military need criteria.

Finally, Congress should continue its interest in and improve its capacity to raise and respond to fundamental questions about the threats to America's national security and how to meet these threats.[75] Congress already has the resources (staff and research capacity) to inform itself on military policy issues, although these are in danger of being retrenched. Congress also has the interest. Since it is unlikely that Congress will revert to its former passive role in defense policy-making, the emphasis should be on improving its capacity to influence military hardware decisions in ways that promote the development and deployment of necessary and workable systems in a cost-effective manner. To do otherwise is to relinquish its role in reshaping America's military position in the post–Cold War period and shirk its responsibilities to the American people to submit matters so important as the instruments of destruction to public debate. Ultimately, it is to the people we look for validation of the foreign and defense policy commitments of a democratic nation, a topic that is addressed in the next chapter.

Notes

1. *U.S. Constitution*, art. 1, sec. 8, clauses 11-14.
2. See *U.S. Constitution*, 10 U.S.C. 138 (a). In 1961 Congress began the process of extending annual authorizations to include first weapons systems, and ultimately all of the R&D, development, testing, and evaluation carried on by the Defense Department.

3. Charles W. Kegley and Eugene R. Wittkopf, *American Foreign Policy: Pattern and Process* (New York: St. Martin's Press, 1987), 415.

4. Donald M. Snow and Eugene Brown, *Puzzle Palaces and Foggy Bottom: U.S. Foreign and Defense Policy-Making in the 1990s* (New York: St. Martin's Press, 1994), chapter 4.

5. Lauren Holland, "The Use of NEPA in Defense Policy Politics: Public and State Involvement in the MX Missile Project," *Social Science Journal* 21 (July 1984): 53-71.

6. See the comments of John Tower, cited in U.S. Congress, *Defense Organization: The Need for Change* (Washington, D.C.: Government Printing Office, 1985), 578.

7. See Fen Osler Hampson, *Unguided Missiles: How America Buys Its Weapons* (New York: W.W. Norton, 1989), 58. Also Steven S. Smith, *Call to Order: Floor Politics in the House and Senate* (Washington, D.C.: The Brookings Institution, 1989), and Amos A. Jordan, William J. Taylor Jr. and Lawrence J. Korb, *American National Security: Policy and Process* (Baltimore: The Johns Hopkins University Press, 1993), 109–111.

8. See *News Release*, House Armed Services Committee, 2 November 1989. Brent Barker suggests that one reason for the expanded scope of legislative involvement in procurement matters has to do with the budget deficit. Defense spending constitutes 75 percent of the 25 percent of the federal budget that is "controllable," which means it is susceptible to reductions as a way to reduce the deficit. Baker, "National Defense and the Congressional Role," *Naval War College Review* 35 (July–August 1982): 4.

9. In this study, the scope of involvement is broad or narrow. The scope is broad when the involvement includes members not formally empowered to participate. It is narrow when action is primarily confined to the armed services committees and the defense appropriations subcommittees in both houses.

10. See George C. Edwards III, "Conclusion: The Constitutional System and National Security," in George C. Edwards III and Wallace Earl Walker, eds., *National Security and the U.S. Constitution: The Impact of the Political System* (Baltimore: The Johns Hopkins University Press, 1988), 305–327.

11. See Barry M. Blechman, *The Politics of National Security: Congress and U.S. Defense Policy* (New York: Oxford, 1990), 9-17.

12. U.S. Congress, "Defense Organization," 591. Also Edwards "Congress and National Security."

13. Smith, *Call to Order*, 2.

14. James M. Lindsay, *Congress and Nuclear Weapons* (Baltimore: The Johns Hopkins University Press, 1991), 32.

15. Ibid., 30.

16. Hampson, *Unguided Missiles*, 57–63. Also see R. Douglas Arnold, *Congress and the Bureaucracy* (New Haven: Yale University Press, 1979), and Les Aspin, "The Defense Budget and Foreign Policy: The Role of Congress," *Daedalus* 104 (Summer 1975).

17. Ronald J. Fox, *The Defense Management Challenge: Weapons Acquisition* (Boston, Mass.: Harvard Business School Press, 1988).

18. Jacques S. Gansler, *Affording Defense* (Cambridge, Mass.: MIT Press, 1989), 116.

19. Congress has exerted influence over defense policy, it is said, when it reduces or raises the administration's budget requests by a "significant" (in most cases by more than 5 percent) amount.

20. Fiscal analysts contend that funding decisions are "the surrogate independent variable for larger policy decisions regarding doctrine. . . ." Asa A. Clark IV, "Interservice Rivalry and Military Reform," in *The Defense Reform Debate: Issues and Analysis*, eds. Asa A. Clark IV et al. (Baltimore: The Johns Hopkins University Press, 1984), 261. The argument is that the act of disaggregating the budget into separate appropriations titles and further into line items inevitably leads Congress to make genuine programmatic and policy distinctions. Thus, by engaging in fiscal oversight, Congress engages in programmatic and policy oversight. By making fiscal changes, Congress exercises influence over military matters. See Arnold Kanter, *Defense Politics: A Budgetary Perspective* (Chicago: The University of Chicago Press,1975).

21. Lindsay, *Congress and Nuclear Weapons*, 146.

22. Paul N. Stockton, "Congress and Defense Policy-Making for the Post–Cold War Era," in *Congress Resurgent: Foreign and Defense Policy on Capitol Hill*, eds. Randall B. Ripley and James M. Lindsay (Ann Arbor, Mich.: University of Michigan Press, 1993), 235.

23. Fox, *The Defense Management Challenge*, 72–80.

24. Lindsay, *Congress and Nuclear Weapons*, 158. The latter law is Congress's response to the 1986 Packard Commission recommendations on the reorganization of the defense policy-making process.

25. Gansler, *Affording Defense*, 109.

26. James H. Dixon et al., *National Security Policy Formulation: Institutions, Processes, and Issues* (New York: University Press of America, 1984). Edward N. Luttwak, *Strategy: The Logic of War and Peace* (Cambridge, Mass.: Belknap Press, 1987). Also, Lindsay, *Congress and Nuclear Weapons*, chapter 5.

27. Stockton, "Congress and Defense Policy-Making."

28. According to confidential interviews with staff and legislators, members of Congress are trying to be more of a decisive voice in policy oversight (in the formulation and articulation of U.S. strategy). The combined tendency to "over-oversight" and defer to the executive branch continues, however. See Randall B. Ripley and Grace A. Franklin, *Bureaucracy and Policy Implementation* (Homewood, Ill.: Dorsey Press, 1982), 236, Hampson, *Unguided Missiles,* chapter 4, and Blechman, *The Politics of National Security,* chapter 2.

29. Interviews with senior senate staff members and Pentagon staff.

30. Lauren Holland and Robert Hoover, *The MX Decision: A New Direction in U.S. Weapons Procurement Policy?* (Boulder, Colo.: Westview Press, 1985), and Hampson, *Unguided Missiles,* chapter 6.

31. Nicholas Swales in Hampson, *Unguided Weapons,* 222.

32. This is not to discount the work of a small group of legislators who have sought (unsuccessfully) to block the deployment of nuclear weapons systems. See, for example, Ronald V. Dellums (with R.H. Miller and H. Lee Halterman), ed., *Defense Sense: The Search for a Rational Military Policy* (Cambridge, Mass.: Ballinger, 1983), and Asa A. Clark IV, Peter W. Chiarelli, Jeffrey S. McKitrick, and James W. Reed, eds., *The Defense Reform Debate: Issues and Analysis* (Baltimore: The Johns Hopkins University Press, 1984).

33. Jordan et al., *American National Security,* 121.

34. Robert J. Art, "Congress and the Defense Budget: Enhancing Policy Oversight," *Political Science Quarterly* 100 (1985): 227–248.

35. Lindsay, *Congress and Nuclear Weapons*, 144.

36. Ibid., 151.

37. Lindsay, *Congress and Nuclear Weapons*, 149.

38. At the time, the defense secretary's reaction to legislative opposition to Osprey was a suggestion that the president be given the power to combat micromanagement through halting spending on defense programs that are supported by the Congress but not by the Pentagon. *Defense News*, 1 January 1990, 7. The Osprey is still in production.

39. Senator Sam Nunn, D-Ga., quoted in *Time*, 21 October 1985, 35.

40. Delays in the weapons acquisition cycle and increases in the costs of military hardware can complicate the process of matching military needs and operational capabilities. As noted in earlier chapters, each weapon system is conceived to meet a real national security threat. Therefore, a delay in its deployment means that the United States continues to be militarily vulnerable. In essence, this was the core of the window of vulnerability argument used by the Reagan administration to justify the procurement of the MX missile system. Too, if the costs of a weapons system grow to the point where fewer units can be afforded, its workability may be jeopardized. Clearly, a certain number of Navy ships, Army tanks, and Air Force fighter planes are needed to insure that the services have the capacity to perform their missions. Moreover, with fewer funds, a defense contractor may compromise in the development and production of a major weapons system. The effects of legislative funding decisions, then, become indirect, but not insignificant ones.

41. Center for Strategic and International Studies (CSIS), *U.S. Defense Acquisition: A Process in Trouble* (Georgetown: Georgetown University Press,1987), 170.

42. U.S. Congress, Congressional Budget Office (CBO), *Concurrent Weapons Development and Production* (Washington, D.C.: Government Printing Office, August 1988).

43. U.S. Congress, *Congressional Record*, 98th Cong., 1st sess., vol. 129, Part 15: 20089.

44. In testimony before the Senate Armed Services Committee in 1985, micromanagement was defined as the practice whereby Congress was "overdefinitive in its legislation and . . . overproductive in terms of the number of [procurement reform] bills that are generated." Quoted in Fox, *Defense Management Challenge*, 74. Fox defines micromanagement as "becoming involved in the day-to-day activities of the [defense] department."

45. Gansler, *Affording Defense*, 116.

46. *Defense News*, 4 June 1990: 3.

47. Stockton, "Congress and Defense Policy-Making," 255.

48. Kosta Tsipis and Penny Janeway, eds., *Review of U.S. Military Research and Development* (Washington, D.C.: Pergamon-Brassey's, 1984).

49. Greg Williams, *The Army's M1 Tank: Has It Lived Up to Expectations?* (Washington, D.C.: Project on Government Procurement, 1990).

50. CSIS, *U.S. Defense Acquisition*, 170.

51. Personal interviews, the Pentagon, Washington, D.C. July 1991.

52. Lindsay, *Congress and Nuclear Weapons*, 164.

53. James W. Reed, "Congress and the Politics of Defense Reform," in *Defense Reform Debate*, Clark et al., 239. Also see Tim Weiner, "The Dark Secret of the Black Budget," *Washington Monthly*, May 1987.

54. See Table 8-1, in Lindsay, *Congress and Nuclear Weapons*, 154–55. Black box programs are those that the Pentagon shields from public and legislative scrutiny for national security reasons.

55. Quoted in ibid., 155. Under penalty of law, no person affiliated with a "black budget" weapon system may publicly discuss any information held. To an increasing extent, the military services are hiding their weapons programs in black boxes

56. See, e.g., Robert A. Bernstein and William W. Anthony, "The ABM Issue in the Senate, 1968–1970: The Importance of Ideology," *American Political Science Review* 68 (September 1974): 1198–1206; Richard Fleisher, "Economic Benefit, Ideology, and Senate Voting on the B-1 Bomber," *American Politics Quarterly* 13 (April 1985): 200–211; James M. Lindsay, "Congress and the Defense Budget: Parochialism or Policy?" in *Arms, Politics, and the Economy: Historical and Contemporary Perspectives,* ed. Robert Higgs (New York: Holms and Meier, 1990); Lindsay, "Parochialism, Policy, and Constituency Constraints: Congressional Voting on Strategic Weapons System," *American Journal of Political Science* 34 (November 1990): 936–960; Lindsay, "Testing the Parochial Hypothesis: Congress and the Strategic Defense Initiative," *Journal of Politics* 53 (August 1991).

57. See, for example, Kenneth Robert Mayer, *The Political Economy of Defense Contracting* (New Haven: Yale University Press, 1991).

58. Lindsay, *Congress and Nuclear Weapons*.

59. Thomas L. McNaugher, *New Weapons Old Politics: America's Military Procurement Muddle* (Washington, D.C.: The Brookings Institution, 1989); James Fallows, *National Defense* (New York: Random House, 1981).

60. Berkely Rice, *C-5A Scandal* (New York: Houghton-Mifflin, 1971), 111.

61. In 1983 the CBO issued an audit that claimed the Navy had improperly transferred several hundred million dollars from other accounts to pay for more Hornets (F/A-18). As a result, several members vowed not to consider any further funding until a legal investigation was conducted. Reported in *Business Week*, 14 February 1983. More recently, Congress empowered an independent panel to evaluate the Pentagon's recent defense review (QDR, 1997) and provide alternative options for meeting projected new threats and international conditions. See Bradley Graham, "Pentagon Faulted for Short-Sighted Plans." *The Washington Post*, 20 May 1997: A17.

62. Lindsay, "Congress and Defense Policy: 1961 to 1986," *Armed Forces and Society* 13 (Spring 1987): 371–401.

63. Kegley and Wittkopf, *American Foreign Policy*, 415.

64. Stockton, "Congress and Defense Policy-Making for the Post–Cold War Era."

65. Fox, *Defense Management Challenge*, 71.

66. Snow and Brown, *Puzzle Palaces*, 116.

67. Lindsay, *Congress and Nuclear Weapons*, 151.

68. Ibid., 152–153.

69. Ibid.

70. Gansler, *Affording Defense.* 122. Also Michael E. Brown, *Flying Blind: The Politics of the U.S. Strategic Bomber Program* (Ithaca: Cornell University Press, 1992), 14–16.

71. Congress engages in oversight micromanagement or "over-oversight" when it makes excessive demands on the Pentagon for information; and in legislative micromanagement when it introduces "detailed restrictions and directions" into defense legislation and committee reports. Fox cites as examples Title IX of the 1986 DoD authorization act, and the Weapon System Warranties Act (10 U.S.C. 2403). *Defense Management Challenge*, 74.

72. DoD Reorganization Act of 1985. Also see President's Blue Ribbon Commission on Defense Management, *Quest For Excellence: Final Report to the President* (June 1986) and Defense Secretary Cheney's *Defense Management Report to the President* (July 1989).

73. McNaugher, *New Weapons Old Politics.*

74. Gansler, *Affording Defense*, 120.

75. Art, "Congress and the Defense Budget," 405.

F/A-18 (Hornet)
Congress Gets Stung

Congressional involvement in the F/A-18 naval strike fighter has been significant. In 1974 Congress passed an amendment to the defense appropriations bill which mandated that the Navy terminate its VFAX (fixed wing fighter attack experimental) program and pick an NACF (Naval Air Combat Fighter) from two existing Air Force designs (the YF-16 and YF-17). Reacting to the soaring costs of the Navy's F-14 fighter plane, Congress sought a less expensive alternative that could fill the low role in the high-low mix concept, and perform as a fighter and attack (bomber) plane. The Navy resisted, and Congress again invoked its appropriations powers to instruct the service this time to choose a derivative of the Air Force's F-16 fighter plane. The Navy sought the protective umbrella of Defense Secretary James Schlesinger, and eventually contracted with Northrop-McDonnell Douglas to build a derivative of the YF-17.

The Navy's actions touched off a heated battle in Congress that highlighted the role of parochialism in decisions on tactical weapons issues. After a bruising legislative confrontation, Congress approved the F/A-18 (Hornet) multirole aircraft. The Hornet's supporters were able to build a coalition of legislative support by first playing upon the parochial needs of key legislative members such as Speaker of the House Tip O'Neill (in whose district the engines would be built), and Senators Alan Cranston, Ted Kennedy, and Thomas Eagleton, who then relied upon the norm of reciprocity (logrolling) to offset the opposition.

Since the program's conception as the Hornet, Congress has fought successfully to save it, despite repeated outside attempts to retrench and even eliminate it. In 1977 Congress, in response to a threat by President Carter to cancel Hornet because of exorbitant costs, joined with Pentagon supporters and successfully lobbied the president and the secretary of defense, Harold Brown. In 1982 military and congressional supporters succeeded in turning back the efforts of Secretary of the Navy John Lehman and HADS Chair Joseph Adabbado (in whose district the A-6 and F-14 planes are built) to drastically cut the purchase of new planes. Despite evidence of performance and cost overrun problems, Congress continues to micromanage the F/A-18, increasing the purchase of planes one year, then decreasing it in other ones.

Primary Sources: Bill Gunston, *The F/A Hornet* (Rummyton, England: Ian Allan, 1985); G. Phillip Hughes, "Congressional Influence in Weapons Procurement," *Public Policy* 28 (Fall 1980): 415–449; U.S. General Accounting Office, *The F/A-18 Naval Strike Fighter: Progress Has Been Made But Problems and Concerns Continue* (Washington, D.C.: Government Printing Office, 18 February 1981).

HIGHLIGHT

M-1
Congress Builds a Tank

The M-1 (Abrams) tank was the third in a series of failed attempts (MBT-70 and XM-803) by the Army to design a weapon acceptable to Congress, which meant neither too costly nor technically risky. Broad and intense congressional involvement in the Abrams program can be attributed to two factors. First was the tank's enormous price tag. According to Fen Hampson, the cost of the M-1 program "has been in the top ten of United States military R&D and Procurement outlays since at least 1984."[1] The Abrams tank also became "something of a test case to affirm [congressional] control over the military on defense procurement [issues]."[2]

Congress's obsession with fiscal matters contributed to but did not cause the tank's performance problems. A legislative ceiling on unit costs encouraged the manufacturer (Chrysler Defense Inc. which was bought later by General Dynamics Corporation) to compromise and use inferior parts in order to stay within the lines of the contract agreement. However, the tank's performance capabilities were also compromised by the absence of quality control during production (which, according to Tsipis and Janeway, could have avoided subsequent RAM-D problems) and the amalgamation of requirements imposed by agencies and actors within the Pentagon, most notably the six-year procurement schedule (set by service chief of staff Westmoreland) and the tank's weight goal (set by chief of staff-designate Abrams).[3]

Legislative interference in the contract decisions also affected the M-1's development, most notably Congress's unprecedented act in 1983 preventing the Army from considering a competing supplier for the tank's engine, despite serious performance failures in the AVCO design. As Stubbing documents, AVCO made generous campaign contributions to key members of HASC and HADS timed to the vote.

Legislative concerns over the M-1 delayed its procurement (it reached its Initial Operational Capability in 1981), and, in so doing, ironically contributed to increases in both the costs and technical uncertainties of the weapon system. Accordingly, despite fiscal and technical concerns by Congress (and the OSD), the M-1 developed into a high-cost, technically sophisticated, and innovative weapons system. As late as 1986, the capacity of the tank to achieve its design requirements for reliability, durability, maintainability, and availability (RAM-D) was still in doubt (Congressional Research Service). By 1987, many of these problems had been resolved. Yet the M-1 tank remains controversial. Considered by its supporters to be an excellent (albeit gold-plated) weapon, critics find the tank unnecessarily sophisticated and expensive and the need for it ambiguous given advances in antitank technology and changes in world politics.

[1]Fen Osler Hampson, *Unguided Missiles: How America Buys Its Weapons* (New York: W.W. Norton, 1989), 222.
[2]Ibid., 199.
[3]Thomas L. McNaugher, *New Weapons Old Politics* (Washington, D.C.: The Brookings Institution, 1989), 73, 125.

Primary Sources: Arthur Alexander, "XM-1," in *Report of the Commission on the Organization of the Government for the Conduct of Foreign Policy*, vol. 4 (Washington, D.C.: Government Printing Office, 1975); Steven R. Bowman, *The M-1 Tank* (Washington, D.C.: Congressional Research Service Issue Brief, 1992 f); Hampson, *Unguided Missiles;* McNaugher, *New Weapons Old Politics.*

HIGHLIGHT

DIVAD
"Sargeant York Can't Shoot"

More than for any other weapons system in this study, Congressional action on the DIVAD (division air defense) automated antiaircraft gun illustrates the complex range of motivations and concerns behind military hardware matters, and the ambiguous nature of legislative influence over them. DIVAD was conceived during the 1970s to meet an undisputed need for a new weapon to replace the outdated Vulcan, in light of the growing military threat that the then new Soviet attack helicopter (Mi-28-HAVOC) posed. Congress, concerned that the new weapons system would be too costly and pose unmanageable technical risks, invoked its funding power to pressure the Army to incorporate only proven technologies and components into their air defense system. According to the Center for Strategic and International Studies (CSIS), Congress's unrealistic demands severely constrained the Army and its contractor, Ford Motors, contributing to the technical problems that ultimately doomed the antiaircraft system. For its part, however, the Army exacerbated the situation by setting unrealistic performance goals that demanded both challenging component integration and new and complex technology (mostly computer-related), and then employing a concurrent management strategy that moved the system into production before the tests were completed and the bugs worked out of the weapon. Congress continued to appropriate funds, at the behest of legislators with a vested stake in the survival of the system who relied upon rigged test results (tests held in unrealistically favorable conditions), seemingly oblivious to evidence of serious technical flaws despite condemning reports by the GAO, CBO, OMB, and the DoD inspector general. Representative Denny Smith (R-Ore.), newly empowered because of the democratization of Congress during the 1970s, used his legislative position to mobilize the Military Reform Caucus (a bipartisan committee in Congress concerned with procurement efficiency) to work to defeat DIVAD. Two years after public revelations, the conventional media (in 1984) exploded with the news, DIVAD being the subject of a special "20/20" broadcast and regular news attention from the *New York Times*,

Washington Post, Time, and *Newsweek,* for example. Eventually, Defense Secretary Weinberger canceled the program (in 1985) after another set of disastrous operational test results, the first major weapons system to be terminated after the start of production since the Cheyenne attack helicopter (which Congress canceled). According to *Science* magazine (10 April 1987, pp. 137–140), the development of FAAD (Forward Area Air Defense), DIVAD's replacement, demonstrates that nothing was learned from the DIVAD experience.

Primary Sources: U.S. General Accounting Office, *Inherent Risk in the Army's Acquisition Strategy Demands Particular Caution in Evaluating the Divad Gun System's Production Readiness* (Washington, D.C.: Government Printing Office, 31 January 1980); Greg Easterbrook, "DIVAD," *Atlantic Monthly* (October 1982): 29–39; Harvey Simon, *Breaking the Bad News: Divad* (Cambridge, Mass.: Case Program, Kennedy School of Government, Harvard University, 1988); Richard Simpkin, "The Infantry Fighting Vehicle: Maid-of-All-Work or Crown Princess? *Military Technology* (October 1985): 48–65.

CHAPTER 6

The Role of the Public

In a democracy, decisions so fundamental as those that involve a nation's capacity to annihilate its enemies must be legitimated by the people. However, debate rages over what constitutes legitimization and, consequently, the nature of the role that the American people should play in military force structure decisions. Advocates of the rational perspective or Guardianship Principle contend that it is in the public interest for decisions on technical matters, such as the choice of military hardware, to be made by an elite group of military experts; the public is neither interested nor informed enough to contribute productively to the defense policy debate.[1] In such cases, legitimacy comes from the confidence that the people have in those to whom they entrust (through the electoral process) policy-making responsibilities. Advocates of the political perspective or Equality Principle counter with the claim that a policy-making process that confines decision-making to an elite violates the principles upon which democracy stands. Democracy's viability is as much contingent upon the nature of the policy-making process as it is on the decisions that process produces. Moreover, military hardware questions raise not only technical and strategic issues, but also moral and ethical concerns that are most effectively resolved in a public forum. Egalitarians do not suggest that all of the people should be involved in weapons decisions all of the time, but only that opportunities should be made available to the public to influence military decisions when the people deem necessary.

In an effort to complete the picture of the decision-making process for military hardware decisions, this chapter assesses the role of the public. The chapter begins with an elaboration of the theoretical debate over the role of the public in making defense and foreign policy. The two theoretical positions are then tested empirically by examining the data gathered on the

nineteen weapons acquisition cases in this study and by comparing decision-making in the United States with that in the late Soviet Union.

A Public Role: The Theoretical Debate

The Guardianship Principle: Antipathy for the People

For advocates of the Guardianship Principle, the public, defined broadly to
include public opinion, the mass media, and interest groups, should not be
involved in the crafting of defense policy. They argue that the public is not
capable of making useful contributions to the defense policy debate and that
public involvement in weapons acquisition discussions is counterproductive.

Regarding individual citizens, advocates of the Guardianship Principle
assume that the average person lacks the technical knowledge to participate
in the defense policy debate as well as the interest to become sufficiently
knowledgeable about defense policy matters. According to Cecil Crabb and
Pat Holt, only about 15 percent of the public are attentive on foreign and
defense policy issues.[2] On nuclear weapons issues, David Meyer found the
public to be "generally opposed to, and ill-informed of, government
policy."[3] Charles Kegley and Eugene Wittkopf note "that most Americans
fail to possess even the most elementary knowledge about their own political system, much less international affairs, [and] often the 'information'
held is so inaccurate that it might better be labeled 'misinformation.'"[4]
They go on to argue that public opinion is "uninformed, uninterested, un-
stable, acquiescent, and manipulable," especially on foreign and defense
policy issues. For this reason, the authors conclude, "public opinion provides neither a clear nor a meaningful guide to policy making."[5] Theodore
Sorensen once asserted that "Public opinion is often erratic, inconsistent,
arbitrary, and unreasonable—with a compulsion to make mistakes . . . It
rarely considers the needs of the next generation or the history of the
last . . . It is frequently hampered by myths and misinformation, by stereo-
types and shibboleths, and by an innate resistance to innovation."[6] Robert
Dahl suggests that the "specialized knowledge" that is required to answer
"crucial" technical and political questions about nuclear weapons and
strategy is "far outside the realm of ordinary experience." Included in this
list are questions about the effects of major weapons systems, the reliability
and accuracy of military hardware, the verifiability of nuclear weapons, the
relative balance of military power between the United States and its enemies, and the military intentions of foreign leaders.[7]

Even the attentive public, the mass media and special-interest groups (collectively the interested public), are prevented from making a useful contribution by two conditions. One condition is the national security imperative that justifies the classification of certain information. The interested public cannot be sufficiently informed because to become so might require access to sensitive military information, the release of which could jeopardize national security. A second condition concerns motivation. Since the attentive public is not necessarily motivated by the principle of the public good but by private needs, a public role can be contrary to good defense policy. In other words, because members of special-interest groups and the mass media are motivated to be involved in defense policy by the personal advantages to be gained, their vision is myopic.

This is particularly the case for special-interest groups. Of those private groups that seek to influence military hardware decisions, defense corporations are considered to be the most onerous. This is even more so because of the reciprocal relationship that they have built with key members of congressional committees and the Pentagon, constituting a military subsystem.[8] The key actors in the military hardware subsystem dynamic are said to come from the fifteen to twenty defense companies that dominate the industry (most notably, McDonnell Douglas, General Dynamics, General Electric, Raytheon, General Motors, Lockheed, United Technologies, Martin Marietta, Boeing, and Grumman), the military services, and the House and Senate Armed Services and House and Senate Appropriations Defense Subcommittees.[9] What enhances the viability of the military subsystem is that defense policy is distributive,[10] the three sets of actors have significant resources to engage in logrolling, the subsystem actors have autonomy, the tripartite alliance controls both policy formulation and implementation, and the actors communicate frequently.[11] The danger of subsystems, according to critics, is that the decisions to build and deploy major weapons are made for political and economic reasons (rather than military ones) that may compromise their military viability.[12]

In addition to derailing the debate over defense issues, the public, by being involved, contributes an additional layer to an already inefficient, protracted policy-making process. While the democratic process may work in the domestic arena, a protracted debate over defense policy may mean the difference between life and death, according to this argument. The bargaining and compromise characteristic of democratic decision-making lengthens the time it takes to produce a weapon, impeding a response to an imminent threat. Additionally, government by democratic procedures, which divides and fragments power and works through bar-

184 WEAPONS UNDER FIRE

gaining, results in compromise decisions that are rarely the best solutions
to military problems, especially when the decisions are forced by special-
interest groups. In some important ways, the military subsystem expedites decision-making by isolating military policy, although the decisions
reached are compromise ones, and not necessarily the best responses to
military threats. As such, weapons are deployed that are redundant, overly
specialized, clumsily hybrid, incomplete, or faulty. Compromise decisions
can also result in certain mission needs not being met and almost assur-
edly increase the costs of procuring military hardware.[13]

Advocates of the Guardianship Principle also fault public involvement
for undermining the American government's ability to produce
coherent defense policies, thus weakening the country's international repu-
tation and power.[14] "The unhappy truth," Walter Lippmann once asserted,

> is that the prevailing public opinion has been destructively wrong at
> the critical junctures. The people have imposed a veto upon the judge-
> ments of informed and responsible officials. They have compelled the
> governments, which usually knew what would have been wiser, or what
> was necessary, or more expedient, to be too late with too little, or too
> long with too much, too pacifist in peace and too bellicose in war, too
> neutralist or appeasing in negotiation or too intransigent. Mass opin-
> ion has acquired mounting power in this century. It has shown itself to
> be a dangerous master of decisions when the stakes are life and death.[15]

Barry Blechman blames public opinion for forcing Congress's "wholly
uncritical support for proposed budget increases that everyone in the
business knew had not been well thought through and could not possibly
be spent efficiently," and for the national legislature's exaggerated reaction to national concern with defense procurement practices in the mid-
1980s—over a hundred pieces of "ill-considered" reform legislation.[16]

The Equality Principle: Praise for a Public Role

For advocates of the Equality Principle, the public (defined narrowly as the
media, public interest groups, and individual citizens) is fully capable of
making a valuable contribution to defense policy-making. Egalitarians first
counter the claim that the average citizen is ill-informed and uninterested
in foreign and defense policy issues. According to Bruce Russett, "Public
opinion on most issues is reasonably stable, not capricious, fickle, or volatile."[17] This proved to be the case during operations Desert Shield and
Desert Storm, according to John Mueller.[18] "Foreign policy issues," assert

Kegley and Wittkopf, "are more important to the American people than are domestic concerns. . . ."[19] Meyer concludes that the apparent ambivalence in public opinion on national security issues in the post–World War II period (antipathy for both nuclear war and the Soviet Union) is an understandable phenomenon, not evidence of a fickle and ignorant mass public.[20] Bruce Russett has found that much of the public does hold clear preferences on nuclear weapons, for example. "Most people have accepted the existential reality of nuclear deterrence, but lack enthusiasm for building specific new nuclear weapons systems." Most people also feel that "deterrence is not defense," that nuclear war is not "a legitimate policy," and that an effective test ban treaty must be a bilateral agreement.[21]

Thomas W. Graham found a high level of functional awareness of nuclear weapons issues among the American public. Over 80 percent of the public was found to be aware of the Strategic Defense Initiative (SDI), MX, the hydrogen and atomic bombs, and the Strategic Arms Limitation Treaty (SALT) II.[22] A large percentage of the population (between 30 percent and 78 percent) also had a detailed knowledge of "specific" nuclear weapons such as the hydrogen bomb (78 percent), SDI/Star Wars (43 percent), and the atomic bomb (50 percent).[23] Robert Shapiro and Benjamin Page found the American public to be rational, attentive to the available information, and capable of registering opinions on foreign policy issues. "The public has not always successfully judged the best interests of the United States or that of people elsewhere, nor have elites and the media always reported truthfully and interpreted correctly. Nevertheless, we maintain that Americans, as a *collective* body, have done well with whatever information has been provided, and that they have formed and changed their policy preferences in a reasonable manner."[24]

Egalitarians also argue that rather than constraining government officials, the public has actually expanded their authority by lending legitimacy to governmental actions. "[W]ithout a genuine public consensus of support," asserts one informed source, "the executive branch cannot legitimately and effectively pursue any foreign policy."[25] Since it is impossible to determine with any certainty the best military solution to a particular foreign policy problem, most decisions rely upon political and moral judgements, on which the people have opinions. If these issues cannot be resolved definitively, then the legitimacy that democracy extends to decisions becomes more compelling. "A national security policy which lacks a broad public consensus as its foundation is more likely to be seen as irresolute by potential adversaries."[26] As an illustration, the Harvard Nuclear Study Group credits "broad public support [for paving] the way for the SALT I treaty [in 1972]" and "public pressure in the United States and among European allies [for hastening] the Reagan administration's pursuit of arms control with the Soviets [in 1982]."[27]

In addition to lending legitimacy to governmental actions, the public has, in important cases, emboldened government officials by advocating certain actions. Crabb and Holt cite the examples of public opposition to Soviet expansionism, which induced the Truman administration to adopt the policy of containment; public disenchantment with the Vietnam War, which led to Nixon's decision to terminate the war; and public support for a strong defense during the late 1970s and the 1980s, which influenced "the Carter and Reagan administrations to stiffen their positions toward Soviet interventionism and to strengthen the American defense establishment . . ."[28] Kegley and Wittkopf include public support as a factor in admitting mainland China to the United Nations, and public outrage as instrumental in shaping government attitudes toward South Africa's apartheid policy and the complicity of American businesses in that country.[29]

According to adherents of the Equality Principle, even the mass media have acted responsibly in notable situations that have served the public interest. Robert Trice credits the media generally for its role in transmitting information to the public and thus stimulating public and governmental debate on crucial issues.[30] Meyer cites the example of CBS's decision to run *The Defense of the United States*, a documentary describing in horrific detail the probable effects of a 15-megaton nuclear warhead on Omaha, Nebraska, as a way to challenge the Reagan administration's buildup.[31] Daniel Kaufman credits "[t]he intense media coverage accorded operational failures—the Iranian hostage rescue attempt in 1980, the destruction of the Marine barracks in Beirut in 1983—[with] focus[ing] public attention on the services' ability to carry out their functions and [raising] questions about command arrangements for deployed operational forces." Kaufman goes on to cite media coverage of and public concern over the Defense Department's scandalous, wasteful, and fraudulent procurement practices (exemplified by the purchase of $600 hammers) as contributing to the reform efforts in the Pentagon.[32] The media also performed an important role in politicizing the MX issue when citizens in Utah and Nevada were organizing to oppose the deployment of the ten-warhead missiles in the Great Basin desert region.

The assertion that the public is motivated by private rather than public concerns is further challenged by the counterclaim that defense experts (scientists, technicians, and military bureaucrats) "are not themselves perfectly neutral technicians dispassionately searching for the policy that would maximize the values affirmed by the electorate."[33] Defense experts are bureaucrats and politicians who act to secure personal and organizational benefits. The "play of bureaucratic dynamics" is most evident in the "service rivalries over budgets, weapons, and strategic plans."[34] The evidence in chapters 3 and 4 rebuts the claim that the governing elite is a rational, virtuous, and omniscient one.

The rise of public interest groups also disputes the claim that public involvement is motivated solely by private concerns.[35] The case of the nuclear freeze movement is a recent example. A broad coalition of groups was mobilized and engaged in civil disobedience and direct action in support of a nuclear test ban treaty. Millions of people were attracted to the movement, and hundreds of cities and towns supported freeze resolutions, drawn by their concerns over the risks of nuclear proliferation and war.[36] While ultimately disbanding, the nuclear freeze movement is credited with influencing Reagan's decisions to soften his "rhetoric" and pursue serious arms control negotiations, widely recognized as a public good. With this motivation, Reagan successfully concluded the treaty on intermediate-range missiles. "This would not have happened without the pressure from the movement, and Mikhail Gorbachev."[37] Congress, too, responded to the nuclear freeze movement, registering more interest in and support for arms control agreements.

To the charge that the public delays and distorts decision-making, Robert Dahl responds that "The president still generally gets the weapons he wants, even if it often takes longer and requires a political struggle with Congress." He cites the example of the MX missile system.[38] Egalitarians also remind advocates of the Guardianship Principle that this country subscribes to democracy regardless of (and in fact well aware of) its inefficiency.[39]

Egalitarians also accuse advocates of the Guardianship Principle of exaggerating the onerous nature of a public role. Rarely is the public mobilized sufficiently to prevent governmental action, is the response. Moreover, since a public role is not a formal part of the defense policy-making process, its effectiveness depends upon the willingness of decisionmakers to translate public preferences into governmental action. Neither the president nor members of the Congress nor the federal bureaucracy are "obliged to abide by the dictates of public opinion."[40] While the democratization of Congress (during the 1970s) has expanded the public role, general public influence is still indirect. Even special-interest groups, which exert the most immediate, direct, and significant impact on policy-making in the United States, lack formal policy authority and must rely upon intermediaries.[41]

Only rarely does the public dictate governmental actions. More likely, "public opinion sets broad limits of constraint, identifying a range of policies within which decisionmakers can choose, and within which they must choose if they are not to face rejection in the voting booths."[42] Additionally, the government is fully capable of reining in public involvement. One need only compare the relative freedom with which the press covered the Vietnam War, and its role in mobilizing opposition to that military engagement, with more recent restrictions on the press reporting on Grenada, Panama, and Desert Storm.[43] Congress can expedite decision-making and foreshorten public involvement, with "fast-track" legislation, and the Pentagon can invoke the national security exemption to the Freedom of Information Act (FOIA) to avoid releasing information to the public. In short, even when the public is involved, it does not necessarily have influence.

Another retort by those who embrace the ideal of democratization is to cite numerous examples of so-called defense experts making bad decisions. The argument is that no amount of technical expertise can guard against wrong decisions. Military experts are capable of vacillation and oscillation and of manufacturing policy harmful to American interests. Dahl cites as examples the decision to place Multiple Independently-Retargetable Renetry Vehicles (MIRVs) on nuclear warheads, the Reagan administration's intervention in Lebanon, and Iran-Contra as elite mistakes made without the benefit of public involvement.[44] It is also important to note that foreshortening the democratic process does not guarantee better-quality military hardware. Both the F-117A fighter plane and B-2 strategic bomber were classified programs, designated "black box" systems because of the national security implications of their development. In such cases, decision-making is confined to a narrow group of elites within the Pentagon, eliminating the democratic virtues of the normal procurement process. The F-117A is considered to be an excellent plane, whereas the B-2 has encountered a number of mechanical problems.

Advocates of an active role for the public do not want to argue that every dimension of every military decision should be decided by the public. It is widely recognized that military hardware decisions raise a multitude of issues, some of which are susceptible to public dialogue and some of which are not. Dahl, for example, distinguishes between the decisions to use nuclear weapons in a specific military situation, which must be made by a small group of elites, and the decisions about the policies that guide launching decisions (such as counterforce, countervalue, and countercity), which can be made in a public forum without compromising national security.[45] A group of Catholic bishops has taken this argument one step further, contending that even the first set of decisions raises moral and ethical (as well as technical, strategic, and political) issues that should be subjected to public debate. These questions include whether it is even appropriate to use nuclear weapons in a certain context, whether owning nuclear weapons is acceptable as a deterrent, and "what targets are morally permissible."[46]

Egalitarians conclude their defense of a democratic military decision-making process by invoking the inherent appeal of democracy to most Americans. "The democratic process is generally believed to be justified on the ground that people are entitled to participate as political equals in making binding decisions, enforced by the state, on matters that have important consequences for the individual and collective interests. Nothing can have more important consequences for so many people, Americans and others alike, as decisions that may prevent or cause the use of nuclear weapons."[47]

A Public Role—Pest or Panacea? An Empirical Test

The primary concern distinguishing the guardianship from the egalitarian perspective is the quality of the role that the public plays in military hardware decisions. The theoretical conflict is over whether the public (meaning public opinion, interest groups, and the media) makes positive, neutral, or negative contributions to military hardware decisions. In short, the dilemma is whether "something as vital to the life and independence of the nation [can] safely be left to popular decision—[or whether] something so central to the lives of individuals [can] be alienated from popular control. . . ."[48]

This dilemma will be addressed systematically by examining data from the nineteen cases of weapons procurement in this study, and by comparing decision-making in the United States with that in the late Soviet Union. The first set of data is used to establish a relationship between the quality of military hardware and the amount of public involvement. The second approach is used to demonstrate that defects in the American military decision-making process are not necessarily a result of the democratic nature of the system but an unavoidable consequence of the difficulties of making defense policy in the nuclear age.

Case Study Data:
Is Too Much Public Participation Detrimental?

To answer the question of whether public involvement in military decisions is detrimental or not, it is first necessary to catalogue the nature and degree of public participation in military hardware decisions. For purposes of this study, the range of activities includes lobbying Congress, taking direct action, getting media attention, registering public opinion, and seeking litigation. Lobbying Congress includes any effort to influence legislation, such as providing information to members of Congress, testifying before congressional committees, bargaining informally, and negotiating with legislators, by either private or public interest groups. "Direct action" is defined to mean any activity that involves the public in an effort to influence decision-making in unconventional ways such as demonstrations, protests, and civil disobedience. Media attention can be either reactive or investigative. Reactive media attention refers to coverage that merely reports events surrounding a weapons system. Investigative attention is coverage that seeks to draw attention to and/or uncover evidence of malfeasance. Public opinion is defined as public beliefs as registered by a reputable polling firm. The implicit assumption is that any situation for which a reputable polling firm has registered public opinion is a significant one. Finally, litigation includes any action taken to use the courts to influence a weapons decision.

Table 6.1 summarizes the nature of public activities surrounding the nineteen cases of weapons procurement studied. What is immediately evident from this table is that in no case is there an absence of public involvement. Not unexpectedly, the most common form of activism is interest group lobbying, primarily by organizations representing the defense industry. In a few cases, such as the MX missile, B-1 bomber, Trident submarine, and M-16 rifle, there is also evidence of public lobbying. And while these cases are clearly the exception to the rule of private, rather than public, group involvement, the level and scope of commitment is astonishing. The case of the B-1 bomber is illustrative. A number of public action groups (the Friends Committee on National Legislation, Environmental Action, Common Cause, Peace Education, SANE, and the Federation of American Scientists) were engaged in an intensive lobbying effort in Congress and a grass-roots level campaign to defeat the strategic bomber. According to Norman Ornstein and Shirley Elder, the B-1 opposition was engaged in distributing pamphlets, mass mailings, and writing letters to Congress and to newspapers, and pressuring legislators to take a public stand.[49] According to Meyer, no movement prior to the anti-B-1 group "had ever made such a clear impact on the fate of a weapons system in development."[50]

Another significant finding is the changing role of the media. In the 1950s and 1960s, with the Skybolt and Thor-Jupiter decisions, the role of

TABLE 6.1

Nature and Scope of Public Involvement/Influence

Weapons	Involvement?	Nature of Involvement	Influence?	Nature of Influence
Skybolt	y (modest)	media (reactive) lobbying (defense industry)	yes	informational
Thor-Jupiter	y (modest)	media (reactive) lobbying (defense industry)	yes	informational/contract decision
TFX	y (modest)	media (investigative) lobbying (defense industry)	yes	informational
Polaris	y (modest)	media (reactive) lobbying (defense industry)	yes	informational/contract decision
MX	y (extensive)	full range	yes	full range
B-1	y (extensive)	full range	yes	full range
Cheyenne	y (modest)	media (minor) lobbying (defense industry)	yes	contract decision
C-5A	y (modest)	media (reactive) lobbying (defense industry/citizens)	yes	informational/contract decision
M16	y (moderate)	media (investigative) lobbying (defense industry/citizens)	yes	design modified
Trident	y (extensive)	full range	yes	informational/design modified
Bradley	y (moderate)	media (investigative)/litigation lobbying (defense industry)	yes	informational/program saved

(continued)

TABLE 6.1 (*continued*)

Weapons	Involvement?	Nature of Involvement	Influence?	Nature of Influence
A-10	y (modest)	media (minor) lobbying (defense industry)	yes	contract decision
F-16	y (modest)	media (minor) lobbying (defense industry)	yes	informational
M-1	y (moderate)	media (investigative) lobbying (defense industry/citizens)	yes	contract decision
Aegis	y (modest)	media (investigative) lobbying (defense industry)	yes	contract decision/informational/procurement practices
ALCM	y (modest)	lobbying (defense industry)	no	n/a
DIVAD	y (moderate)	media (investigative) lobbying (defense industry)	yes	information/program canceled/ contract decision
F/A-18	y (modest)	media/litigation lobbying (defense industry)	yes	informational
Skipper	y (modest)	media lobbying (defense industry)	no	n/a

the media was exclusively reactive. The media provided a vehicle for transmitting information about a particular military decision. For example, the national press became interested in Thor-Jupiter first in 1957 because of the intensity of the interservice rivalry, and again in 1958 when a successful launching of Thor marked a U.S. Intermediate Range Ballistic Missile (IRBM) capability. Media coverage of Skybolt was limited almost exclusively to the diplomatic faux pas committed by the United States when it canceled a weapon that Great Britain assumed would give it a nuclear capability. With the TFX/F-111 decision during the mid-1960s, however, the national and regional (especially commercial) media began to perform an important investigative function, delving into and helping expose questionable government practices. The *Washington Post* was particularly attentive first to the charges of favoritism in the award of the TFX contract to General Dynamics instead of Boeing (the former under investigation by Congress during the McClellan hearings), and then to evidence of cost overruns and schedule delays provided in congressional transcripts (House Appropriations Defense Subcommittee). What is particularly interesting about the media is that its sources of information are public ones, employees who blow the whistle (A. Ernest Fitzgerald and the C-5A jumbo transport plane, "Mr. Boisvert" and the Bradley)[51] or unclassified government documents (the M-1 tank, the GAO, and press releases from Representative Les Aspin, D-Wis.). Congress has used its statutory powers to encourage revelations of government wrongdoing by protecting whistle-blowers (Civil Service Reform Act of 1978), and increasing access to government documents (Freedom of Information Act of 1966). The FOIA in particular has strengthened the hand of the media, allowing it to serve more effectively as a conduit of government information.

A third important finding is that there is little public interest in most weapons systems. In the majority (63 percent) of the cases, public involvement was modest, confined almost exclusively to perfunctory media attention and to defense industry lobbying. Those systems that generated the most interest were the enormously expensive and strategically threatening ones. Not unexpectedly, the largest amount and widest scope of participation were found on the three strategic weapons that make up the nuclear triad—the Trident submarine and missile system, the B-1 bomber, and the MX missile system. But these constitute only 16 percent of the total.

While interesting, the information about the scope and nature of public involvement does not answer the question that frames the debate: whether the public performs a negative, positive, or neutral role in military hardware decisions. For an answer to this question, the data included in columns four and five of Table 6.1 are illuminating. Here again the effects of public involvement are clear. In only two cases is there an absence of evidence that public involvement influenced a decision to build and deploy a major weapons system. Notice, however, that the nature of influence is primarily of two types, defense contract decisions and the dissemination of information. This finding is not totally unexpected, since the predominant nature of involvement is defense industry lobbying and media attention.

In terms of the impact of media attention, anecdotal evidence suggests that the mere dissemination of information has had some substantive policy consequences. However, demonstrating a direct relationship between the media and the nature of the policy changes is difficult. It can be assumed that the availability of information does have some politicizing effects, serving to broaden the debate and perhaps the scope of participation. Press attention can also prod (although not compel) policymakers to take some action. In the case of Aegis, the press drew much attention to the test results of the 1983 operational sea-trials in which Aegis scored only a 33 percent success factor. In response, Congress held investigative hearings, leading to another operational testing period in April 1984. In the case of the division air defense gun (DIVAD), the media is credited with influencing (although not dictating) Secretary of Defense Weinberger's decision to cancel the air defense gun.

The case of the M-16 rifle presents further anecdotal evidence. When servicemen in Vietnam began writing letters home asking for ramrods and power lubricant to offset the malfunction rate of the rifle, their parents began writing and phoning their representatives in Congress demanding that action be taken. The national press picked up the story and began publishing articles recounting the tragedy of the rifle failures. In May 1967 the House Armed Services Committee (HASC) created a special subcommittee to review the M-16 program. Anticipating a public reaction, the Pentagon tried to block the release of information from Vietnam about the rifle. In a letter to Representative James J. Howard of New Jersey, a young Marine stationed in Vietnam recounted the efforts of the Pentagon to prevent the publication of photos taken by a newswoman documenting the failure rate of the standard issue Army rifle.[52] In the end, Congress released a report highly critical of the development of the rifle, without implicating specific individuals, and the rifle was redesigned and improved, but not necessarily in line with legislative recommendations. In short, the media do have an influence, albeit an indirect one.

While the effects of media information are generally indirect, the same cannot be said for the consequences of defense industry lobbying. A mass of, again, anecdotal evidence links questionable contract decisions to subsystem relations. One such decision is the awarding of a contract to Fairchild Industries (located in the congressional district of the defense appropriations subcommittee chair, Joseph Addabbo) in 1973 to build the A-10 transport plane. Another decision awarded a contract to RCA Missile and Surface Radar (later General Electric) and Ingalls Shipbuilding (a division of Litton Industries located in Senate Armed Services Committee (SASC) Chair John Stennis's senatorial district) to build Aegis. Yet another decision helped financially beleaguered Lockheed (located in SASC Chair Richard Russell's senatorial district), when that company was awarded a contract to build the C-5A. Additional examples include the contract decisions for the Cheyenne helicopter (Lockheed), the M-1 tank (Chrysler), the ammunition for the M-16 (Olin Mathieson Corporation), and the F-111/TFX (General Dynamics). Perhaps the most blatant example is the B-1 bomber for which Rockwell subcontracted with 5,200 companies in forty-eight states.

The obvious question is whether a contract decision can be said to have broader strategic or military consequences. In other words, while it is clear that the defense industry can influence contract decisions, do contract decisions in turn influence the viability of military hardware? For example, if Boeing had received the contract instead of General Dynamics, would the TFX (F-111) fighter-bomber have evolved into a successful dual-mission plane? Or can the Air Force and Navy be faulted with making demands on the contractors that ultimately doomed the biservice tactical aircraft? While it is impossible to answer this question, it is clear that the questionable practices associated with some defense industries in building military hardware have contributed to (although not singularly caused) problems with major weapons systems. For example, while fault can be found with Lockheed for cutting corners in the manufacturing of the C-5A jumbo transport plane and for general malfeasance, blame can also be placed on the fixed-price contract that the Pentagon dictated that subsequently failed to allow for flexibility in funding when technical problems were inevitably encountered during the production of the plane. While no defense contractor is blameless for the technical errors in a weapons system of their manufacture, neither is any defense contractor totally at fault for these errors. As should be evident from the discussion in this book, building weapons systems is a case of compounding errors. The defense industry is an important actor, but only one of a number of different actors in the defense procurement game.[53]

More important for making a qualitative judgment is the finding that
production contract awards constitute a limited set of decisions made at
an advanced stage of the procurement process. During the preliminary
stages of the procurement process (concept formulation, demonstration,
and validation), the evidence in chapter 3 establishes the military services
as clearly the dominant party. This means that if there is a subsystem operating, it does not make (although it may certainly contribute to) the
potentially risky military and strategic decisions regarding which weapons systems America should build. More likely, a military subsystem influences subsequent decisions (during the production and deployment
and operation stages) regarding specific design features, manufacturing
choices, and, of course, contract selections.

Determining whether public involvement has been positive or
negative in those few cases where influence registers as design modifications (Trident, M-16), cancellation or restoration of a weapon
(DIVAD, Bradley), or changes in procurement practices (B-1, Aegis) is
an evaluation that at its core is ideological. For example, it is evident
that public involvement contributed to (although was not solely responsible for) the delays in the development and deployment of the
MX missile system. The public was critical in altering the system (because of its role in opposing certain basing modes) and in some cases
redirecting the political debate. The MX was transformed by public
concerns over the environmental, cultural, and socioeconomic, as well
as the strategic, consequences of its deployment. Public concerns by
citizens and local/ state officials (in the South Platte region of Kansas,
Nebraska, and Colorado to multiple aim point [MAP] basing, and in
the Great Basin region of Utah and Nevada to multiple protective
shelter [MPS] basing) over the impact of MX deployment influenced
the Carter administration's decision to abandon MAP and the Reagan
administration's decision to abandon MX/MPS. The Reagan administration's recommendations for subsequent basing modes (interim
silo-basing, dense pack, rail garrison basing) were all gauged to avoid
the recurrence of the type of public opposition that emerged over
MPS, by eliminating the political and legal viability of key domestic
legislation as vehicles for defeating MX. These included the National
Environmental Policy Act (NEPA) and the Federal Land Policy
and Management Act (FLPMA) in addition to various clean air and
water statutes.[54]

Determining whether the unprecedented level of public involvement in the MX missile debate resulted in the delay of a strategically
necessary weapons system during a period of military weakness depends upon the viability of the "window of vulnerability" argument
promoted by the Reagan administration during the 1980s. While a significant portion of the attentive public and defense community embraced the argument that the successful deployment of the ten-warhead
missile was critical to insuring nuclear parity with the Soviets and sustaining America's retaliatory capability, others countered with the argument that a sufficient number of sea- and air-based ballistic missiles
would survive a Soviet first strike to compensate and that an inadequately protected MX was highly provocative. The fact that changes in
international relations invalidated the need for the MX missile system,
conceived as a highly accurate, relatively invulnerable Intercontinental
Ballistic Missile (ICBM) system, in part resolved the ideological dispute.

The relative merits of public involvement in the DIVAD and B-1
bomber debates are ambiguous as well for reasons that have to do with
the fundamental differences that divide people at both the elite and mass
levels. While press coverage and congressional concerns are credited
with influencing (although not dictating) Defense Secretary Casper
Weinberger's decision to cancel DIVAD, it is still not clear whether the air
defense gun could have been further modified and turned into a viable
weapons system. In other words, did public "interference" prematurely
terminate a weapon that had great potential? Similarly, does one condemn or applaud the fact that the anti-B-1 coalition was instrumental in
delaying the production of the B-1 bomber now that the end of the Cold
War has invalidated its original mission?

In sum, the evidence in Table 6.1 and elsewhere shows that military
hardware decisions do get a lot of public attention, but only a small seg-
ment of the public is involved. The primary actors are private interest
groups and the media. That these actors are important forces in making
military decisions is established by the data. The data also show that
lobbying and reporting influence weapons decisions, but at an advanced stage of the procurement process. The most important
questions, those regarding the make-up of America's military
force structure, are not decided by the public or a military subsystem. Subsequent decisions, those concerning the design features,
performance capabilities, and management strategy, do appear to be
made in a more public manner. And these secondary decisions can be
made in such a way that they do contribute to (although rarely cause)

the distortion of the original intent of a weapon, compromising its military viability in the end. Whether public involvement is decisive in weapons decisions, however, is difficult to prove. And, finally, whether public involvement is valuable or detrimental is mostly a subjective determination.

In one final effort to use Table 6.1 to assess the value of public involvement, the data in that table are combined with the information in Table 1.1, and a simple correlation run between public involvement (characterized as modest, moderate, or extensive) and performance problems. Table 6.2 contains the results. Again, what is immediately evident from the data is the relatively small number of weapons systems on which there is more than modest involvement (42 percent). In only five cases could the public's involvement be described as moderate (26 percent) and in only three cases as extensive (16 percent). The data in Table 6.2, while not significant, do point to a higher incidence of performance problems in cases of moderate involvement, and a smaller number of performance problems in cases of modest (and, ironically, extensive) involvement. In other words, there is some limited support for the argument that public participation disrupts the development of viable weapons.

Is there evidence that public involvement contributes to delays in the procurement process or to increases in the costs of building a weapon? Tables 6.3 and 6.4 contain the results from a simple correlation between cost overruns/schedule delays and public involvement. The data in Table 6.3 again are not significant, but do point to a higher incidence of cost overruns in cases of moderate and modest, but not extensive, involvement, challenging the assertion of a relationship. The data in Table 6.4, while significant, are similar to the data in Table 6.3. In all five situations in which the public was involved moderately in the development of a weapons system, the program experienced schedule delays. However, in cases of modest involvement, the chances of delay are slightly less likely, and in cases of extensive public involvement, the findings are counterfactual. In sum, drawing upon the data in the three tables, the presumed associations do show up in cases of moderate involvement, are counterfactual in cases of extensive involvement, and are reversed in (two) cases of modest involvement, challenging the claim that a public role in defense decision-making is a detrimental or disruptive one.

TABLE 6.2

Public Involvement by Performance Problems

	Public Involvement		
	Modest	Moderate	Extensive
Performance Problems			
Yes	36%	80%	33%
No	64%	20%	67%
(N)	(11)	(5)	(3)

TABLE 6.3

Public Involvement by Cost Overruns

	Public Involvement		
	Modest	Moderate	Extensive
Cost Overruns			
Yes	55%	80%	33%
No	45%	20%	67%
(N)	(11)	(5)	(3)

TABLE 6.4

Public Involvement by Schedule Delays

	Public Involvement		
	Modest	Moderate	Extensive
Schedule Delays			
Yes	45%	100%	33%
No	55%	0%	67%
(N)	(11)	(5)	(3)

Does Democracy Distort Decision Making?

Another approach to resolving the same issue of whether too much public participation is counterproductive is to consider whether it is democracy that is the culprit. If it is the democratic nature of the American decision-making process that distorts military hardware decisions, then nondemocratic systems ought not to encounter the same problems. An examination of military hardware decision making in the late Soviet Union thus may be illuminating.[55]

Authoritarianism should create the conditions for a more rational, expedient, and timely process of decision-making. In theory, authoritarian governments reduce those qualities that foster dissent by imposing uniformity, controlling conflict, and subordinating the parochial interests of government officials to the interests of the state. Yet despite minimizing the very conditions that are said to complicate weapons acquisition in the United States, the former Soviet Union did not necessarily have a better record of accomplishment. What is known about the Soviet inventory of military hardware reveals amazingly similar problems—weapons systems with redundant, inadequate, or uncertain performance capabilities. Examples of redundant weapons include the SS-18 and SS-19 missiles; weapons with inadequate or uncertain performance capabilities include the MIG-23 fighter plane and several Soviet missiles (including the SS-4 medium range ballistic missile, the SS-5 intermediate range system, and the SS-17 ICBM); and militarily unnecessary weapons include ground-launched cruise missiles.

How can this irony—two structurally polar political systems encountering similar technical and strategic problems in their weapons systems—be explained? Obviously, it is not the political process alone that distorts military decision-making, a finding that calls into question reform efforts in the United States to attenuate the military process. If the cause is not solely a political one, then what is it? One contributing factor (discussed often in this study), which is not confined to democracies but is evident in any country, relates to the conditions necessary for rationalism. Regardless of the nature of the distribution of power, neither the United States nor the Soviet Union had the resources needed to make optimal policy. Where the pluralist nature of budgetary politics restricted defense resources in the United States, the reclusive nature of the Soviet economy restricted defense resources in that nation. In addition, both countries were hampered by the difficulties associated with acquiring information that was not readily available about other nations.[56] As such, misperceptions and misjudgments were common in both systems. Moreover, no country is able to eliminate or adequately compensate for the uncertainties that abound in the international environment. Neither democratic nor authoritarian systems bring with them crystal balls that predict how other countries will behave in the future. Authoritarian systems do provide more methods for minimizing conflict and forcing the consensus that is a prerequisite to efficient governmental action. But these methods are artificial ones and have a dampening effect on creativity and innovativeness, thus ultimately burdening the decision-making process.

In addition to the common nature of the constraints that affected rational policy-making in the Soviet Union and United States, both countries experienced similar organizational and process problems, but for different reasons. For example, both the American and Soviet systems encountered delays in decision-making, which contributed to military inventory problems. In the United States, weapons systems were delayed by the process of bargaining and compromise characteristic of democracies. In the Soviet Union, programs were delayed by the process of relying upon technology borrowed from the United States.[57] Two notable examples are MIRVs and the Tu-4 bombers (replicas of the American B-29). In both cases progress in the Soviet Union was contingent upon access to and the application of technology developed in the United States. Moreover, neither the United States nor the Soviet Union provided a foolproof method for correcting errors of judgment before they became faults in a weapons system. In the American system, the fragmentation of power allowed for some faulty ideas to reach fruition as similarly faulty weapons. In the Soviet system, the concentration of power made it possible for the personal biases of one man or a group of individuals to dictate decision-making. In the absence of shared powers, there was no way to correct errors of judgment made at the top. Stalin's resistance to development of military rockets ultimately crushed that program during the 1930s.[58] A number of design experts who pursued weapons research in conflict with expressed state priorities were dismissed, imprisoned, or executed. In short, neither democratic nor authoritarian systems can guard against the development and deployment of faulty weapons systems. To improve military decision-making, therefore, requires a holistic approach that considers organizational and structural characteristics as only one set of possible reform targets.

Conclusion

In the end, despite concerted efforts (that began in the 1970s) by advocates of democratization to expand the opportunities for public involvement, the weapons acquisition process is still a relatively closed system. Most weapons decisions are not subject to public debate. Most citizens are not interested in weapons decisions, unless those decisions affect their immediate interests. The defense industry continues to play a major role in contract decisions. The media continue to perform an important (albeit mostly perfunctory) informational function.

For adherents of the Equality Principle, the status of public involvement is disconcerting, especially the predominant influence of the defense industry. More efforts should be made, according to egalitarians, to offset the disproportionate advantage that special-interest groups have in the defense area by encouraging, even legislating, more involvement from nondefense groups. As examples, egalitarians point to statutory efforts such as the FOIA and more widespread use of public hearings.

For advocates of the Guardianship Principle, the influence of the defense industry is also troublesome because it disrupts what could be a rational process guided by military (not economic) concerns. Thus, efforts should be made to regulate more effectively the defense industry—and in some cases the mass media of communications—while discouraging any more efforts at widespread public involvement. Suggested policy recommendations aimed at the defense industry include legislation mandating greater disclosure of information, placing more restrictions on the revolving door (through which military, business, and congressional personnel go in a continuous rotation of jobs), tightening loopholes in laws on lobbying, mandating greater competition among defense firms at every stage of the procurement process, including production (after both prototypes and early production models have been rigorously tested), and punishing defense-spending waste and fraud that, according to the GAO, account for between ten and thirty percent of the monies spent on defense contracts.[59] As noted in chapter 5, Congress already has addressed the problems raised by the Pentagon's penchant for sole-source contracts and concurrent management strategies, and approved the creation of the position of assistant secretary of defense for procurement and acquisitions to coordinate and standardize contracting practices.

Despite these concerns, there are few empirical disadvantages in having the public involved in defense decisions and a lot of traditional advantages. Therefore, it seems appropriate to conclude with support for the idea of a more (not less) democratic process for making military hardware decisions. Although the details of this process will be more fully explored in the concluding chapter, a few comments are in order.

Inspiration and the brief contours of such a process come from Robert Dahl, who advocates an "extended adversarial process," in which the government's task, during the initial stages of weapons decisions, is to clarify the debate and reduce important issues to two opposing policies, one supported by the administration and another supported by an opposition. The public, then, is confronted with a narrowly construed choice, but a choice nonetheless, that will thus define the boundaries of permissible government action and lend legitimacy to policy decisions. For Dahl, the electoral process is the best forum for people to register an opinion on policy choices. However, the same process can be extended to include opportunities for public response to governmental dilemmas even when there is not an election at stake. In order for this process to work effectively, the government must make as much information available as possible.[60] It is likely that interest groups and the media will continue to perform their important informational functions, digesting, analyzing, and transmitting information to the public. The wider availability of information and the greater politicization of the defense debate will empower nondefense groups, whose involvement will serve ideally to counteract the disproportionate power now exercised by the defense industry. What maintains the system as a public one is that the government (the president, military, Congress, and so on) must constantly seek the support of the people for their policies. This does not mean that the public ought to dictate defense policy. Rather, the public should be allowed to "set basic and stable principles to guide public policy."[61]

This, the pluralist ideal, has guided students of the American political system for years, meeting with practical and theoretical opposition throughout. The viability of such an adversarial process is contingent upon its ability to respond to and thus offset those forces that have distorted the system for making military hardware decisions. In the next chapter, evidence from the preceding chapters is pulled together, and some overall conclusions are drawn to answer the questions of why the United States builds the weapons it does; why some of these weapons encounter performance problems, cost overruns, and schedule delays; and what can be done to improve the weapons acquisition process.

Notes

1. These are the distinctions that Robert F. Dahl makes in *Controlling Nuclear Weapons: Democracy Versus Guardianship* (New York: Syracuse University Press, 1985).
2. Cecil V. Crabb Jr. and Pat M. Holt, *Invitation to Struggle: Congress, the President, and Foreign Policy* (Washington, D.C.: Congressional Quarterly Press, 1992), 290.
3. David S. Meyer, *A Winter of Discontent: The Nuclear Freeze and American Politics* (New York: Praeger, 1990), 85.

4. Charles W. Kegley Jr., and Eugene R. Wittkopf, *American Foreign Policy: Pattern and Process* (New York: St. Martin's Press, 1987), 287.

5. Ibid., 305.

6. Theodore C. Sorensen, *Decision-Making in the White House: The Olive Branch or the Arrow* (New York: Columbia University Press, 1963), 45–46.

7. Dahl, *Controlling Nuclear Weapons*, 14.

8. For a discussion of the military subsystem see Lauren Holland, "Who Makes Weapons Procurement Decisions? A Test of the Subsystem Model of Policy-Making," *Policy Studies Journal* 24 (1997): 607–624. Also see Gordon Adams, "The Iron Triangle: Inside the Defense Policy Process," in *The Domestic Sources of American Foreign Policy*, eds. Charles W. Kegley Jr. and Eugene R. Wittkopf (New York: St. Martin's Press, 1988); James Kurth, "The Military-Industrial Complex Revisited," in *American Defense Annual*, ed. Joseph Kruzel (Lexington, Mass.: D.C. Heath, 1989); Kenneth R. Mayer, *The Political Economy of Defense Contracting* (New Haven: Yale University Press, 1991); and Randall B. Ripley and Grace A. Franklin, *Bureaucracy and Policy Implementation* (Homewood, Ill.: Dorsey Press, 1982).

9. During the 1990s, many of the defense companies mentioned in this study have merged or been acquired by larger conglomerates. Examples include the mergers of Northrop, Grumman, and General Dynamics Space Division, Raytheon and E-Systems, and Martin Marietta and Lockheed; the acquisition of Teledyne by Litton, Unisys by Loral (then purchased by Lockheed-Martin Marietta), Magnavox by Hughes Aircraft, and Westinghouse's Electronic Systems by Northrop-Grumman; and the formation of Alliant (formerly Hercules).

10. According to the conventional wisdom, defense policy, because it is distributive, is ideally suited to a subsystem arrangement since there are more opportunities for tangible benefits to be generated and distributed. Of course, defense policy is distributive only if you discount the broader national security benefit derived from workable military hardware. See chapter 3.

11. Daniel McCool, "Subgovernments As Determinants of Political Viability," *Political Science Quarterly* 105 (1990): 278; and Norman C. Thomas, "Bureaucratic-Congressional Interaction and the Politics of Education," *Journal of Comparative Administration* 2 (1970): 56.

12. McCool, ibid., and Holland, "Who Makes Weapons Decisions?"

13. Jacques S. Gansler, *Affording Defense* (Cambridge, Mass.: MIT Press, 1989.) Also see Steven E. Miller, who argues that the democratic process of decision-making has prevented the passage of truly viable arms control agreements. "Politics over Promise: Domestic Impediments to Arms Control," *International Security* 8 (Spring 1984): 67–90.

14. Amos A. Jordan et al., *American National Security: Policy and Process* (Baltimore: The Johns Hopkins University Press, 1989), 43–36, 104–105, 115–116.

15. Walter Lippmann, *The Public Philosophy* (Boston: Little, Brown, 1955), 267. Also see Alexis de Tocqueville, *Democracy in America*, vol. 1 (N.Y.: Vintage, 1945), 240–245; George F. Kennan, *American Diplomacy, 1900–1950* (Chicago: University of Chicago Press, 1951); and Ronald J. Terchek, "Foreign and Domestic Policy Linkages: Constraints and Challenges for the Foreign Policy Process," in *Interaction: Foreign Policy and Public Policy*, eds. Don C. Piper and Ronald J. Terchek (Washington, D.C.: American Enterprise Institute, 1983), 51–96.

16. Barry M. Blechman, *The Politics of National Security: Congress and U.S. Defense Policy* (New York: Oxford University Press, 1990), 58.

17. Bruce Russett, *Controlling the Sword: The Democratic Governance of National Security* (Cambridge: Harvard University Press, 1990), 155.

18. John E. Mueller, "American Opinion and the Gulf War: Trends and Historical Comparisons." Paper presented at Political Consequences of War Workshop sponsored by the National Elections Studies, Center for Political Studies, and the Brookings Institution, 11 February 1992.

19. Kegley and Wittkopf, *American Foreign Policy*, 288–289.

20. Meyer, *Winter of Discontent*, 86–87. Meyer cites studies by Daniel Yankelovich and John Doble, "The Public Mood: Nuclear Weapons and the USSR," *Foreign Affairs* 63 (Fall 1984): 33–46.

21. Russett, *Controlling the Sword*, 152–153.

22. Thomas Graham, "The Pattern and Importance of Public Awareness and Knowledge in the Nuclear Age," *Journal of Conflict Resolution* 21 (1988): 322.

23. Ibid. The author distinguishes between functional awareness and "functional knowledge [which] exceeds understanding of abstract concepts or terms." While between 5 and 10 percent of the public "can be considered very knowledgeable about nuclear or arms control issues," 83 percent can be considered to be "functionally literate." For example, 83 percent of those polled know that the United States has not "given up the right to use nuclear weapons under any circumstances," 327.

24. Robert Y. Shapiro and Benjamin I. Page, "Foreign Policy and the Rational Public," *Journal of Conflict Resolution* 32 (June 1988): 211. Emphasis in the original.

25. House Committee on International Relations, *Congress and Foreign Policy*, 94th Cong., 2d sess., 1976, 19. Also see Meyer, who concludes that "access to the arenas of decision making for all groups is critical to establish and maintain political legitimacy in a democracy." *Winter of Discontent*, xiv.

26. From the Harvard Study Group, *Living with Nuclear Weapons* (Cambridge, Mass.: Harvard University Press, 1983), 200–202.

27. Ibid. Although the authors also concede that public action has influenced American policy in the other direction as well. In 1976, for example, President Ford chose not to attempt to finish negotiations for a SALT II agreement with the Soviet Union because he was afraid that an agreement would damage his chances of winning the Republican nomination.

28. Crabb and Holt, *Invitation to Struggle*, 273–274.

29. Kegley and Wittkopf, *American Foreign Policy*, 307.

30. Robert H. Trice, "The Policymaking Process: Actors and Their Impact," in *American Defense Policy*, eds. John F. Reichart and Steven R. Sturm (Baltimore: The Johns Hopkins University Press, 1982), 506.

31. Meyer, *Winter of Discontent*, 119–121.

32. Daniel J. Kaufman, "National Security: Organizing the Armed Forces," *Armed Forces and Society* 14 (Fall 1987): 85–112.

33. Dahl, *Controlling Nuclear Weapons*, 11–12. The pervasive attachment that the services have to their roles and missions makes them reluctant to embrace weapons that jeopardize existing doctrines or established roles and missions. Consider, for example, the Air Force's resistance to Remotely Piloted Vehicles (RPVs) and cruise missiles, and all three services' resistance to mines and

minefields. Richard Garwin explains that the Navy has ignored mine warfare because "no one can command a mine. You don't get promoted for procuring them, there's no glamour to them." According to Stubbing, the Army and Air Force assign a low priority to mines because they threaten the value of armor on the battlefield, and support a low priority mission for the Air Force (to provide close air support for ground forces), respectively. Richard Stubbing, *The Defense Game* (New York: Harper and Row, 1986), 151.

34. Dahl, *Controlling Nuclear Weapons*, 11–12.

35. The Project on Military Procurement states as its goals "to reform the Pentagon procurement system by exposing the ongoing waste, fraud, and abuse to the press, Congress, and the public; to provide an effective and reliable defense while saving the taxpayer as much money as possible; and to assist whistleblowers in the military establishment during their struggles to expose those abuses." The Defense Budget Project "provides a regular analysis of the president's and Congress's annual defense budget requests." The organization networks with other groups to promote the dissemination of defense spending information.

36. See Bruce M. Russett, "Ethical Dilemmas of Nuclear Deterrence," *International Security* 8 (Spring 1984): 36–54; Meyer, *Winter of Discontent*; L. Bruce van Voorst, "The Critical Masses," *Foreign Policy* 48 (Fall 1982): 82–86; and Douglas C. Waller, *Congress and the Nuclear Freeze: An Inside Look at the Politics of a Mass Movement* (Amherst: University of Massachusetts Press, 1987).

37. Comment made by Sanford Gottlieb in a review of Waller, *Congress and the Nuclear Freeze*, in *Arms Control Today* (March 1988): 29.

38. Dahl, *Controlling Nuclear Weapons*, 22.

39. See, for example, Samuel P. Huntington, "American Ideals versus American Institutions," *Political Science Quarterly* 97 (Spring 1982): 16, 24. Also see Huntington in Michael J. Crozier, Samuel P. Huntington, and Joji Watanuki, *The Crisis of Democracy: Report on the Governability of Democracies to the Trilateral Commission* (New York: New York University Press, 1975), 59–118.

40. Sorensen, *Decision-Making in the White House*, 45-46. Sorensen actually made this comment with reference to the president. The full text asserts that "No president is obliged to abide by the dictates of public opinion . . . He has a responsibility to lead public opinion as well as respect it—to shape it, to inform it, to woo it, and win it. It can be his sword as well as his compass."

41. See Meyer, *Winter of Discontent*, 243, 269; Dixon, *National Security Policy Formulation*, 132; Terchek, "Foreign and Domestic Policy Linkages," 56; James M. Lindsay, *Congress and Nuclear Weapons* (Baltimore: The Johns Hopkins University Press, 1991); and Sean M. Lynn-Jones, "Democratizing U.S. Defense Policy," paper delivered at the 1990 Annual Meeting of the American Political Science Association, San Francisco, California, 1990. According to Ripley and Franklin, to compensate, interest groups seek to formalize their influence by operating as part of a regular, entrenched cozy triangle or subsystem arrangement. Randall B. Ripley and Grace A. Franklin, *Congress, the Bureaucracy, and Public Policy*, 4th ed. (Homewood, Ill.: Dorsey Press, 1987), 10.

42. Russett, *Controlling the Sword*, 110. Also see Dixon, *National Security Policy Formulation*, 129. President Eisenhower warned in his farewell address to the nation that "only an alert and knowledgeable citizenry can compel the proper meshing of the huge industrial and military machinery of defense with our peaceful methods and goals, so that security and liberty may prosper together."

43. Kegley and Wittkopf, *American Foreign Policy*, 322. "In the extreme, the government effectively censors the news, as the Reagan administration did

when it denied reporters permission to observe the Grenada assault force in 1983, an intervention later revealed to be fraught with mistakes."

44. Dahl, *Controlling Nuclear Weapons*, 20, 45.

45. Ibid., 34.

46. Bruce M. Russett, "Ethical Dilemmas of Nuclear Deterrence," 8 *International Security* (Spring 1984): 36–40. According to Russett, the National Conference of Catholic Bishops of the U.S. "Pastoral Letter on War and Peace" issued in May 1983 challenges "contemporary American military policy, significantly contributes to a de-legitimization of nuclear weapons as an instrument of war-fighting or even in some ways of deterrence, and demands far-reaching changes in thought and action." The letter underscores the fact that issues of nuclear weaponry are not "esoteric technical matters" but "moral issues" that "ordinary citizens" have a right and an obligation to be concerned about, and to have their views aired. Central to their argument are three principles. The first is that intentional killing of innocent people, even in order to accelerate the termination of a war (such as bombing Dresden, or Nagasaki and Hiroshima), is morally unacceptable. This invalidates counterpopulation strategies as well. The second principle dictates that "the harm done by an act, even unintentionally, may not be disproportionate to the good intended to be achieved or the evil to be avoided." The "proportionality" principle also challenges the use of counterpopulation warfare. A third principle suggests that the means used to defend against aggression "must themselves be at least morally neutral," and "offer a reasonable chance of success."

47. Dahl, *Controlling Nuclear Weapons*, 20.

48. Russett, *Controlling the Sword*, 146.

49. See Norman J. Ornstein and Shirley Elder, *The B-1 Bomber: Organizing at the Grass Roots* (Washington, D.C.: National Defense University Press, 1983).

50. Meyer, *Winter of Discontent*, 144.

51. Importantly, the story about Boisvert and FMC appeared on the obituary page of the *New York Times*, 21 September 1986, 44.

52. See Edward Clinton Ezell, *The Great Rifle Controversy* (Harrisburg, Pa.: Stackpole Books, 1981), 208.

53. For a detailed discussion of the defense contracting issue see Kenneth R. Mayer, *The Political Economy of Defense Contracting* (New Haven: Yale University Press, 1991).

54. See Lauren Holland, "The Use of NEPA in Defense Policy Politics: Public and State Involvement in the MX Missile Project," *Social Science Journal* 21 (July 1984): 53–71. Also see Lauren H. Holland and Robert A. Hoover, *The MX Decision: A New Direction in U.S. Weapons Procurement Policy?* (Boulder, Colo.: Westview Press, 1985), chapter 8.

55. See, for example, Robert P. Berman and John C. Baker, *Soviet Strategic Forces: Requirements and Responses* (Washington, D.C.: The Brookings Institution, 1982); Andrew Cockburn, *The Threat: Inside the Soviet Military Machine* (New York: Random House, 1983); David Holloway, *The Soviet Union and the Arms Race* (New Haven: Yale University Press, 1983); Matthew Evangelista, *Innovation and the Arms Race: How the United States and the Soviet Union Develop New Military Technologies* (Ithaca: Cornell University Press, 1988); and Lauren Holland, "Democracy and Decision-Making: Generating Political Solutions to Technical Problems," paper presented at Moscow University, Moscow, March 1992.

56. See Herbert Simon, *Administrative Behavior: A Study of Decision-Making Processes in Administrative Organization* (New York: The Free Press, 1976); and

Charles E. Lindblom, "The Science of Muddling Through," *Public Administration Review* 19 (Spring 1959): 79–88.

57. In the Soviet Union, weapons decisions either responded to external threats as perceived by the Communist party leadership, or to technological advances by the Soviet Union's "enemies," or both. Evangelista, *Innovation and the Arms Race*. Examples include Soviet decisions concerning the atomic bomb in 1945, thermonuclear weapons during the 1940s and 1950s, strategic forces during the 1960s, ABM prior to the SALT I agreements, and the development of the SS-20 intermediate range missile and MiG-15 fighter plane.

58. Because of the highly centralized and controlled nature of the Soviet process, it was possible for the personal biases of one man or a group of individuals to dictate decision-making. In the absence of shared powers, there was no way to correct errors of judgment made at the top. Stalin's resistance to development of military rockets during the 1930s delayed that program. Soviet leaders' interest in reaching military parity with the United States as a way to achieve political power fueled weapons development after Stalin's death. Personal biases were evident not only in the preferred weapons priorities of Party leaders, but in favoritism extended toward certain groups in the system. One author claims that favoritism sustained a military-industrial complex in the Soviet Union. See Cockburn, *The Threat*. This is unlikely. Favoritism, while extant, never came to be institutionalized in the Soviet Union. The armed forces and defense industry enjoyed privileged positions "as a result of the high priority the Soviet leaders [gave] to building up military power." However, they were never successful in building an independent power base or establishing a "clearly defined lobby." Holloway, *The Soviet Union and the Arms Race*, 158. Both groups continued to be subordinated to government directive. The exception was the period between 1957 and 1963 when the defense industry successfully resisted Khruschev's economic plans. Holloway, *The Soviet Union and the Arms Race*, 159.

   Control, even in the Soviet Union, was imperfect, though. Although the Communist Party dictated weapons decisions, it did so through the uncertain vehicle of establishing military doctrine. Lacking scientific and technical expertise, and needing to reach a consensus, Party leaders could do no more than provide broad guidelines. This meant that the initial design requirements for weapons were set and preliminary development was dominated by the weapons design bureaus. Granted, more control was secured through the regular supervision that Party leaders provided, and the punitive nature of their power. The Party dominated the formulation of military doctrine and deployment and resource allocation decisions. Ultimately the Soviet bureaucratic infrastructure was responsible for approving the design priorities of the bureaus. See Berman and Baker, *Soviet Strategic Forces*, 3.

59. Sam Marullo, *Ending the Cold War at Home: From Militarism to a More Peaceful World Order* (New York: Lexington Books, 1993), 144, 149, 164-175.

60. Otis Pike even suggests that the annual defense guidance be subjected to public debate. *Deseret News*, Salt Lake City, Utah, 20 February 1992, 14A.

61. Russett, *Controlling the Sword*, 157–158.

HIGHLIGHT

B-1
The Bomber That Couldn't Be One

On 1 October 1986, the B-1 officially became part of America's nuclear arsenal after thirty years of controversy, having survived a veritable obstacle course of public, legislative, and presidential opposition. In the end, the environmental and peace groups (and their allies in the White House and Congress) that mobilized to defeat the new strategic bomber program were no match for the financial superiority of, the sophisticated tactics employed by, and the persistence exhibited by a coalition of labor, manufacturing, and military interests.

Economic, ideological, environmental, and strategic concerns provided the impetus for the extensive lobbying campaign organized by public interest groups such as Environmental Action, Common Cause, Peace Education, The National Taxpayers Union, SANE, The Women's International League for Peace and Freedom, and Federation of American Scientists. While the incentives varied, the goal was the same—defeat of the B-1 bomber program. With limited resources, this coalition engaged in an educational campaign directed at Congress and the general public that portrayed the B-1 as "economically unsound, environmentally harmful, and militarily irrelevant."[1] A small coterie of devotees distributed pamphlets, conducted mass mailings, wrote letters to members of Congress and the editors of major national newspapers, and lobbied tirelessly. Poised in opposition were the Air Force and its allies in the defense industry, labor, the science community, and Congress (particularly senior members serving on the House and Senate Armed Services Committees and Defense Appropriations Subcommittees). With enormous financial backing and an inside track, these groups blanketed the country with information on economic benefits (defense contracts to 5,200 companies in 48 states), threatened recalcitrant legislators with retaliation, and exaggerated the military threat to which the B-1 would respond (an argument bolstered by international events such as the death of SALT II, the Iranian hostage crisis, and the Afghanistan invasion, which turned public opinion in a prodefense direction). While the bomber program survived in the end, the countervailing forces impeding its expeditious production

(continued)

B-1 *(continued)*

and deployment served to broaden the arena and agenda of public debate on the B-1. Today, B-1B bombers are used as carriers for conventional bombs and cruise missiles, their original mission having been invalidated with the end of the Cold War.

[1]Norman J. Ornstein and Shirley Elder, "The B-1 Bomber: Organizing at the Grass Roots," in *Studies in Defense,* ed. Eston T. While (Washington, D.C.: National Defense University Press, 1983).

Primary Sources: Nick Kotz, *Wild Blue Yonder* (New York: Pantheon, 1988); Norman J. Ornstein and Shirley Elder, "The B-1 Bomber: Organizing at the Grass Roots," in *Studies in Defense,* ed. Eston T. White (Washington, D.C.: National Defense University Press, 1983).

HIGHLIGHT

MX
A Missile in Search of A Home

When President Ronald Reagan announced in October of 1981 that his administration was abandoning the Carter proposal to deploy MX missiles in a multiple protective shelter basing scheme (MPS) in Nevada and Utah, the influence of public involvement was readily admitted. "While it is not the determining factor," Reagan asserted, "it should be noted that MPS basing has strong environmental opponents who would use every available tactic, and there are many, to delay MX deployment."[1] What the administration was alluding to was the creative use that residents in the Great Basin region were making of federal and state environmental and land-use legislation to delay through litigation the construction of the mammoth military project. What Reagan's comments failed to mention, however, was the broad-based nature of the coalition that defeated MPS basing. Cattle and sheep ranchers, faithful followers of the Mormon Church, Native Americans, and recreationists joined with environmentalists in an odd coalition that presented an especially powerful public force. The demonstrations and lobbying that followed made it difficult for the congressional delegations from Utah and Nevada to ignore the social, environmental, and cultural threats raised by MPS deployment.

The dramatic and unprecedented impact that this public force had on the MX missile system was due only in part to the dilatory tactics made available by NEPA, FLPMA, the FOIA, and various other environmental and land-use legislation at the federal and state levels. Contributing greatly to the coalition's success was the fact that the opposition did not confine itself to concerns about the enormous costs of and devastation resulting from the construction of the project. As citizens began examining the Air Force arguments for MX/MPS in public hearings and the Environmental Impact Statement (EIS) documents, they began questioning the very logic of a highly accurate, ten-warhead missile. Too, the use of MX as a bargaining chip in the SALT II agreements meant that the system was of interest to advocates of arms control. The sheer enormity and costliness of the system made it attractive as a public works proj-

(continued)

MX (*continued*)

ect and national budgetary issue. By expanding debate beyond the self-interest of those directly affected by MPS deployment, a momentum built across the country with significant results for public opinion. According to Harris polls, by 1985, 59 percent of the public supported congressional efforts to cut back and even delay funds for the MX missile program despite the contrary position of President Reagan.[2]

Although the public cannot be credited with defeating the MX (which was canceled by President Bill Clinton after its mission was invalidated by the warming of relations between the United States and Russia), it contributed immeasurably by broadening the scope of debate and forcing issues of public concern onto the legislative agenda. As a participant in the movement, I found the politicizing effect that involvement in the anti-MX movement had for citizens in Nevada and Utah most rewarding, a feeling only recently marred by the failure of the same groups to negotiate their differences over public lands.

[1]"President's Remarks on Weapons Plan and Background Statement." *New York Times*, 3 October 1981.
[2]Robert Y. Shapiro and Benjamin I. Page, "Foreign Policy and Public Opinion," in *The New Politics of American Foreign Policy*, ed. David A. Deese (New York: St. Martin's Press, 1994), 223.

Primary Sources: Lauren Holland and Robert Hoover, *The MX Missile System: A New Direction in Weapons Procurement Policy?* (Boulder, Colo.: Westview Press, 1985); Lauren Holland, "The Use of NEPA in Defense Policy Politics: Public and State Involvement in the MX Missile Project," *The Social Science Journal* 21 (July 1984): 53–71; and Matthew Glass, *Citizens Against MX: Public Languages in the Nuclear Age* (Urbana, Ill.: University of Illinois Press, 1993).

HIGHLIGHT

M-16 Rifle
The Army's Attack on Democracy

The case of the M-16 rifle demonstrates boldly the indisputable benefits of a democratic system in which open and free discussion is valued, citizens are encouraged to share their concerns with their elected representatives, and elected representatives actually respond to these concerns. It also demonstrates the powerful forces working to impede democracy, in this case, the unconscionable efforts by the U.S. Army, blinded by concerns over their organizational survival and attachment to traditional values.

Until the Vietnam War (from the period following the Civil War), every rifle that the Army developed was based on the premise that combat reality meant soldiers shooting at targets several hundred yards distant. Thus, rifles were designed for accuracy and precision (marksmanship), were heavy (due in part to the large caliber bullet), and were not intended to be fired fully automatic (a tactical innovation that did not fit in with the marksmanship tradition, even when the changing face of twentieth-century warfare seemed to demand it).

Under the impetus of the traumatic circumstances of Vietnam, the Army Infantry Board (AIB), representing the needs of the infantry, concluded that a lightweight weapon capable of controlled automatic fire would be more effective. The Army Ordinance Department, a traditional cadre of powerful army officers oriented toward tradition, resisted the innovation. Surreptitiously, AIB developed an M-16 prototype and secured the support of Air Force General Curtis LeMay and eventually Secretary of Defense Robert McNamara, under whom the Army was compelled to adopt the M-16. The Army took the prototype and made over 130 technical changes so that the rifle would conform to traditional standards. The M-16 then was sent to Vietnam (in lieu of the M-14) where it was discovered that the changes made by the Army's Technical Coordinating Committee (TCC) caused the once-reliable rifle to fail at a high rate in combat. Servicemen began writing letters home asking for ramrods and powder lubricant to offset the rate of malfunc-

(continued)

M-16 Rifle *(continued)*

tions. Upon receiving such letters, the families began writing and phoning their representatives in Congress demanding that action be taken. The national press picked up the story, and several articles were published recounting the tragedy of the rifle failures. In May 1967, the House Armed Services Committee authorized a special subcommittee on the M-16 Rifle Program to hold hearings and conduct an extensive study of the weapon. Under pressure, the Army repaired the rifle. The M-16 continues to serve as the Army's standard service rifle even today.

Primary Sources: Thomas L. McNaugher, *The M16 Controversies: Military Organizations and Weapons Acquisition* (New York: Praeger, 1984); Edward Clinton Ezell, *The Great Rifle Controversy* (Harrisburg, Pa.: Stackpole Books, 1981).

CHAPTER 7
Conclusion

In chapter 1, a promise was made that the findings of this study would be used in the concluding chapter to formulate a preliminary theory of the weapons acquisition process. To avoid skewing the findings toward one of the several alternative theories and conceptual frameworks popular in the military policy literature, four broadly construed explanations were applied and used as heuristics throughout this study. As expected, each perspective was helpful in offering clues on where to look for evidence of the forces and actors that combine to drive the weapons process in the United States. Each explanation also was useful in suggesting reasons why so many weapons are deployed that exceed their cost and schedule estimates and fall short of their performance requirements. Alone, none of the perspectives is able to adequately describe and explain the weapons acquisition system. The process for making military hardware decisions is simply too complex and multifaceted to be amenable to description and explanation by one theory or conceptual framework. Together, however, the four explanations highlight some of the most important elements that drive the weapons procurement process and thus contribute to a more complete picture. In short, each of the perspectives has some validity for every weapons system, either simultaneously or at different points in the procurement life of a program.

Every weapons system in this study can trace its origin to a strategic or military need, even if this was not the primary impetus for the program, underscoring the importance of the rational perspective. The utility of the rational perspective can also be seen in the important role that the president plays in weapons procurement, within the organizational and political constraints anticipated by the pragmatic and political explanations. The pragmatic perspective also correctly anticipates the critical role that uncertainty plays in the procurement process, most dramatically in the way the absence of certitude fuels the disagreements that divide actors at all stages of the process, from defense analysts, military experts, and technicians, to actors in the legislative and executive branches of government. The political perspective is complementary, directing our attention to the bureaucratic, economic, and political incentives that motivate each set of actors, and the operable countervailing forces, one of which is the driving force of technology. Moreover, the technology argument contributes to our understanding of why so many weapons systems in the military inventory are gold-plated ones.

Despite the intricate and entangled nature of military procurement, there are some general patterns that can be illuminated, providing the basis for some generalizable propositions or hypotheses. Theory building requires at a minimum that a set of propositions be established that are plausible and empirically testable by others. Since each chapter contains a discussion of the findings and implications for reform specific to its scope, the propositions listed below (and the findings and reform recommendations that follow) are by intent broadly construed.

General Propositions

Proposition 1. *Every weapon can trace its origin to strategic or military need, even if this was not the original impetus.* Although weapons do not always originate for military or strategic reasons alone (often also being the product of technical or organizational forces), ultimately every weapon can be justified as performing an important mission or meeting a military need, even if that need is projected to be vaguely defined and distant. The ease with which a justification can be fashioned for almost any weapon is a product of the difficulty of reaching a consensus on what constitutes a military threat or mission need and the uncertainties that abound in the security realm. Too often, the absence of certainty and consensus appears to be exploited by those who use strategic preferences and intelligence projections to support weapons for technical, political, economic, or bureaucratic reasons. More likely, military and nonmilitary forces are indistinguishable to actors who must respond to multiple pressures that are not exclusively rational ones.

Proposition 2. *While individual presidents, in most cases, do not make weapons decisions, presidential guidance of military hardware decisions is considerable, and provides the rationale requisite to building a meaningful force structure.* American presidents command enormous formal and informal powers with which to dictate and direct military matters, including decisions about America's force structure. For both practical and personal reasons, however, most presidents defer to their advisors and the Pentagon on matters of military procurement, until the nature of America's force structure becomes a matter of political concern. Presidents Nixon and Carter, for example, were forced by circumstances surrounding their desire to win congressional and military support for arms control agreements (SALT I and SALT II, respectively) to support weapons systems (Trident and the MX) that they opposed in principle. President Reagan's relative indifference to the details of his force modernization program was challenged with public revelations detailing the performance inadequacies of division air defense gun (DIVAD), which was canceled by Defense Secretary Weinberger. President Kennedy was brought into the fray surrounding the cancellation by Defense Secretary McNamara of the Skybolt missile program only when the action threatened to compromise relations with Great Britain.

Because a president's involvement in military matters is intermittent, actual influence over military procurement matters is not solely a function of his willingness to invoke his national security prerogative, something Carter discovered when he tried (unsuccessfully) to cancel production funds for the B-1 bomber. Rather, to succeed means to overcome or offset the bureaucratic advantages that the Pentagon has, which entails a combination of an effective management style and strategy, competent advisors, and luck. Carter, despite highly competent advisors, was unable to fashion a coherent policy agenda, making him even more vulnerable to the repercussions from the Soviet invasion of Afghanistan and Iranian hostage debacle. Reagan was able to compensate for a detached management style with aggressive advisors who exploited the tensions with the Soviets to promote a world view they shared with their president, assisted in their efforts by a Soviet economy on the brink of collapse and favorable American public opinion. Regardless of the extent to which a president is active and successful in influencing military hardware decisions, a legacy is guaranteed by the role he plays in establishing foreign and defense policy goals and strategies that provide the context for military decisions.

Proposition 3. *The military services are the defense planners most in control of weapons procurement, at least during the preliminary stages of the acquisition process.* In most cases, weapons programs originate with a military service (or a subunit within a service) that continues to dominate the process up to full-scale development, after which point a military program is almost impervious to termination (for reasons that relate to the institutional, personal, and fiscal stakes that have accumulated). Ironically, the scope of participation tends to broaden at just this point when a weapon is being considered for development. For this reason, even systems that become the object of congressional, executive, and public concern are rarely felled even by aggressive opposition after a development decision is made.

The military services, while preeminent, are not autonomous, however, even during the preliminary stages of the Milestone process. Given the important stakes involved in building a weapon, the services confront a narrow range of competition at the outset from within and outside the Pentagon that builds to become continuously broader throughout development. The concessions that the services make to other actors in order to build a coalition of support for their preferred system impact the weapon in ways that rarely compromise its survival. More often, the concessions on a particular weapons system result in modifications in the design features and performance requirements, the time designated for production, the funds available for support, and/or the defense companies that receive the contracts to build it.

Proposition 4. *While technology is not the sole determinant (first cause) in the conception of major weapons systems, it is a critical factor in a weapon's subsequent development.* Technology is rarely the only determinant, but it plays a profound role during the procurement process, influencing the design, development, testing, and ultimate workability of a weapons system. During the development stage in particular, technology is an important source of component and model improvements. Problems are most likely to arise in weapons procurement when the technology being promoted is uncertain and risky, or when technology becomes a tool to promote other political, organizational, or personal interests. For the military services, technically sophisticated weaponry can compensate for limits on the force structure and thus provide a way to protect a service's stature. Technical modifications can also be used to appease opponents whose support is critical to the survival of a weapon, as occurred in the bizarre case of the M-2 Bradley personnel carrier. Advanced technology also holds out the promise of unimagined military achievements, as did Star Wars for President Reagan, who saw a way to neutralize America's vulnerability to nuclear attack. The uncertainties associated with developing and then applying advanced technology to military hardware carry with them the risks that weapons will not perform as expected, will cost too much, and will take too long to develop. The policy implications of this finding are significant, particularly as they are contrary to the prerogatives of the impending military technology revolution. Where the inherent risks of advanced technology recommend investments in moderate developments, the military technology revolution depends in part on new and innovative weapons systems for its success.

Proposition 5. *Members of Congress have the will and extensive means by which to influence weapons decisions.* Legislators have broad and substantial national security powers and are enormously involved in procurement matters, albeit unevenly. When engaged, Congress devotes its attention to the funding, management, and design of major weapons systems, and, less often to the strategic debates over the rationale for and performance of military hardware, with varying degrees of influence. Congress is most successful in stretching out the production of major weapons systems, altering the number of units to be procured, modifying the performance parameters, altering the management strategy, and influencing the system's mission capabilities. For institutional and political reasons, Congress rarely is able to build the broad-based support (winning coalition) requisite to forcing a decision onto the Pentagon (or even the president, for that matter). The result is that congressional action seldom results in the origination, cancellation, or resurrection of a weapons system, with some important (albeit infrequent) exceptions such as Midgetman (which originated with the congressionally authorized Scowcroft Commission) and the Cheyenne helicopter (which Congress terminated). In short, Congress is a decidedly junior player in military hardware decisions.

While Congress seldom poses a serious obstacle to the military and executive branch on weapons procurement matters, when it does act, its contributions to the military debate have been useful and helpful ones. Examples include DIVAD, Thor-Jupiter, the M-1 tank, the MX missile system, and the M-16 rifle. Despite the cloud of reelection concerns that hangs over legislators, most congressional votes are ideologically and not parochially motivated. It is a rare (if unprecedented) situation when legislative action has seriously compromised the security of the United States, an important finding since national security matters are increasingly becoming a more prominent item on the legislative agenda. The fundamental disagreements that Congress and the president have over America's future role in global relations are likely to further politicize military matters.

Proposition 6. *The general public lacks the interest and means to play an important role in weapons decisions.* Despite successful efforts since the 1970s by advocates of democratization to increase the opportunities for public involvement, the process for making military hardware decisions remains a relatively closed one. With some important exceptions—the media, the defense industry, and labor unions—the scope of public involvement is a narrow one. The general public exhibits a knowledge of but little interest in major weapons systems, until their immediate interests are impacted by deployment. Nonetheless, when engaged, the public (like Congress) does contribute productively to the military debate. Of equal importance, there are few empirical disadvantages in having the public involved in defense decisions and a lot of advantages that derive from the inherent (normative) appeal of democracy and pluralism.

Proposition 7. *The decision to develop and deploy a major weapons system is ultimately a political one.* Although weapons can originate for technical, strategic, and/or organizational reasons (i.e., reasons other than political ones), in the end they cannot survive without political support. Even when the president, Congress, and the public are not actively participating in a weapons decision, ultimately their consent (even if tacit) is mandatory. Regardless of the clarity of his directives, the president is accountable for weapons decisions that are made by his advisors and political appointees, supported by his budget, and validated as the tools he uses or threatens to use to secure the integrity of the United States. Regardless of the scope and depth of their involvement, Congress is accountable for weapons decisions whose survival depends upon its funding approval. Regardless of the intensity of their interest and level of their activity, the public is accountable for any unclassified weapons decision that it does not consciously oppose (even if that opposition is inadequate for terminating the program). In short, this final proposition is a recognition that governmental decisions that commit public resources and engage policymakers either elected by the public or accountable to it are subject to the dictates of the democratic prerogative in the United States. Regardless of the policy area, decision-making in the United States is political.

Implications

What are the important implications or lessons that are associated with these findings, particularly as they pertain to the future of weapons procurement? Foremost, the end of the Cold War will not necessarily result in dramatic changes in the weapons procurement process. Since the forces that drive the procurement process are not exclusively strategic or military, the end of the Cold War, with the accompanying changes in the strategic environment, will not necessarily alter the way in which military hardware decisions are made or the outputs of this process. This explains the current fascination with expanding the B-2 bomber and Seawolf submarine programs (originally conceived for use against the Soviet Union). If changes in military procurement are to be made, they will require a comprehensive effort that recognizes (and can penetrate) the interlocking nature of the multiple forces that drive procurement. This recognition is the essence of the argument for a military technology revolution that envisions a successful revolution in America's military force structure only if complementary changes are accomplished in three areas—technology, doctrine, and organizational structure.

Given this complexity, change in one set of forces (such as the way technology is used) will be fruitless without accompanying changes in the other forces (such as the way the Pentagon and Congress make decisions). Recognizing this, successful reform will be a long and protracted process that will lag behind global changes, making the United States ever vulnerable to the volatile international scene in which new threats arise and old threats reemerge daily. Accordingly, isolated attempts now being made to redefine and then restructure the nature of America's force structure in the aftermath of the Cold War will be frustrated by the challenges attendant to interpreting the context of the global threats that the new international dynamic presents. Until defense analysts and foreign policy experts grasp the implications of a multipolar world characterized by regional conflict, a clear mandate for procurement change will be elusive. Before America's military force structure changes, therefore, the nature of the political debate must be defined and resolved. How Americans resolve these questions will partially influence the nature of the weapons procurement process during this decade and into the next century.

Less profound policy changes are likely with the end of the Cold War, however. For example, the absence of an imminent Soviet threat means that weapons decisions can be made in a less hectic manner; no longer is there a need to rush weapons through development and into production. The absence of the Communist imperative will challenge the rationale for applying an expedited management strategy, that is, the concurrent approach currently favored by the military services. The application of a sequential planning scheme would insure a more deliberate procurement process, offering greater assurance that weapons would not be approved without adequate consideration of the feasibility of their performance and technology requirements and would not move into production without proper testing. A more balanced and thoughtful development process could neutralize many of the measures currently used to expedite weapons development that are responsible for the pervasive performance flaws and cost and schedule excesses. Placing weapons programs in the black box category to shelter them from public view is one possible example.

The disintegration of the Soviet Union and Warsaw Pact and improvements in Russian-American relations, with the accompanying arms agreements (such as START I, INF, etc.), mean that global nuclear war is less likely, although not unthinkable, signaling a requisite shift in military priorities toward a more flexible and less strategic force structure. Regardless of how one defines them, future threats are likely to require less technically complex (although not necessarily less technically advanced) weapons. Computer- and cyber-technology can be directed more broadly to improving existing military hardware rather than to inventing new weapons. Since the technical challenges that retrofit development raises are less compelling than those posed by new scientific discoveries, both the uncertainties and the costs that accompany advanced technology can be reduced.

A second important lesson gleaned from the findings relates to the impact that budgetary concerns will have on weapons procurement in the future. Since weapons decisions are political ones, they invariably are balanced against other political needs, such as domestic ones. During the Cold War, the threat of nuclear annihilation made foreign and defense policy concerns preeminent over domestic policy needs. In the absence of an imminent nuclear threat, it will be more difficult to rationalize sacrifices to the nation's infrastructure, for example, to support a bloated national security apparatus. While America's "safety net" has already been compromised by congressional efforts to balance the budget, reduce taxes, and maintain a high level of defense spending all at the same time, public opinion polls show that citizens are beginning to resent efforts to sacrifice social programs (such as Medicare and Social Security) to weapons systems even the Pentagon does not want (such as additional B-2 bombers). Understanding the relative trade-offs of domestic programs to increases in defense spending could further politicize significant portions of the electorate in ways that place the national security debate more prominently on the public agenda. According to Sam Marullo, "$4 billion in cuts in Medicare services equals the cost of an antisatellite weapon [and] $1.5 billion in cuts in housing for the elderly and the handicapped equals the cost of one U.S. Marine amphibious assault ship."[1] Ironically, the Republican commitment to balancing the budget without cutting taxes may force legislators to look to defense spending, which now constitutes the largest source of discretionary funds in the federal budget. During this time, Republicans would do well to remember the words of President Dwight D. Eisenhower, who once warned the nation: "Every gun that is made, every warship launched, every rocket fired signifies in the final sense a theft from those who hunger and are not fed, those who are cold and are not clothed. The world in arms is not spending money alone. It is spending the sweat of its laborers, the genius of its scientists, the hopes of its children."[2]

A third insight that derives from the findings in this study concerns the forces that are most likely to resist reform efforts. The most obvious are the four military services that benefit from the current levels of spending. Fueling efforts by the services to retain their preeminent position in weapons procurement are ongoing efforts by the current administration to redefine and reassign mission responsibilities and tighten budgets. Together, service dominance, fiscal constraints, and uncertain mission assignments are likely to provoke efforts (even collusive ones) by the services to protect their turf by resisting comprehensive reform efforts. The defense industry and its organized labor force are likely to coalesce around opposition to reform efforts that compromise their currently privileged economic standing. When combined with the efforts of sympathetic members of Congress, the military subsystem could prove a formidable obstacle to the implementation (but not necessarily the conception) of reform.

These three lessons, of course, do not exhaust the insights one can extract from the findings in this study. It is doubtful, however, that more probing would alter the unflattering image of a weapons procurement process in the United States that is not only flawed but perhaps impervious to change. Does this mean that one should become resigned to the status quo and abandon reform options? On the contrary, the insights hold within them the seeds of realistic and viable change, but only if we abandon the assumption that the military policy-making process must be rationalized and depoliticized to operate effectively. In fact, it may be the case that the process actually would benefit from more politics, an assertion that is addressed in the next section.

A Reform Impetus

Students of weapons procurement continue to view the process with derision and scorn, mostly for its failure to produce in an efficient, judicious, and timely fashion weapons systems that are the optimal solutions to military threats in the global environment. As such, much reform effort is directed toward rationalizing the process for making military hardware decisions. In short, most studies of America's weapons acquisition process begin and end with the assumptions that rationalism is the preferred discourse; that decisions that carry with them significant consequences and inherent risks such as those that involve America's national security, deserve to be made in a reasoned and objective manner by a small group of skilled and specially trained elites; and that to do otherwise is contrary to the national or public interest.

While appealing, the argument for rationalism can be faulted on three grounds. Foremost, the conditions of rationality are impossible to achieve in any political system, but especially in a democracy where many of the provisions for a free and open government are at odds with the demands of rational decision making, such as secrecy, expediency, and elite rule. More pointedly, people disagree about what is rational, and democracy encourages and legitimates divergences of opinion. Democracy also endorses politics (and its attendant tools of bargaining and negotiation) as the medium through which disagreements should be resolved. The current and ongoing debate over the nature of the threats posed by the post–Cold War global situation reaffirms a basic democratic reality that what constitutes rationalism in politics depends upon who dominates the national security discourse.

During the Cold War there was a consensus that the Soviet Union constituted the preeminent threat against which America's military forces ought to be directed. In retrospect, we know that the Soviet threat was exaggerated, but it did provide a convenient impetus for organizing what would otherwise have seemed a confusing and unpredictable world.[3] Today, while international relations are described as being more dangerous and volatile than before, in reality it may be that we merely lack the language for transforming the world into neat and manageable categories such as was done during the post–World War II period. A language is evolving, some of which is new (such as "The New World Order") and some of which is old (such as "collective security"). But it is a language that reflects the perceptions of those who control the debate, the political winners. There is no definitive notion of a political reality, only a consensus that emerges through a process of bargaining and negotiation. And the consensus that is emerging is that the global situation, while more unpredictable and volatile, does not pose the imminent and immediate threats to America's vital national interests that the post–World War II period did. This alone challenges the rationale for the relaxation of democratic principles in national security policy-making during the Cold War.

A second attack on rationalism points to the military capabilities achieved by the United States in the post–World War II period. Despite a messy, dirty, and sometimes chaotic and protracted policy-making process, America's military force structure was and continues to be the best in the world. For the forty-five years that constitute the time frame for this study, the United States has made weapons decisions in a decidedly nonrational and political manner. For the most part, however, the weapons systems procured have been workable ones (even if they exhibit some performance problems), justifiable given a particular military need (even if some defense analysts and military experts disagree with this need), technically superior to the weapons of America's enemies (even if some of the technical sophistication has compromised the weapon in other ways), and politically legitimate (even if some citizens and policymakers oppose the system). The policy-making process is by no means perfect. As the findings in this study suggest, the democratic ideal of an open decision-making process is not always corrective (see chapters 3 and 4). But are these democratic forces sufficiently disruptive to justify attacks on democracy? Democracy rarely results in the termination of weapons systems. And in balance with the benefits that accrue from maintaining an open dialogue on military matters, the flaws in weapons procurement are not sufficiently onerous to justify the attenuation of America's political system. The most extreme case in this study, the M-16 rifle, is the exception, a weapon deployed that did pose risks to its users. In short, the conditions conducive to producing optimal military hardware in some instances are at odds with what are taken to be major benchmarks of democracy.

A third attack on rationalism points up the important advantages of politics to military policy. Those who embrace rationalism condemn politics for being inefficient and wasteful; for crediting too many actors and agencies with a role in the decision-making process; and for promoting bargaining, negotiation, and ultimately, compromise policies that undermine the security of the United States. Are the benefits of politics sufficiently dramatic to compensate for its limitations? More importantly, can a case for politics be made that is grounded in anything more substantial than the "feel good" arguments of its advocates? The answer is yes, since politics can compensate for the inadequacies of rationalism in policy-making. More precisely, politics enlivens policies, legitimates the ethical issues that weapons procurement raises, and can substitute for the inability to achieve a definitive consensus.

In the first case, politics can be creative, an impetus to political innovation. In his book on weapons innovation in the Soviet Union and United States, Matthew Evangelista credits American ingenuity in military matters largely to the open, porous, and informal structure of the national security system.[4] In this sense, then, politics is a counterweight to narrowness and bias in decision-making, which can result when the scope of participation is so narrowly construed that weapons development reflects the opinions or views of a small group of same-thinking experts.

Secondly, weapons decisions are ultimately moral ones. Rationalism wants to neutralize opportunities for normative concerns to disrupt reasoned judgement. But military hardware decisions raise all sorts of ethical questions that need to be resolved before weapons are conceived and deployed. Weapons have no inherent value other than their potential use as tools of devastation and destruction. The use of political power to take life raises moral questions to which a democratic people have a right to contribute. To make decisions that carry with them the consequences of life and death in a moral vacuum is to distance ourselves from those decisions.

As a final consideration, a political consensus can substitute for strategic uncertainty. In the absence of a true consensus, political compromise can compensate, and ultimately prove more expeditious when policy-making is stymied by the inability to reach an agreement on such fundamental matters as what constitutes the threats to America's security and how to respond to these threats. But more importantly, and especially today, citizens are more likely to view as credible the resources committed to weapons procurement if the decisions have been validated through a process in which their views are credited. When citizens rail against the biases in what is perceived to be a system controlled by a military subsystem, their discontent is with the absence of sufficient countervailing measures that could balance out the excessive influence by those with a vested stake.

Reform Measures

Can anything be done to reconcile the need for a more efficient and judicious process for making weapons decisions with the desire to preserve the democratic and political nature of the procurement process? Can ways be found to reform the process and improve the product without attenuating pluralism and the representative system of government? These are obvious questions that take on more significance in the post–Cold War period as America struggles with ways to insure it has the capacity to make the important changes to take the country into the twenty-first century.

One reform recommendation that appeals both to those who advocate more and those who advocate less democracy is the need for extended competition beyond the earliest stages of the procurement process, which means including the full-scale development and production phases. The logic behind this reform is to offset the advantages that accrue to those who, early on, employ optimism and deceit as tools to promote their preferences. Without a guarantee that an R&D contract will lead to a production contract, or that a Milestone I decision will automatically lead to Milestone II and Milestone III approval, there would be more of an incentive for privileged actors to continue to be diligent and conscientious. The hope would be that extended competition would discourage the buy-in phenomenon, whereby a defense company bids intentionally low at the development stage, knowing that it will also get the production contract. As Thomas McNaugher has suggested, "Competition should end only after early production models of competing new designs have been subjected to operational as well as technical testing."[5] Extended competition might require longer lead times, additional short-term funds, the elimination of sole-source contracts following prototype competitions, and/or the delay of contract awards until full-scale development, operational testing, and early production have been completed. According to its advocates, extended competition would encourage innovation and creativity, promote a more realistic assessment of a weapon's cost, and offer greater assurances of a workable system. In short, extended competition would allow the Milestone process to function as it was intended.

A more controversial recommendation is to make additional information available to the public and members of Congress. Examples include more statutory efforts, such as the Freedom of Information Act and the more widespread use of public hearings. There is a certain irony insofar as those who condemn congressional and public involvement as disruptive of the procurement process and distracting to defense experts cite as one reason nonexperts' lack of knowledge and understanding. The logical solution, it seems, would be to share more of this information so that legislative and public input is more substantive and essential. The concern that further democratizing the procurement process would overwhelm the system with citizen input seems unfounded. Most citizens and legislators are not interested enough to take the time to inform themselves on matters of military policy. Those who are, generally have a vested economic or political stake in a weapons decision. Expanding the base of information could level the playing field by providing critical resources by which nonprivileged groups and legislators could (if they wanted to) balance out the advantages that are held by the defense industry and members holding key positions in Congress. Broadening the scope of participation does not mean eliminating the national security exemption, however (although in the absence of a Soviet threat it could mean relaxing it). Besides fueling pluralism, enlarging the scope of participation could increase the opportunities for "fire-alarms" to be rung that focus public attention on cases of malfeasance. This could then provide a basis for more aggressive enforcement of criminal and civil codes to punish fraud, waste, and abuse.

Importantly, making more opportunities available to the public, even if they are not used, could result in less frustration with military spending on the part of citizens if they feel that they have more of a say in how those decisions are made. Capitalizing on this advantage is the suggestion proffered by Robert Dahl that the government assume responsibility for translating issues of military concern, including military hardware ones, into dichotomous positions that provide the context for a public dialogue which can then translate to electoral decisions. Given the obvious advantages that accrue to politicizing the military process, actions by Congress to cut its resource and information base raise serious concerns about motives. Plans to strengthen the party leadership, weaken the committee and subcommittee system, and carry out related procedural changes could more narrowly circumscribe the arena of debate on military hardware matters.

A third important, albeit ambiguous, suggestion is to implement more comprehensive campaign reform. If one concern is with the perceived parochial tendencies of some members of Congress, then the solution is to eliminate one potential incentive for hypocritical voting—PAC and campaign contributions. Campaign reform would also help balance the disproportionate influence of the defense industry and labor unions in the military debate by eliminating an important source of their power. By cutting the thread that connects the defense industry and members of Congress, an important leg of the military subsystem would be neutralized. The argument for campaign reform is ambiguous because the findings cited in this study challenge the independent impact of PAC contributions and lobbying on congressional voting behavior. Nonetheless, any reform that liberates policymakers from indecorous forces has normative appeal.

Finally, democracy is contrary to the most commonly cited military reform recommendation, that is, to insulate the Pentagon from political control so as to eliminate the bureaucratic forces that feed organizational behavior in military policy. In America, military personnel are bureaucrats first and fighting men and women second. Democratic means, however, are available to modify the incentive structure, most notably to eliminate the competition over budgets that drive the fight for more glitzy, expensive, and, in some cases, nonessential military hardware. Given the previous recommendation for extended competition, the objective is not to repudiate competition per se, but to discourage (provide disincentives for) disingenuous behavior. In other words, something needs to be done to reverse the phenomenon of budgets driving weapons, and break the connection between funding and organizational stature. This means briefly isolating these decisions, while still retaining some political control, however.

At no time since the end of World War II has the United States been in a better position to accomplish this sort of policy segmentation. Currently, a reassessment is being made of the contribution that the military establishment can make to the nation's security now that the global environment has been fundamentally changed and the assumptions that underlie roles and missions have been profoundly challenged. Military planners and foreign policy analysts are rethinking the nature and scope of America's vital national interests, available military capabilities, mission needs, and military force requirements. At the same time, a fundamental reexamination of budgetary priorities is going on, a topic of legislative-executive battles. As well, a procurement dispute is afloat as many preeminent weapons systems in America's force structure are reaching the end of their military viability, a condition traditionally and automatically met by approving follow-on systems.[6] While a significant number of weapons systems already have reached a point in their development where they are relatively immune to political attack, the largest (nuclear) components of the procurement budget are vulnerable, providing a windfall to defense planners rethinking America's military hardware needs.

In addition to the policy opportunities that the end of the Cold War provides, the requisite organizational mandates are already in place to support the reassessment that is going on. The chairman of the Joint Chiefs of Staff (CJCS) and the defense secretary have been given more power to make independent decisions; an under secretary of defense, acquisition, is in place to supervise and coordinate procurement activity; the Defense Acquisition Board has been newly empowered; and the Pentagon is working to simplify and streamline the procurement process. In short, the complexity and lack of coordination that traditionally have worked to the advantage of the military services are being addressed.

The challenge is to prevent these three sets of policy opportunities from being exploited politically as in the past, while retaining the uniquely political nature of America's policy-making process. This effort entails insuring that influence is sufficiently balanced so that the interests that have traditionally benefited from the status quo of procurement will be offset by other less privileged concerns. The most visible example is the federal budget, decisions about which must be made by a broader scope of political interests than those that currently dominate the debate. The reform recommendations for extended competition, more information, and campaign reform are all geared toward promoting more balance in American politics.

An effective force structure is essential to protect the democratic values and principles venerated by the American people. Yet the production of the best military hardware is sometimes stymied by these same democratic virtues. This book has argued that the solution to this dilemma is not less democracy but more balance in American politics. In short, the best way to organize the process for making military hardware decisions is a democratic governing structure, the essence of which is political balance.

Notes

1. Sam Marullo, *Ending the Cold War at Home: From Militarism to a More Peaceful World Order* (New York: Lexington Books, 1993).

2. Quoted in ibid., 158.

3. In a series of revelations during 1995, the CIA admitted to Congress that it knowingly circulated dubious intelligence to the president and the Pentagon about the Soviet threat and its military capabilities, passed by double agents, that was used to justify the purchase of advanced weapons systems.

4. Matthew Evangelista, *Innovation and the Arms Race* (Ithaca, N.Y.: Cornell University Press, 1988).

5. Thomas L. McNaugher, *New Weapons Old Politics: America's Military Procurement Muddle* (Washington, D.C.: The Brookings Institution, 1989), 182–185. According to McNaugher, in order for extended competition to work to promote efficiency and creativity, defense planners and industry personnel must be given more freedom to operate without the suffocating constraints imposed by detailed performance and design requirements.

6. The most visible examples are the Seawolf nuclear submarine, B-2 (Stealth) bomber, and F-22 fighter plane, all systems intended to replace what their promoters claim are their soon-to-be-obsolete predecessors.

F-22
Business as Usual

More than any other weapons system currently being developed, the F-22 fighter plane illustrates how formidable the factors and actors are that influence America's force-structure decisions. The plane's military need is under dispute (controversial) both within and outside the Pentagon (particularly from the Army, which resents its reduced role in avionics), and a concurrent management strategy is being applied to its development, even though the technology demanded is ambitious (according to the Pentagon's Defense Science Board).

Conceived during the 1980s to meet the Soviet threat and sustain America's air superiority (by performing the air-combat mission), the F-22 is still being justified by an Air Force that views Russian advances in surface-to-air and air-to-air missiles and fighter aircraft technology as threatening. The General Accounting Office (GAO) has argued consistently that the existing F-15 is fully capable of meeting any existing enemy threat until 2015, especially since the potential adversary forces that the United States is likely to confront have few fighters with the capability to challenge the F-15. The Defense Resources Board has advised the Air Force to delay the F-22 until a less costly alternative can be evaluated, in order to reduce the defense budget. Army General Jay Garner, deputy chief of staff for operations and plans (force development), contends that "given the limited air-to-air capability of plausible Third World opponents, it is highly questionable that 442 F-22 fighters, at a price of $17.5 billion, are justified." For its part, the Army is looking at a $20 billion funding shortfall over its six-year budget plan, and the research and development budget for the F-22 is "twice the level of total Army aviation procurement." Most important, the two- (regional) war strategy that bolsters the F-22 is being challenged by defense experts both within and outside the Pentagon. According to Pentagon cost analyst Franklin Spinney, "the two-war strategy is just a marketing device to justify a high budget." Air Force Chief of Staff Merrill McPeak notes that "neither our historical experience nor our common sense leads us to think we need to be [prepared for a two-war plan.]. We've had to fight three major regional contingencies in the

past forty-five years. . . . One comes along every fifteen years or so—
two have never come along simultaneously."

Until the Army attack, the F-22 had few opponents, despite its
exorbitant cost. Clinton Defense Secretary Perry and Congress consistently have supported the plane as a way to insure America's air
superiority. Congress has gone so far as to eliminate the Pentagon's
requirement that the F-22 undergo two sets of flight tests to demonstrate its air superiority against the F-15 fighter before going into
production.

The plane entered full-scale development in 1991, after the fall
of the Berlin Wall and the breakup of the Soviet Union. By 1994 the
Air Force admitted the program was risky because of the technological advances that are critical to its operational success. Nonetheless, the F-22 program is being developed under a highly concurrent
management program that will allow the plane to enter production
"well before commencement of IOT&E [Initial operational testing
and evaluation]," in violation of two federal laws. Already, the F-22
has encountered several problems with its engine, stealth characteristics, integrated avionics, and software.

[1]GAO/NSAID-94-118, 25 March 1994.

Primary Sources: U.S. GAO, *Tactical Aircraft: F-15 Replacement Is Prema-
ture as Currently Planned.* (Washington, D.C.: GPO, 25 March 1994);
Defense News, 22–24 September 1994, 22–28 August 1994; U.S. GAO,
*Tactical Aircraft: Concurrency in Development and Production of F-22
Aircraft Should Be Reduced* (Washington, D.C.: GPO, 19 April 1995).

Methodology

The study involved four major steps. First, the theoretical literature was used to generate three explanations for weapons outcomes, from which the dependent and independent variables were derived. Second, a group of nineteen major weapons decisions since World War II was selected. Third, bibliographic sources describing the policy-making process for each decision were collected. Finally, the source materials were used as data sets, and relevant information was extracted relying upon "a set of standardized, general questions."[1]

Dependent and Independent Variables

An extensive survey of the defense policy-making literature was conducted from which three common explanations for military hardware development and weapons performance were derived. The three theoretical perspectives (discussed in chapter 1) were used to generate the dependent and independent variables. Each perspective asserts a relationship between some condition of policy-making (independent variables), and the nature and quality of the policy decision (dependent variables). The pragmatic argument emphasizes the uncertainty and complexity associated with the making of military procurement decisions. From this perspective, then, weapons decisions invariably are affected by the degree to which the uncertainties in the policy-making environment can be controlled. Accordingly, the more exact and contrived the decision-making process, the greater the likelihood that the weapon will be procured in a timely, cost-effective manner, and will perform well. The technical argument emphasizes the importance of the technological requirements of building a military system. From this perspective, then, the degree of technical challenge affects weapons decisions. Accordingly, the less ambitious and more certain the technology required by the newly conceived weapon, the greater the likelihood that the completed weapon will be procured in a timely, cost-effective manner, and will perform well. The political argument emphasizes the importance of a coalition in support of a weapons system. From this perspective, then, political dynamics affect weapons decisions. Accordingly, the narrower the scope of participation, the less the degree of conflict over a weapons system and, therefore, the more likely that the weapon will be procured in a timely, cost-effective manner, and will perform well.

Selecting the Cases

A master list of major weapons decisions since World War II was compiled from government publications and the relevant defense policy literature.[2] According to the U.S. General Accounting Office, major systems are "those over $200 million in research and development or $1 billion in production."[3] The decision to examine only major weapons decisions was made for two reasons. For one, the information about major weapons is more readily available. For another, the external (systemic level) and internal (bureaucratic and organizational level) factors influencing major weapons decisions are roughly similar.

This resulted in an initial universe of close to a hundred cases. Of these, nineteen cases were selected in a random fashion. The decision to study nineteen cases was influenced by two additional considerations (other than those that generally dictate sample selection judgments). One consideration was whether the information requisite to compiling a complete case study was available. Given the application of a case survey method of analysis, it was imperative that there be a complete case history available for each weapons decision. A second concern was a sample size that was manageable given the demands of the research in this study. To narrow the sample size, the universe was manipulated to provide a stratum that would reflect variety in the dependent and independent variables. As Alexander George asserts, "the desideratum that guides se-

lection of cases in the controlled comparison approach is not numbers
but variety, that is, cases belonging to the same class that differ from each
other. Thus, the investigator in designing the study will either seek cases
in which the outcome of the dependent variable differed or cases having
the same outcome but a different explanation for it."[4]

While small by survey research standards, the nineteen cases constitute
a compilation that is large in comparison with those used for previous research in the area of military procurement. Other studies of weapons procurement either have been limited to a study of one weapons system or a
set of related weapons (such as strategic bomber programs), or have used
evidence from any number of cases of weapons procurement for illustrative (rather than for evidential) purposes. This study draws upon the available data on a diverse set of weapons procurement decisions in the post–
World War II period to both illustrate and systematically test prevailing
assumptions about military hardware development.

The database is also justified as being expedient given the experimental nature of the research in this study. Gathering complete data for even
one case history is an enormously complicated and time-consuming task.
Examining a small number of programs in considerable detail, rather
than a large number in less detail, has two advantages. First, it is likely
that a more complete understanding of the factors that influence weapons procurement and quality will occur. Second, it also means that some
of the methodological problems that occur can be resolved before one
commits exorbitant amounts of time and resources in constructing an
expanded database. The database can always be expanded later. While this
approach does limit to some degree the ability to generalize findings to a
national level, the study covers enough programs to test the prevailing
theoretical perspectives. According to Yin, "Case studies, like experiments,
are generalizable to theoretical propositions and not to populations or
universes. In this sense, the case study, like the experiment, does not represent a 'sample,' and the investigator's goal is to expand and generalize
theories (analytical generalization) and not to enumerate frequencies
(statistical generalization)."[5] Similarly, Alexander George has concluded
that the application of the "disciplined-configurative" mode of analysis in
a comparison of a few case studies can make important contributions to
theory development.[6]

Given the caveats cited above, the hypotheses are stated as relations
between conditions rather than as correlations. This sets up a less ambitious task. If these cases do yield some useful relationships between the
variables, then we are justified in recommending the addition of more

case histories, and that more rigorous tests than the cross-tabulations done here be conducted.

Collecting the Bibliographic Sources

Various literature guides were employed to compile a list of bibliographic sources for each weapons decision. The bibliographic sources included existing (scholarly) case studies (which formed the basis for the data set), government documents, and press reports. For example, data on the Trident submarine and missile system were compiled drawing upon scholarly works and case studies such as *Trident* by D. Douglas Dalgleish and Larry Schweikart and "Trident: Setting the Requirements" by Mary Schumacher; government documents such as the CRS Issue Brief series on Trident (IB73001) and GAO reports such as "Status of the Trident Submarine and Missile Programs," PSAD-77-34 (8 March 1977); and various stories in the *New York Times* and *Aviation Week and Space Technology*.[7] Additional information was obtained through personal interviews.

Generating the Data

This study uses the case survey methodology to examine the weapons acquisition decision-making process.[8] This method allows the researcher to regard already published case studies as "data sets." These case studies, then, become the basis upon which additional information is generated particular to the scope of this study. Existing case studies have been supplemented with original data generated through personal interviews and document analysis.

By using case studies as data sets, it is possible to use the insights contained in each case study to generalize about the studies as a whole, to enumerate frequencies, and to make simple statements of association and nonassociation. Drawing upon George's method of structured, focused comparison, this study uses a uniform list of questions to "interrogate" each case. (The list of questions and coding form are contained in appendix B.) By using a fixed set of questions, reliability can be measured by having more than one person answer each question for a single case study. Reliability was further insured by having at least two researchers conduct each interrogation. The major limitation of relying upon this method is that the analyst is dependent upon the accuracy of the original studies.

Notes

1. Alexander L. George, "Case Studies and Theory Development: The Method of Structured, Focused Comparison," in *Diplomacy: New Approaches in History, Theory, and Policy*, ed. Paul Gordon Lauren (New York: Free Press, 1979), 62.

2. See, for example, Franklin C. Spinney, *Defense Facts of Life: The Plans/ Reality Mismatch* (Boulder, Colo.: Westview Press, 1985).

3. U.S. General Accounting Office, *Weapons Testing: Quality of DOD Operational Testing and Reporting* (Washington, D.C.: Government Printing Office, 1988).

4. Emphasis in the original. George, "Case Studies and Theory Development," 60.

5. Robert K. Yin, *Case Study Research: Design and Methods*, rev. ed. (Beverly Hills, Calif.; Sage, 1989), 53.

6. George, "Case Studies and Theory Development."

7. Dalgleish and Schweikart, *Trident* (Carbondale, Ill.: Southern Illinois University Press, 1984); Mary Schumacher, "Trident." (Cambridge: Kennedy School of Government Case Program, 1987).

8. For a more complete discussion see George, "Case Studies and Theory Development"; Robert K. Yin and Karen A. Heald, "Using Case Survey Method to Analyze Policy Studies," *Administrative Science Quarterly* 20 (September 1975): 371–381; and Yin, *Case Study Research*.

List of Questions and Coding Form

1. Type of weapon?
   ○ missile   ○ aircraft   ○ ship   ○ missile system   ○ combat hardware
   ○ air defense   ○ bomb   ○ other (specify)

2. Military service with jurisdiction?
   ○ Navy   ○ Army   ○ Air Force

3. Dependent variable. Performance. Is the system operationally sound or flawed?
   a. According to government test results?
      ○ sound   ○ flawed   ○ unclear
   b. According to other written accounts (such as books, articles, and press reports)?
      ○ sound   ○ flawed   ○ unclear
   c. According to personal interviews?
      ○ sound   ○ flawed   ○ unclear

4. Dependent variable. Cost.
   a. How much was the projected cost for the weapons system? Specify.
   b. How much did the weapon actually cost to produce? Specify.
   c. Did the weapons system encounter cost overruns sufficient to compromise its performance?
      (1) According to government test results?
         ○ yes   ○ no   ○ unclear
      (2) According to other written accounts (such as books, articles, and press reports)?
         ○ yes   ○ no   ○ unclear
      (3) According to personal interviews?
         ○ yes   ○ no   ○ unclear

5. Dependent variable. Schedule.

a. Delineate the acquisition life cycle of the weapons system.

b. Did the weapons system encounter schedule delays sufficient to compromise its performance?

(1) According to government test results?

○ yes ○ no ○ unclear

(2) According to other written accounts (such as books, articles, and press reports)?

○ yes ○ no ○ unclear

(3) According to personal interviews?

○ yes ○ no ○ unclear

6. Independent variable. Military (Pragmatic)

a. With which agency or group did the weapons system originate?

○ military service ○ OSD ○ defense industry ○ Congress

○ government research group (specify) ○ President

○ Secretary of Defense ○ other (specify)

b. Did the originating agency make concessions to other groups (specify) in order to build a coalition of support for the weapons system? Open-ended (specify).

c. What was the operational mission of the weapon system at its conception? Open-ended (specify).

d. How well established was the military (mission) need for the weapons system at the time of its conception?

(1) According to government reports?

○ well established ○ not well established ○ unclear.

(2) According to other written accounts (such as books, articles, and press reports)?

○ well established ○ not well established ○ unclear.

(3) According to personal interviews?

○ well established ○ not well established ○ unclear.

e. Was there agreement among defense analysts in the Pentagon and NSC on the military (mission) need for the weapons system at the time of its conception?

(1) According to government reports?

○ yes ○ no ○ unclear. Specify groups in agreement/ disagreement.

(2) According to other written accounts (such as books, articles, and press reports)? Specify groups in agreement/ disagreement.

○ yes ○ no ○ unclear.

(3) According to personal interviews? Specify groups in agreement/ disagreement.

○ yes ○ no ○ unclear

f. At the time of its conception, were the weapon's design specifications compatible with its mission requirements?

(1) According to government reports?

○ yes ○ no ○ unclear

(2) According to other written accounts (such as books, articles, and press reports)?

○ yes ○ no ○ unclear

(3) According to personal interviews?

○ yes ○ no ○ unclear

  g. Was the weapons system's military need consistently maintained throughout its acquisition life? (Or was the need for the weapon redefined?)

(1) According to government reports?

○ yes ○ no ○ unclear

(2) According to other written accounts (such as books, articles, and press reports)?

○ yes ○ no ○ unclear

(3) According to personal interviews?

○ yes ○ no ○ unclear

7. Independent variable. Technical.

  a. Was the weapon a product of "technology push" or "user pull"?

(1) According to government reports?

○ technology push ○ user pull ○ unclear

(2) According to other written accounts (such as books, articles, and press reports)?

○ technology push ○ user pull ○ unclear

(3) According to personal interviews?

○ technology push ○ user pull ○ unclear

  b. What was the nature of the technology necessary to actually produce the weapons system?

(1) According to government reports?

○ ambitious ○ moderate ○ modest ○ unclear

(2) According to other written accounts (such as books, articles, and press reports)?

○ ambitious ○ moderate ○ modest ○ unclear

(3) According to personal interviews?

○ ambitious ○ moderate ○ modest ○ unclear

8. Independent variable. General Support (Political).

  a. What sorts of agencies and groups supported the weapons system? Open-ended.

  b. What sorts of agencies and groups opposed the weapons system? Open-ended.

  c. What are the reasons given for their support for the weapons system?

○ military need ○ organizational reasons ○ constituent benefit
○ economic reasons ○ technical reasons ○ other (specify)

  d. What are the reasons given for their opposition to the weapons system?

○ military need ○ organizational reasons ○ constituent benefit
○ economic reasons ○ technical reasons ○ other (specify)

  e. Overall, given the number and types of groups involved in the weapons decision, is the scope of participation broad or narrow?

○ broad ○ narrow ○ unclear

9. Independent variable. Congress (Political).

a. Briefly describe the nature and degree of involvement by members of Congress, with particular emphasis on key individuals and committees. Open-ended.

b. How would you classify the nature of congressional involvement in the weapons decision?

○ fiscal ○ programmatic ○ policy ○ unclear

c. How would you classify the scope of congressional involvement in the weapons decision?

○ broad ○ narrow ○ unclear

d. Did Congress support the president's recommendations for this weapon?

○ yes ○ no ○ varied

e. If varied, then specify roll call or committee decisions, and Congress' position vis-à-vis the administration.

10. Independent variable. Defense Industry (Political).

a. Which companies received the contract and subcontracts to design and build the weapons system? Specify state of location. Open-ended.

b. Was there any evidence of malfeasance or misconduct on the part of the defense industry in the development of this weapons system?

○ yes ○ no ○ unclear

11. Independent variable. Public (Political).

a. Did the public play a role in the weapons procurement decision?

○ yes ○ no ○ unclear

b. If yes, what was the nature of the role that the public played?

○ interest groups ○ other group action (e.g., protests) ○ testimony (specify)
○ electoral ○ other (specify)

12. What was the management strategy that guided the acquisition of the weapons system?

○ concurrent ○ sequential ○ unclear

13. What was the primary factor(s) affecting the decision to build the weapon?

○ military ○ technical ○ political ○ other (specify) ○ unclear

ACRONYMS AND GLOSSARY

ABM Antiballistic missile. Systems to intercept and destroy or neutralize hostile ballistic missiles. Used interchangeably with BMD (ballistic missile defense).

ABM Treaty A treaty negotiated in 1972 between the U.S. and Soviet Union limiting to one site ballistic missile defense systems with 100 ABM launchers and missiles in each country. The treaty also limits the location and future development of ABM systems.

ALCM Air-launched cruise missile. Small drones that carry nuclear weapons.

AMRAAM Advanced medium-range air-to-air missile.

ANSA Assistant to the President for National Security Affairs.

ASW Antisubmarine warfare. Operations developed to destroy or interfere with enemy submarines.

Brilliant Pebbles One of several SDI schemes that would destroy enemy warheads by kinetic energy generated by thousands of orbiting minimissiles.

Buy-in Phenomenon The strategy employed by a defense company to secure a sole-source production contract by submitting an unrealistically low bid during the development stage. Once a company acquires the production contract it raises prices to recoup previous losses.

CBO Congressional Budget Office.

CINCs Commanders-in-chief. Unified and specified commanders.

CJCS Chairman of the Joint Chiefs of Staff.

Conventional weapons Weapons other than nuclear, biological, and most chemical ones.

Countercity strategy The targeting of the urban populations of the enemy.

Counterforce strategy The targeting of the nuclear and conventional military forces (including strategic command and control systems) of the enemy, rather than their industrial and population centers. Counterforce targeting is the foundation of nuclear warfighting strategies.

Countervalue strategy The targeting of the industrial and population centers in order to destroy the enemy through disrupting their social structure. The foundation of mutually assured destruction.

CRS Congressional Research Service.

C³I Command, control, communications, and intelligence. The systems and procedures used to ensure that civilian and military personnel remain in communication during peacetime and wartime operations.

Defense policy Describes those foreign policies whose objective is the protection of the territory of the United States, its values and beliefs, and its vital interests abroad such as oil. These can include military policies to deter, or if deterrence fails, to win a war, diplomatic policies such as arms control agreements, or economic policies such as embargoes. "National security policy" is used interchangeably with "defense policy." *See* **Foreign policy.**

Detente Formal or informal efforts to reduce tensions among foreign nations.

Deterrence Efforts to discourage opponents from initiating or escalating existing military action against the United States.

DoD Department of Defense.

First strike A preemptive strategic nuclear attack on an opponent.

Force structure The way in which the various parts of a nation's military strength are arranged such as the array of weapons systems.

Foreign policy Refers to the full range of policies defining our relationships with other nations.

FY Fiscal year.

GAO General Accounting Office.

Gold plating Refers to the practice of loading a weapon with exotic and expensive components to improve performance which prove not to be cost-effective.

HADS House Appropriations Defense Subcommittee.

Hard target A site built to withstand a nuclear attack, and sometimes a chemical, biological, or radiological attack.

HASC House Armed Services Committee. Now the House National Security Committee.

ICBM Intercontinental ballistic missile. A land-based ballistic missile with a range of about 3,000 to 8,000 nautical miles.

INF Treaty A treaty negotiated between the United States and Soviet Union in June 1988 eliminating nuclear delivery systems with a range of between 500 and 3,500 kilometers. Included in this treaty were the U.S. Pershing II missiles, ground-launched cruise missiles, and the Soviet SS-4s, SS-5s, and SS-20s.

IRBM Intermediate-range ballistic missiles.

JCS Joint Chiefs of Staff.

JROC Joint Requirements Operational Committee.

Milestone Review Process The series of chronological stages that a weapons system undergoes during which it is reviewed at critical stages in its life cycle by the secretary of defense and DSARC (now DAB) for performance and cost. A weapon can be terminated at any stage during the Milestone process.

Military policy A subset of defense policies that deal exclusively with military solutions such as weapons decisions and war plans.

MIRV Multiple independently targetable reentry vehicle. Two or more reentry vehicles carried by a single ballistic missile and directed to separate targets.

MRBM Medium-range ballistic missile.

National security policy *See* **Defense policy.**

NIE National intelligence estimate.

NSC National Security Council.

OMB Office of Management and Budget

OSD Office of the Secretary of Defense.

PPBS Planning, Programming, and Budgeting System. The process developed by Secretary of Defense Robert McNamara during the 1960s for defense budget planning in the Pentagon.

R&D Research and development.

SADS Senate Appropriations Defense Subcommittee.

SALT An acronym for the bilateral negotiations between the United States and the Soviet Union during the 1960s and 1970s on the subject of Strategic Arms Limitation Talks.

SASC Senate Armed Services Committee.

SDI Strategic Defense Initiative. Also called "Star Wars." A form of ballistic missile defense conceived during the Reagan administration.

Second strike The use of strategic nuclear weapons in reprisal for a nuclear first strike by an opponent.

SIOP Single Integrated Operational Plan. The strategic nuclear war plan of the United States.

START An acronym for the bilateral negotiations between the United States and U.S.S.R. during the 1980s on Strategic Arms Reduction Talks.

War-fighting strategy A strategy by which a nation is prepared to fight (rather than deter) any kind of war at any level in the conflict spectrum.

Warhead That part of the missile, bomb, or munition that contains the explosive materials that inflict damage.

SELECTED REFERENCES

Books

Allison, Graham, and Gregory F. Treverton. *Essence of Decision: Explaining the Cuban Missile Crisis*. Boston: Little, Brown, 1971.

————. *Rethinking America's Security: Beyond Cold War to New World Order*. New York: W.W. Norton, 1992.

Armacost, Michael H. *The Politics of Weapons Innovation: The Thor-Jupiter Controversy*. New York: Columbia University Press, 1969.

Arnold, R. Douglas. *Congress and the Bureaucracy*. New Haven: Yale University Press, 1979.

Art, Robert J. *The TFX Decision: McNamara and the Military*. Boston: Little, Brown, 1968.

Art, Robert J., and Robert Jervis, eds. *International Politics: Anarchy, Force, Political Economy, and Decision-Making*. New York: HarperCollins, 1985.

Barr, James, and William E. Howard. *Polaris!* New York: Harcourt, Brace, 1960.

Baucom, Donald B. *The Origins of SDI, 1944–1983*. Lawrence: University Press of Kansas, 1992.

Berman, Robert P., and John C. Baker. *Soviet Strategic Forces: Requirements and Responses*. Washington, D.C.: The Brookings Institution, 1982.

Betts, Richard K., ed. *Cruise Missiles: Technology, Strategy, Politics*. Washington, D.C.: The Brookings Institution, 1981.

Blechman, Barry M. *The Politics of National Security: Congress and U.S. Defense Policy*. New York: Oxford University Press, 1990.

————, and William J. Lynne, eds. *Toward a More Effective Defense: Report of the Defense Reorganization Project.* Cambridge, Mass.: Ballinger, 1985.

Boll, Michael M. *National Security Planning: Roosevelt Through Reagan.* Lexington: The University Press of Kentucky, 1988.

Brown, Harold. *Thinking About Security: Defense and Foreign Policy in a Dangerous World.* Boulder, Colo.: Westview Press, 1983.

Brown, Michael E. *Flying Blind: The Politics of the U.S. Strategic Bomber Program.* Ithaca: Cornell University Press, 1992.

Center for Strategic and International Studies. *Military Technology Revolution: A Structural Framework.* Washington, D.C.: Georgetown University, 1993.

————. *U.S. Defense Acquisition: A Process in Trouble.* Washington, D.C.: Georgetown University Press, 1987.

Chubb, John E., and Paul E. Peterson, eds. *The New Direction in American Politics.* Washington, D.C.: The Brookings Institution, 1985.

Clark, Asa A. IV, Peter W. Chiarelli, Jeffrey S. McKitrick, and James W. Reed, eds. *The Defense Reform Debate: Issues and Analysis.* Baltimore: The Johns Hopkins University Press, 1984.

Cockburn, Andrew. *The Threat: Inside the Soviet Military Machine.* New York: Random House, 1983.

Coulam, Robert F. *Illusions of Choice: The F-111 and the Problem of Weapons Acquisition Reform.* Princeton: Princeton University Press, 1977.

Crabb, Cecil V., and Pat M. Holt. *Invitation to Struggle: Congress, the President, and Foreign Policy.* Washington, D.C.: Congressional Quarterly Press, 1992.

————, and Kevin V. Mulcahy. *American National Security: A Presidential Perspective.* Pacific Grove, Calif.: Brooks/ Cole Publishing Co., 1991.

Cronin,Thomas E., ed. *Rethinking the Presidency.* Boston: Little, Brown, 1982.

Crozier, Michael J., Samuel P. Huntington, and Joji Watanuki. *The Crisis of Democracy: Report on the Governability of Democracies to the Trilateral Commission.* New York: New York University Press, 1975.

Dahl, Robert F. *Controlling Nuclear Weapons: Democracy Versus Guardianship.* New York: Syracuse University Press, 1985.

Dalgleish, D. Douglas, and Larry Schweikart. *Trident.* Carbondale, Ill.: Southern Illinois University Press, 1984.

Deese, David A., ed. *The New Politics of American Foreign Policy*. New York: St. Martin's Press, 1994.

Dellums, Ronald V., ed. *Defense Sense: The Search for a Rational Military Policy*. Cambridge, Mass.: Ballinger, 1983.

Dicerto, J.J. *Missile Base Beneath the Sea: The Story of Polaris*. New York: St. Martin's Press, 1967.

Dixon, James H. et al. *National Security Policy Formulation: Institutions, Processes, and Issues*. New York: University Press of America, 1984.

Edwards, George C. III et al. *The Presidency and Public Policy Making*. Pittsburgh, Pa.: University of Pittsburgh Press, 1985.

Endicott, John E., and Roy W. Stafford, eds. *American Defense Policy*. Baltimore: The Johns Hopkins University Press, 1977.

Enthoven, Alain C., and K. Wayne Smith. *How Much Is Enough? Shaping the Defense Program, 1961–1969*. New York: Harper and Row, 1971.

Etzold, Thomas H. *Defense or Delusion? America's Military in the 1980s*. New York: Harper and Row, 1982.

Evangelista, Matthew. *Innovation and the Arms Race: How the United States and the Soviet Union Develop New Military Technologies*. Ithaca: Cornell University Press, 1988.

Ezell, Edward Clinton. *The Great Rifle Controversy*. Harrisburg, Pa.: Stackpole Books, 1981.

Fallows, James. *National Defense*. New York: Random House, 1981.

Feld, B.T. et al. *Impact of New Technologies on the Arms Race*. Cambridge, Mass.: MIT Press, 1970.

Fox, Ronald J. *The Defense Management Challenge: Weapons Acquisition*. Boston: Harvard Business School Press, 1988.

Gaddis, John Lewis. *How Relevant Was American Strategy in Winning the Cold War?* Carlisle Barracks, Pa.: Strategic Studies Institute, 1992.

Gansler, Jacques S. *Affording Defense*. Cambridge, Mass.: MIT Press, 1989.

Gentry, Jerauld R. *Evolution of the F-16 Multinational Fighter*. Washington, D.C.: Industrial College of the Armed Forces, 1976.

Glass, Matthew. *Citizens Against MX: Public Languages in the Nuclear Age*. Urbana, Ill.: University of Illinois Press, 1993.

Gleditsch, Nils Petter, and Olav Jnolstad, eds. *Arms Races: Technological and Political Dynamics*. London: Sage, 1990.

Goodwin, Jacob. *Brotherhood of Arms: General Dynamics and the Business of Defending America.* New York: Times Books, 1986.

Gray, Colin S. *Weapons Don't Make War: Policy, Strategy, and Military Technology.* Lawrence: University Press of Kansas, 1993.

Greenwood, Ted. *Making the MIRV: A Study of Defense Decision Making.* Cambridge, Mass.: Ballinger, 1975.

Gunston, Bill. *The F/A Hornet.* London: Motorbooks International, 1985.

Halperin, Morton. *Bureaucratic Politics and Foreign Policy.* Washington, D.C.: The Brookings Institution, 1974.

————, and Arnold Kanter, eds. *Readings in American Foreign Policy.* Boston: Little, Brown, 1973.

Hampson, Fen Osler. *Unguided Weapons: How America Buys Its Weapons.* New York: W.W. Norton, 1989.

Hartmann, Frederick H., and Robert L. Wendzel. *Defending America's Security.* New York: Brassey's, Inc., 1990.

Harvard Study Group. *Living with Nuclear Weapons.* Cambridge: Harvard University Press, 1983.

Higgs, Robert, ed. *Arms, Politics, and the Economy: Historical and Contemporary Perspectives.* New York: Holmes and Meier, 1990.

Hilsman, Roger. *The Politics of Policy Making in Defense and Foreign Affairs: Conceptual Models and Bureaucratic Politics.* Englewood Cliffs, N.J.: Prentice-Hall, 1993.

Holland, Lauren H., and Robert A. Hoover. *The MX Decision: A New Direction in U.S. Weapons Procurement Policy?* Boulder, Colo.: Westview Press, 1985.

Holloway, David. *The Soviet Union and the Arms Race.* New Haven: Yale University Press, 1983.

Huntington, Samuel P. The *Common Defense: Strategic Programs in National Politics.* New York: Columbia University Press, 1961.

Jordan, Amos A., William J. Taylor Jr., and Lawrence J. Korb. *American National Security: Policy and Process,* 2nd ed. Baltimore: The Johns Hopkins University Press, 1993.

Jordan, Amos A. et al. *American National Security: Policy and Process.* Baltimore: The Johns Hopkins University Press, 1989.

Kanter, Arnold. *Defense Politics: A Budgetary Perspective.* Chicago: University of Chicago Press, 1975.

Kegley, Charles W., Jr., and Eugene R. Wittkopf. *American Foreign Policy: Pattern and Process*. New York: St. Martin's Press, 1987.

————. and Eugene R. Wittkopf, eds. *The Domestic Sources of American Foreign Policy*. New York: St. Martin's Press, 1988.

Kellerman, Barbara, and Ryan J. Barrilleaux. *The President As World Leader*. New York: St. Martin's Press, 1991.

Kennan, George F. *American Diplomacy 1900–1950*. Chicago: University of Chicago Press, 1951.

Kissinger, Henry. *Years of Upheaval*. Boston: Little, Brown, 1982.

Koenig, Louis W. *The Chief Executive*, 5th ed. New York: Harcourt Brace Jovanovich, 1986.

Korb, Lawrence. *The Fall and Rise of the Pentagon: American Defense Policies in the 1970s*. Westport, Conn.: Greenwood Press, 1979.

Kotz, Nick. *Wild Blue Yonder: Money, Politics, and the B-1 Bomber*. New York: Pantheon Books, 1988.

Kozak, David C., and James M. Keagle, eds. *Bureaucratic Politics and National Security: Theory and Practice*. Boulder, Colo.: Rienner, 1988.

Kruzel, Joseph, ed. *American Defense Annual*. Lexington, Mass.: D.C. Heath, 1989.

Lapp, Ralph. *Arms Beyond Doubt: The Tyranny of Weapons Technology*. New York: Cowles, 1970.

Lauren, Paul Gordon, ed. *Diplomacy: New Approaches in History, Theory, and Policy*. New York: The Free Press, 1979.

Lindsay, James M. *Congress and Nuclear Weapons*. Baltimore: The Johns Hopkins University Press, 1991.

Liske, Craig, and Barry Rundquist. *The Politics of Weapons Procurement: The Role of Congress*. Denver, Colo.: University of Denver, 1974.

Long, Franklin A., and George W. Rathjens, eds. *Arms, Defense Policy, and Arms Control*. New York: W.W. Norton, 1976.

Lord, Carnes. *The Presidency and the Management of National Security*. New York: The Free Press, 1988.

Luttwak, Edward N. *Strategy: The Logic of War and Peace*. Cambridge, Mass.: Belknap Press, 1987.

Mandelbaum, Michael, ed. *America's Defense*. New York: Holmes and Meier, 1989.

Mansfield, Edwin. *Problems of the Modern Economy: Defense, Science, and Public Policy*. New York: W.W. Norton, 1968.

Marullo, Sam. *Ending the Cold War at Home: From Militarism to a More Peaceful World Order.* New York: Lexington Books, 1993.

Mayer, Kenneth R. *The Political Economy of Defense Contracting.* New Haven: Yale University Press, 1991.

McLean, Scilla, ed. *How Nuclear Weapons Decisions Are Made.* New York: St. Martin's Press, 1986.

McNaugher, Thomas L. *The M16 Controversies: Military Organizations and Weapons Acquisition.* New York: Praeger, 1984.

———. *New Weapons Old Politics: America's Military Procurement Muddle.* Washington, D.C.: The Brookings Institution, 1989.

Meyer, David S. *A Winter of Discontent: The Nuclear Freeze and American Politics.* New York: Praeger, 1990.

Mintz, Morton. *America Inc.: Who Owns and Operates the United States.* New York: Dial Press, 1972.

Mullen, Michael G. *Choppers Grounded: The Supply-Demand Problem.* Washington, D.C.: National Defense University Press, 1988.

Ornstein, Norman J., and Shirley Elder. *The B-1 Bomber: Organizing at the Grass Roots.* Washington, D.C.: National Defense University, 1983.

Piper, Don C., and Ronald J. Terchek, eds. *Interaction: Foreign Policy and Public Policy.* Washington, D.C.: The AEI Press, 1983.

Posen, Barry R. *The Sources of Military Doctrine.* Ithaca: Cornell University Press, 1984.

Reichart, John F., and Steven R. Sturm, eds. *American Defense Policy.* Baltimore: The Johns Hopkins University Press, 1982.

Rice, Berkely. *C-5A Scandal.* New York: Houghton-Mifflin, 1971.

Ripley, Randall B., and Grace A. Franklin. *Bureaucracy and Policy Implementation.* Homewood Ill.: Dorsey Press, 1982.

———, and Grace A. Franklin. *Congress, the Bureaucracy, and Public Policy,* 4th ed. Homewood, Ill. Dorsey Press, 1987.

———, and James M. Lindsay. *Congress Resurgent: Foreign and Defense Policy on Capitol Hill.* Ann Arbor, Mich.: University of Michigan Press, 1993.

Rosati, Jerel A. *The Politics of United States Foreign Policy.* New York: Harcourt Brace Jovanovich, 1993.

Rosen, Steven, ed. *Testing the Theory of the Military-Industrial Complex.* Lexington, Mass.: Lexington Books, 1973.

Rossiter, Clinton. *The American Presidency*. New York: Harcourt, Brace and World, 1960.

Russett, Bruce M. *Controlling the Sword: The Democratic Governance of National Security*. Cambridge: Harvard University Press, 1990.

———, and Bruce G. Blair, eds. *Progress in Arms Control?* San Francisco: Freeman, 1979.

Sapolsky, Harvey M. *The Polaris System Development: Bureaucratic and Programmatic Success in Government*. Cambridge: Harvard University Press, 1972.

Scherer, F.M. *The Weapons Acquisition Process: Economic Incentives*. Cambridge: Harvard University Press, 1964.

Simon, Herbert. *Administrative Behavior: A Study of Decision-Making Processes in Administrative Organization*. New York: The Free Press, 1976.

Smith, Steven S. *Call to Order: Floor Politics in the House and Senate*. Washington, D.C.: The Brookings Institution, 1989.

Snow, Donald M. *National Security: Defense Policy for a New International Order*, 3rd ed. New York: St. Martin's Press, 1995.

———, and Eugene Brown. *Puzzle Palaces and Foggy Bottom: U.S. Foreign and Defense Policy-Making in the 1990s*. New York: St. Martin's Press, 1994.

Sorrels, Charles A. *U.S. Cruise Missile Programs: Development, Deployment and Implications for Arms Control*. New York: McGraw-Hill, 1983.

Spinney, Franklin C. *Defense Facts of Life: The Plans/Reality Mismatch*. Boulder, Colo.: Westview Press, 1985.

Stein, Jonathan B. *From H-Bomb to Star Wars: The Politics of Strategic Decision Making*. Lexington, Mass.: D.C. Heath, 1984.

Steinbrunner, John. *The Cybernetic Theory of Decision*. Princeton: Princeton University Press, 1974.

Stone, Deborah A. *Policy Paradox and Political Reason*. Glenview, Ill.: Scott, Foresman and Co., 1988.

Stubbing, Richard A. *The Defense Game: An Insider Explores the Astonishing Realities of America's Defense Establishment*. New York: Harper and Row, 1986.

Tammen, Ronald L. *MIRV and the Arms Race: An Interpretation of Defense Strategy*. New York: Praeger, 1973.

Trout, B. Thomas, and James E. Harf, eds. *National Security Affairs: Theoretical Perspectives and Contemporary Issues.* New Brunswick, N.J.: Transaction Books, 1982.

Tsipis, Kosta, and Penny Janeway, eds. *Review of U.S. Military Research and Development.* Washington, D.C.: Pergamon-Brassey's, 1984.

Walter, Douglas C. *Congress and the Nuclear Freeze: An Inside Look at the Politics of a Mass Movement.* Amherst: University of Massachusetts Press, 1987.

Waltz, Kenneth N. *Theory of International Politics.* Reading, Mass.: Addison-Wesley, 1979.

White, Eston T., ed. *Studies in Defense.* Washington, D.C.: National Defense University Press, 1983.

Wirls, Daniel. *Buildup: The Politics of Defense in the Reagan Era.* Ithaca: Cornell University Press, 1992.

Yin, Robert K. *Case Study Research: Design and Methods,* rev. ed. Beverly Hills, Calif.: Sage, 1989.

York, Herbert F. *Race to Oblivion: A Participant's Guide to the Arms Race.* New York: Simon and Schuster, 1970.

Zuckerman, Solly. *Nuclear Illusion and Reality.* New York: Viking Press, 1982.

———. *Scientists and War: The Impact of Science on Military and Civil Affairs.* New York: Harper and Row, 1966.

Articles

Art, Robert J. "Congress and the Defense Budget: Enhancing Policy Oversight." *Political Science Quarterly* 100 (1985): 227–248.

Aspin, Les. "The Defense Budget and Foreign Policy: The Role of Congress." *Daedalus* 104 (Summer 1975): 155–174.

Bernstein, Robert A., and William W. Anthony. "The ABM Issue in the Senate, 1968–1970." *American Political Science Review* 68 (September 1974): 1198–1206.

Carter, Ralph G. "Congressional Foreign Policy Behavior: Persistent Patters of the Postwar Period." *Presidential Studies Quarterly* 16 (Spring 1986): 329–359.

Fialka, John J. "Army Fighting Vehicle." *Washington Monthly* 14 (April 1982): 22–29.

Fleisher, Richard. "Economic Benefit, Ideology, and Senate Voting on the B-1 Bomber." *American Politics Quarterly* 13 (April 1985): 200–211.

Goure, Dan. "Is There a Military Technology Revolution in America's Future? *Washington Quarterly* 16 (Fall 1993): 175–196.

Graham, Thomas. "The Pattern and Importance of Public Awareness and Knowledge in the Nuclear Age." *Journal of Conflict Resolution* 32 (1988): 319-334.

Harlich, Lord. "Suez Snafu, Skybolt Sabu." *Foreign Policy* 2 (Spring 1971): 38–50.

Head, Richard. "Technology and the Military Balance." *Foreign Affairs* 56 (April 1978): 544–563.

Holland, Lauren. "The Use of NEPA in Defense Policy Politics: Public and State Involvement in the MX Missile Project." *Social Science Journal* 21 (July 1984): 53–71.

Hughes, G. Phillip. "Congressional Influence in Weapons Procurement." *Public Policy* 28 (Fall 1980): 415–449.

Huntington, Samuel P. "American Ideals versus American Institutions." *Political Science Quarterly* 97 (Spring 1982): 1–38.

Kaldor, Mary. "The Weapons Succession Process." *World Politics* 38 (July 1986): 577–595.

Kaufman, Daniel J. "National Security: Organizing the Armed Forces." *Armed Forces and Society* 14 (Fall 1987): 85–112.

Kendall, Frank. "Exploiting the Military Technical Revolution: A Concept for Joint Warfare." *Strategic Review* 20 (Spring 1992): 23–30.

Kennan, George F. "The Sources of Soviet Conduct." *Foreign Affairs* (July 1947): 566-582.

Krasner, Stephen D. "Are Bureaucracies Important? (Or Allison Wonderland)." *Foreign Policy* 7 (Summer 1972): 159–179.

Lindblom, Charles E. "The Science of Muddling Through." *Public Administration Review* 19 (Spring 1959): 79–88.

Lindsay, James M. "Congress and Defense Policy: 1961 to 1986." *Armed Forces and Society* 13 (Spring 1987): 371–401.

———. "Parochialism, Policy, and Constituency Constraints: Congressional Voting on Strategic Weapons System." *American Journal of Political Science* 34 (November 1990): 936–960.

———. "Testing the Parochial Hypothesis: Congress and the Strategic Defense Initiative." *Journal of Politics* 53 (August 1991), 860–876.

McCool, Daniel. "Subgovernments As Determinants of Political Viability." *Political Science Quarterly* 105 (1990): 269–294.

McNaugher, Thomas L. "Break a Few Rules." *International Defense Review* (February 1994), 23–29.

———. "Weapons Procurement: The Futility of Reform." *International Security* 12 (Fall 1987): 63–104.

Miller, Steven E. "Politics over Promise: Domestic Impediments to Arms Control." *International Security* 8 (Spring 1984): 67–90.

Reppy, Judith. "Research and Development of Arms: Military R&D. Institutions, Output, and Arms Control." *Policy Studies Journal* 8 (Autumn 1979): 84–91.

Rosecrance, Richard. "Reply to Waltz." *International Organization* 36 (Summer 1982): 682–685.

Russett, Bruce M. "Ethical Dilemmas of Nuclear Deterrence." *International Security* 8 (Spring 1984): 36–54.

Shapiro, Robert Y., and Benjamin I. Page. "Foreign Policy and the Rational Public." *Journal of Conflict Resolution* 32 (June 1988): 211–247.

Simpkin, Richard. "The Infantry Fighting Vehicle: Maid-of-All-Work or Crown Princess?" *Military Technology* (October 1985): 48–65.

Tarr, David. "Military Technology and the Policy Process." *Western Political Quarterly* 18 (March 1965): 135–148.

Van Evera, Stephen, and Barry R. Posen, "Reagan Administration Defense Policy: Departure from Containment." *International Security* 8 (1983): 3–45.

Voorst, L. Bruce van. "The Critical Masses." *Foreign Policy* 48 (Fall 1982): 82–86.

Yankelovich, Daniel, and John Doble. "The Public Mood: Nuclear Weapons and the USSR." *Foreign Affairs* 63 (Fall 1984): 33–46.

Yin, Robert K., and Karen A. Heald. "Using Case Survey Method to Analyze Policy Studies." *Administrative Science Quarterly* 20 (September 1975): 371–381.

Government Documents and Rand Publications

Aspin, Rep. Les. *Searching for a Defense Strategy.* Washington, D.C.: House Armed Services Committee, September 1987.

Dews, Edmund et al. *Acquisition Policy Effectiveness*. Santa Monica, Calif.: Rand Corporation, 1979.

Drezner, Jeffrey A., and Giles K. Smith. *An Analysis of Weapon System Acquisition Schedules*. Santa Monica, Calif.: Rand Corporation, 1990.

Perry, Robert et al. *System Acquisition Strategies*. Santa Monica, Calif.: Rand Corporation, 1971.

President's Blue Ribbon Commission on Defense Management. *A Quest for Excellence: Final Report to the President*. Washington, D.C.: Government Printing Office, 1986.

Rich, Michael, and Edmund Dews. *Improving the Military Acquisition Process: Lessons from Rand Research*. Santa Monica, Calif.: Rand Corporation, 1986.

U.S. Congress. *Defense Organization: The Need for Change*. Washington D.C.: Government Printing Office, 1985.

U.S. Congressional Budget Office. *The B-1B Bomber and Options for Enhancements*. Washington, D.C.: Government Printing Office, August 1988.

————. *Concurrent Weapons Development and Production*. Washington, D.C.: Government Printing Office, 1988.

U.S. Department of Defense. *Conduct of the Persian Gulf War, Final Report to Congress*. Washington, D.C.: Government Printing Office, 1992.

U.S. General Accounting Office. *Defense Weapons Systems Acquisition*. Washington, D.C.: Government Printing Office, 1995.

————. *The F/A-18 Naval Strike Fighter: Progress Has Been Made but Problems and Concerns Continue*. Washington, D.C.: Government Printing Office, 1981.

————. *Implications of Highly Sophisticated Weapon Systems on Military Capabilities*. Washington, D.C.: Government Printing Office, 1980.

————. *Inherent Risk in the Army's Acquisition Strategy Demands Particular Caution in Evaluating the Divad Gun System's Production Readiness*. Washington, D.C.: Government Printing Office, 1980.

————. *Major Acquisitions: Summary of Recurring Problems and Systemic Issues: 1960–1987*. Washington, D.C.: Government Printing Office, 1988.

————. *Tactical Aircraft: Concurrency in Development and Production of F-22 Aircraft Should Be Reduced*. Washington, D.C.: Government Printing Office, 1995.

————. *Tactical Aircraft: F-15 Replacement Is Premature as Currently Planned*. Washington, D.C.: Government Printing Office, 1994.

————. *Weapons Acquisition: A Rare Opportunity for Lasting Change*. Washington, D.C.: Government Printing Office, 1992.

————. *Weapons Testing: Quality of DOD Operational Testing and Reporting*. Washington, D.C.: Government Printing Office, 1988.

Werrell, Kenneth P. *The Evolution of the Cruise Missile*. Washington, D.C.: Government Printing Office, 1985.

INDEX

ABM Treaty, 28, 208n
Aegis, 80, 110
    media and, 194
    problems with, 138–139
    Vincennes disaster and, 167
Afghanistan, Soviet invasion of, 41, 52, 217
Air-launched cruise missiles (ALCMS), 41, 88, 149
    development of, 142–143
Albright, Madeleine, 49
Antisubmarine Warfare (ASW), 112, 113
Apache helicopter (AH-64), xxi, 124, 156
Armed services committees, 146
    See also House Armed Services Committee; Senate Armed Services Committee
Aspin, Les, 49, 50, 160

B-1 bomber, 18, 84, 209
    cancellation of, 7, 28, 41, 42, 82, 149, 158, 217
    Congress and, 149, 157, 158
    criticism of, 4, 7, 12, 20n
    public opposition to, 190, 197, 209–210
B-1B bomber, 7, 44, 113, 115, 149
B-2 (Stealth) bomber, 44, 56n, 188
    B-1 bomber and, 7, 20n, 231n
    Congress and, 149, 151, 153, 167, 222
    current use of, 74, 221
    debate over, 8, 29n, 50, 81
    testing of, 114
Baker, James, 47
Berger, Samuel, 49

Black budget (classified) programs, 73, 127, 166, 188, 222
Bradley fighting vehicle, 16, 42
    Congress and, 151, 153, 155, 157
    costs and, 13
    debate over, 8, 16–17, 18, 81, 89, 103–104
    technology and, 13, 125, 218
    TOW missiles and, 17, 122
Brown, Harold, 11, 40, 42–43, 75, 110, 174
Brzezinski, Zbigniew, 44
Bundy, McGeorge, 35
bureaucratic politics, xx, xxvii, 6, 70, 108, 109
Bush, George, xxviii, 51, 56n, 60, 95n
    Congress and, 150
    foreign policy and, 46, 47, 165,

C^3I, 41, 44, 56n, 60
Carter Doctrine, 41
Carter, Jimmy, 36, 42, 51, 52, 217
    B-1 bomber and, 7, 28, 41, 42, 75, 82, 209, 217
    Congress and, 42, 154
    F/A-18 and, 42, 174
    foreign policy and, 40, 41, 43, 48, 217
    MX missile system and, 41, 52, 154, 211, 217
    national security policy and, 28, 40, 42, 55n, 46, 101
    SALT II and, 217
    weakness on defense, 42
Central Intelligence Agency, 66, 67, 94n, 230n

Cheney, Richard, 47, 48, 95n, 156–157
    V-22 Osprey and, 158
Cheyenne helicopter:
    cancellation of, 154, 164, 219
    Kennedy administration and, 36, 99
    problems with, 89, 99–100
    technology and, 130
Christopher, Warren, 49
Clinton, Bill, 48, 49–50, 51, 148
    B-2 bomber and, 20n, 3
    Congress and, 150
    foreign policy and, 47, 49
    MX missile system and, 212
    national security policy and, 48, 50, 91,
        156, 223
    organizational style, 49–50
    weakness on defense, 49
Cohen, William, 49
Commanders-in Chief (CINCs), 76, 91, 93,
    94n
Commission on Roles and Missions of the
    Armed Forces, 92
Communism, containment of, 17, 30, 38, 43,
    54n
Concurrency. See Production concurrency
Congress, 42, 145, 156
    B-1 bomber and, 12, 149
    campaign reform and, 228
    Carter and, 42, 75, 154
    constituents and, 18, 160–161
    defense powers of, 26, 147, 152, 166, 219,
        246
    Department of Defense and, 149–150,
        160, 166
    F-22 and, 233
    F/A-18 (Hornet) and, 155, 157, 161, 174–
        175
    interest groups and, 160–161
    MX missile and, 12, 149
    nuclear freeze and, 187
    policy oversight and, 150, 162–164, 167,
        228
    Reagan and, 44
    role of, xxvii, 163
    Trident and, 61, 147, 151, 159
    use of legislative veto, 151
    in weapons acquisition, 153–155, 158–
        159, 164–165, 176–177, 219, 220
    criticism of role, 155–156

Congressional Budget Office, 84
    technology and, 130
    in weapons acquisition, 7, 146, 155, 163,
        178
Congressional Research Service, 84, 146
Countervailing (counterforce) strategy, 30, 40

defense budget, 42–43,
Defense, Department of, 35, 46, 48, 50, 51, 52
    Congress and, 147, 149–150, 160, 166
    changes in, 91, 92
    criticism of, 4, 79
    M-1A1 and, 16
    organization of, 66, 71, 77, 83, 92, 101
    role of, xxvi, 65, 67, 75, 92
Defense industry, 76, 93, 110, 202, 223
    as part of a subsystem, 111, 123, 183, 223
    democracy and, 121, 203
    follow-on imperative and, xx, 6, 121, 229
    in weapons acquisition, 227
    individual companies, 183
    lobbying by, 190, 195
    reform of, 228
    regulation of, 123
Defense Management, President's Blue
        Ribbon Commission on, 67, 75, 92,
        95n, 126
defense planning guidance document, 56n,
        70, 91
    preparation of, 67, 94n, 96n
defense policy, 41, 43, 53n
    linkage to foreign and military policy,
        29, 80
    presidential role in, 27, 37, 40, 46–47
Defense Reorganization Act of 1958, 33, 58
Defense Resources Board (DRB), 67, 95n, 232
Defense Systems Acquisition Review Council
        (DSARC), 67, 94n, 230
democracy, 14, 181, 225
    inefficiency of, 15, 16, 52
    normative value of, 189, 220
    Pentagon and, 71
    weapons acquisition and, 199–201, 225
Department of Defense Reorganization Act
        (1986), 74, 92, 94n, 95n, 149
deterrence theory, 32, 34, 38, 40, 45
    public opinion and, 185
    technology and, 112
    weapons acquisition and, 32–33

DIVAD (Division Air Defense Gun), 117
  cancellation of, 154, 159, 164, 217
  Congress and, 153, 157, 159, 178–179, 219
  media and, 194
  public and, 197
  Reagan administration and, 45, 82
  technology and, 12, 178
Dulles, John Foster, 22, 33, 54n

Eisenhower, Dwight D., 42, 51, 109, 206n, 223
  defense policy and, 30
  foreign policy and, 33
  on a military-industrial complex, 111
  New Look and, 31, 32, 40
  organizational style of, 33–34
  Polaris submarine and, xxx
Equality Principle, xxviii, 181, 184–189, 202
  Guardianship Principle, debate with, 187–188
  See also Guardianship principle

F-14 fighter plane, 85, 101, 115, 120
  Congress and, 18, 154
  Kennedy administration and, 36
  TFX controversy and, 63, 88
F-15 fighter plane, 36, 70, 80, 88
  competition with F-16, 105, 150
  F-22 and, 232–233
  technology and, 13, 115
  TFX controversy and, 63
F-16 fighter plane, 81, 88, 105–106
  Congress and, 150
  F/A-18 and, 155
  technology and, 13, 113, 115, 123
F-22 fighter plane, 48, 50, 92, 231n
  controversy and, 232–233
F-111 fighter plane, 81, 88
  Congress and, 157
  controversy and, 62–63, 75, 88
  McNamara and, 36, 62
  media and, 193
  technology and, 130
  Vietnam and, xx, 88
F-117A fighter plane, 188
F/A-18 (Hornet), 85, 101, 174
  Carter administration and, 42, 161, 174
  Congress and, 155, 157, 161, 174–175

Congressional Budget Office report on, 163
  technology and, 123
flexible response, xxx, 58, 99
Ford, Gerald, 39, 51, 60, 205n
foreign policy:
  defined, 53n
Freedom of Information Act (FOIA), 188, 202, 227
  MX missile and, 163, 211

General Accounting Office, 84, 91, 236
  Congress and, 4, 79
  review of weapons systems and, 16, 23n, 116–117, 138, 178, 232
  on technology, 120, 130
  weapons procurement process and, 146
Goldwater-Nichols Defense Reorganization Act of 1986. See Department of Defense Reorganization Act of 1986
Gorbachev, Mikhail, 44
guardianship principle, xxvii-xxxviii, 181, 182–184, 202

House Appropriations Defense Subcommittee (HADS), 148, 174, 176, 183
House Armed Services Committee (HASC), 17, 147
  Bradley and, 104, 111, 183, 228
  democratization of, 147
  M-1 tank and, 176
  M-16 rifle and, 194, 214
  MX missile and, 147–149, 154
  Skipper and, 88, 101, 163
  as subsystem, part of, 111, 183, 228
  See also Congress
House National Security Committee. See House Armed Services Committee

interest groups, 160–161, 183, 190, 203
interservice rivalry, 74, 75, 76, 87, 92
  arms race and, 79
  as a cultural phenomenon, 78
  Thor-Jupiter and, 140, 193
  under Truman, 31–32
Iran-Contra scandal 27, 44, 188

Johnson, Lyndon B., 34, 35, 51
Joint Chiefs of Staff (JCS), 27, 33, 35, 66

weapons acquisition and, 66–67, 70, 74, 75, 229–230
Jupiter missiles. *See* Thor-Jupiter

Kennedy, John F., 34–35, 58–59, 82, 99, 217
Kennedy, Robert F., 27, 35, 51
Key West Agreement of 1948, 99
Kissinger, Henry, 37, 38, 39–40, 142

Laird, Melvin, 39, 161
Lake, Anthony, 49

M-1 (Bradley) tank, 70, 152, 155, 219
    Bradley and, 17, 103
    as compromise decision, 15–16, 89
    controversy and, 8, 23n, 117, 176–177
    performance in Gulf War, 16
    RAM-D of, 123, 158, 176
    technology and, 116, 123
M-1A1 tank, 12, 23n, 124
M-16 rifle, 162, 219
    controversy and, 213–214
    media and, 194
    Vietnam and, xx, 87, 162, 194
mass media, 190–193
    equality principle and, 186, 202
    restrictions on, 188, 202, 206n
massive retaliation, xxx, 32, 33, 34, 58
McNamara, Robert, 36, 75
    Cheyenne and, 99
    M-16 rifle and, 213
    national security policy and, 34, 36– 37, 58
    reorganization of the Pentagon and, 35, 36, 58, 96n
    Skybolt missile and, 36, 58, 217
    TFX and, 36, 62, 75, 88, 97n
milestone review process, 84, 91, 93n, 121, 218, 227
    stages of, 66, 70, 73, 76
    technology and, 11
military, U.S.
    in budgetary process, 73, 160
    bureaucratic politics and, xx, 74
    presidential relations with, 33, 39, 45
    role of, 66
    in subsystem, 76, 110, 123, 183
    technology and, 115, 118, 218
    TFX controversy and, 62

weapons acquisition and, 70–73, 76–77, 82, 89, 90, 96n, 217–218
    Congress and, 160
    future of, 223
    technology and, 125, 132
Military Technology Revolution, 119–120, 124, 221
Minuteman (ICBM), 34, 37, 59, 129
MIRV, 38, 81, 112, 200
    decision to develop, 10, 188
mutual assured destruction (MAD), 34–35, 36, 37, 38, 43
MX missile system, 7–8, 81
    cancellation of, 8, 50
    Carter administration and, 41, 52
    Congress and, 147, 149, 150, 163, 219
    cost overruns and, 12
    debate over, 8–9, 17–18, 196, 211
    environmental issues (NEPA) and, 147, 152, 163, 196, 211
    Mormon Church and, 17, 79, 186, 196, 211
    multiple aim point basing (MAP) and, 196
    multiple protective shelter (MPS) basing and, 17, 41, 79, 186
    public land issues (FLPMA) and, 147, 167, 196, 211
    Reagan administration and, 56n, 159, 171n, 196

National Intelligence Estimate (NIE), 66, 70, 91
National Security Act of 1947, 31
National Security Council (NSC), 27, 53n
    NSC-68, 31
    presidential relations and, 33, 35, 39
    weapons acquisition and, 66, 67, 94n, 122
National security policy. *See* defense policy
National Security Restoration Act, 149
NATO, 31, 34, 39, 43, 49
Nixon Doctrine, 37, 39, 55n
Nixon, Richard, 38
    China and, 37
    national security policy and, 37, 38, 217, 242
    organizational style, 38
nuclear triad, xxx, 34–35, 150
    critics of, 79

modernization of, 56n, 80
nuclear weapons, 32, 34–35, 38, 40

Office of Management and Budget (OMB),
    27, 66–67, 103, 178
Office of the Secretary of Defense (OSD), 66,
    71, 75
    relationship with military services, 88,
        105, 154
Operation Desert Storm. *See* Persian Gulf War

Packard Commission. *See* Defense
    Management, President's Blue
    Ribbon Commission on
Patriot (SAM-D) missile system, xxi, 36, 116
Pentagon. *See* Defense, Department of
Perry, William, 49, 93, 233
Persian Gulf War, 9, 46, 47, 124, 184
    performance of military hardware and,
        16, 124, 116–117, 143
Planning, Programming, and Budgeting
    System (PPBS), 36, 66, 93n, 94n,
    96n, 121, 160
Polaris submarine, xxx–xxxi, 33, 113
    Great Britain and, 58
    technology and, 130
    Trident submarine and, 60
policy-making process, 15, 52, 200
    conflict and, 15, 203
    democracy and, 14, 16, 18, 120–121
    public role, 181
Powell, Colin, 47, 48
pragmatic perspective (argument), 9, 81
    contentions of, 6–9, 65, 215–216, 235
    cultural factors and, 77–81
    presidential decisions and, 51–52, 215
    structural factors and, 70–77
    on weapons acquisition, 67–70, 79, 80, 88
President:
    advantages over Congress, 166
    advisors and, 27, 37, 44, 47, 217
    constraints on, 28–29, 52
    foreign and defense policy and, 29, 217
    power of, 51, 216–217
        budgetary, 26, 30, 36, 39–40
        constitutional, 26–29
        organizational, 28, 30
    weapons acquisitions and, xxv, 25, 29, 30,
        215, 216–217, 220

See also individual presidents
Production concurrency, 73, 114, 118–119,
    221–222
    B-1B and, 115
    comparison with sequential strategies,
        119
    DIVAD and, 155, 159
    F-22 and, 92, 233
Project on Military Procurement, 206n
public, 27, 182, 183, 197
    Equality principle on, 184–189
    Guardianship principle on, 181, 183
    MX missile and, 28, 196, 197, 211–212
    nuclear freeze movement and, 187, 209
    role of, xxvii, 187, 188, 189
    weapons acquisition and, xviii, 183, 190,
        196, 219–220
public opinion, 182, 184, 195, 222
    defined, 190
public policy, xviii, 3, 52

RAM-D, 116
    M-1 tank and, 158
rational analysis, xxv, xxx
    Congress and, xxvii, 145, 165
    limitations of, 6–9, 200, 224–226
    Pentagon and, 66–67, 71
    policy-making process and, 95n, 200
    president and, 25, 51, 215
    theories of, xxii, xxvi, 3, 6, 20n, 65, 78, 83,
        181
Reagan Doctrine, 43
Reagan, Ronald, 43, 44, 51, 187
    B-1 bomber and, 7
    criticism of, 42, 56n, 116, 206n
    foreign policy and, 43, 44
    military buildup and, xxi, 124
    MX missile and, 44, 56n, 80, 159, 163,
        171n, 196, 211
    national security policy and, 43, 45, 80, 82
    organizational style of, 44, 217
Rostow, W.W., 35
Rusk, Dean, 35

SAC (Strategic Air Command), 34–35
SALT I, 38, 142, 208n
    MIRV and, 11
    public support and, 185–186

SALT II, 40, 52, 60, 205n
    MX missile and, 211
    U.S. Senate and, 41
Schlesinger, James, 17, 39, 75, 105
scientific community, 109, 110
    role of, xxvi, 107
    weapons acquisitions and, 120, 127, 128
Scowcroft, Brent, 47
Scowcroft Commission,
    Midgetman and, 154, 219
    report of, 80
Seawolf submarine, 149, 157, 221, 231n
Senate Appropriations Defense Subcommit-
        tee (SADS), 148, 183
Senate Armed Services Committee, 147, 148,
        183
    SDI and, 149
SIOP (Single Integrated Operational Plan),
        37
Skipper missile, 85, 101
    HASC and, 88, 101, 163
    testing of, 152, 155
Skybolt missile, 58
    cancellation of, 58–59, 82, 217
    McNamara and, 36, 217
    media and, 190–193
Soviet missiles:
    SS-18, 10, 200
    SS-19, 200
Special Projects Office, xxx
Stalin, Joseph, 201, 208n
START, 44, 46, 185, 222
Strategic Defense Initiative (Star Wars),
        xxviii, 28n
    cancellation of, 156
    Congress and, 149, 156
    Soviet Union and, 124
    technology and, 12, 117, 125, 218
subsystem, 110, 111, 184, 223
    weapons procurement as, 111, 197, 204n

technological determinism, 108
technological imperative, 107, 108, 109
    criticism of, 112–113, 117–118, 132–133
    nuclear weapons and, 109
    weapons acquisition and, xx, xvi, 6, 107,
        216
technology, 119, 218

arms race and, 112–113
costs of, 11–12, 115
future developments in, 11, 13, 114, 120
weapons acquisition and, 10, 12–13, 93n,
        107, 118, 218
    effects of, 11, 110
Thor-Jupiter, 27, 219
    McNamara and, 36
    media and, 190–193
    problems with, 140–141, 157, 164
    technology and, 126
Tower Commission, 44–45
Trident missile and submarine system
    missile (D-5), 7–8, 44, 81
        Congress and, 150
        debate over, 8–9, 159
    submarine, 61, 79
        Carter administration and, 41, 52, 60
        as compromise decision, 18, 60–61, 89,
            160
        Congress and, 147, 151, 153, 161
        Electric Boat Division of General
            Dynamics and, 77
        environmental concerns and, 159
        Nixon administration and, 38, 52, 60
Truman, Harry S, 27, 51
    foreign policy and, 30, 31
    weapons acquisitions and, 31–32
TFX, see F-111 fighter plane

uncertainty:
    efforts to overcome, 78, 79, 110, 218
    in politics, xx, xxi, xxvi, 95n
    in post-Cold War era, 46, 52
    technology and, 13, 114, 122, 131, 218
    in weapons acquisitions, xix, 51, 78, 80,
        215, 226, 235
unconventional warfare, 35, 43, 99
United Nations, 35, 49

V-22 Osprey tilt-rotor aircraft:
    Cheney and, 48, 158
    Clinton administration and, 50
    Congress and, 18, 150, 154
    debate over, 29n, 81
Vietnam War, 35, 37, 88
    Congress and, 166–167
    M-16 rifle and, 87, 162, 213–214

weapons acquisition:
    budgetary concerns and, 222–223
    cultural factors and, 77–81
    dilemmas of, 4, 67, 78, 215
    end of Cold War and, 220–221, 225, 229
    public and, 189, 219–220
    reforms in, 227, 230, 230n
    Soviet Union and, 200–201

weapons systems:
    as compromise decisions, 3, 15, 18, 80
    problems with, 115, 116
    as rational responses, 6, 84
    See also individual weapons systems
Weinberger, Casper, 45, 75
    DIVAD and, 154, 160, 164, 179, 194, 197, 217
    Weinberger Doctrine, 49